W9-BGG-586

THE DISTORTED IMAGE

THE DISTORTED IMAGE

CHANGING CONCEPTIONS OF THE AMERICAN CHARACTER SINCE TURNER

THOMAS L. HARTSHORNE

GREENWOOD PRESS, PUBLISHERS

WESTPORT, CONNECTICUT

Library of Congress Cataloging in Publication Data

Hartshorne, Thomas L
   The distorted image.

   Reprint of the 1968 ed. published by Press of
Case Western Reserve University. Cleveland.
   Bibliography: p.
   Includes index.
   1. National characteristics, American.
2. United States--Civilization--20th century.
I. Title.
[E169.1.H278 1979]   973.9   79-28120
ISBN 0-313-22220-7 lib. bdg.

Reprinted in 1980 by Greenwood Press, Inc.
51 Riverside Avenue, Westport, CT 06880

Printed in the United States of America

10 9 8 7 6 5 4 3 2 1

To Joan

FOREWORD

Addressing himself to a central issue in American thought—the nature of the national character as leading intellectuals and scholars of the late nineteenth century and the first decades of the twentieth envisioned and interpreted it—Dr. Hartshorne has made a noteworthy contribution to American intellectual history. The subject is one of the thorniest a scholar could choose. This is partly because the very existence of national character as a substantive reality or even as a valid concept is open to question. It is also because, as Dr. Hartshorne shows, most of those who concerned themselves with the problem were ill-equipped to do so; few of the earlier writers in this account, for example, even troubled to define the term with any rigor. Yet this is a distinguished group of thinkers and writers. Without succumbing to the temptation of presenting a descriptive catalogue, Dr. Hartshorne has succeeded in giving us an impressive analysis of the positions taken by such older leaders of thought as Frederick Jackson Turner, Josiah Royce, Herbert Croly, Jane Addams, H. L. Mencken, Charles and Mary Beard, and Horace Kallen. Since one focus of the inquiry is on the degree and character of change in thought about national character, we have, as well, sensible and often illuminating analyses of such contemporaries as Margaret Mead, Robert and Helen Lynd, David Riesman, W. W. Rostow, Lewis Mumford, Reinhold Niebuhr, Clyde Kluckhohn, and Erik Erikson.

Dr. Hartshorne nicely balances what, a great many years ago, I called the major approaches to the history of thought: an analysis of "the interiors of ideas" and the relating of ideas to social and cultural contexts. Many have recognized the desirability of combining the two approaches; Dr. Hartshorne has succeeded better than a great many who have tried their hand at this difficult task. The first approach is here exemplified in skillful analysis and sensitiveness to nuances of thought and to logical inconsistencies; the second, in the relationships uncovered between the "interiors of ideas" and such major social realities as agrarianism, immigration, urbanism, industrialism, economic depression, war, and conflicts of power and ideology, as well as such patterns of thought as neo-Freudianism, neo-Marxism, and the culture-personality concept. In the main, the inclusion of several humanists notwithstanding, the emphasis is on social thinkers and social scientists. The humanists will approve the clean and strong writing and the avoidance of what has been called "social science jargon"; the social scientists, if not always agreeing with what has been said, will approve the writer's control of his material and his candid and often original judgments.

The Distorted Image may be further commended for the rewards it offers both to scholars and to educated laymen concerned with the way intellectuals in the last seventy years perceived the national character. Dr. Hartshorne's synthesis and interpretations provide a vantage point for everyone interested in the bearing of shifting views on the subject to discussions certain to be forthcoming in the years ahead.

MERLE CURTI
University of Wisconsin

PREFACE

It has become almost a national sport among American intellectuals to examine and criticize American life and institutions. Everything Americans do, everything foreigners say about us, is examined for the light it may shed on the American character. The American national character has become an American national obsession. Though I am concerned with the American character in this study, I make no attempt to describe, define, or explain that character. Rather, my goal is to determine what American intellectuals have offered in the way of descriptions, definitions, and explanations. My raw material, in other words, is not the national character itself, but the opinions people had and have about it.

Nor do I make an attempt to establish or to deny the theoretical validity of the concept of national character. The concept will be taken as given, and discussion and analysis should not be mistaken for either advocacy or condemnation. I do, however, have an opinion on the subject, and I feel I should state it in the interests of clarity. It seems to me that the concept of national character, especially when it is applied to a large, heterogeneous nation like the United States, is useful only as a large-scale generalization to cover the prominent characteristics of the national culture—not the traits of any supposedly typical individual personality. Thus, we may regard a particular collection of cultural traits as "typically American" if it is exhibited more often or more intensely in America than in any other nation. In other words, the concept may prove useful as a semi-metaphorical descriptive device for a whole national culture, but it has no predictive value. One cannot with certainty assign an individual to any particular national group solely on the basis of his observed behavior, nor can one predict with any degree of accuracy how an individual member of a national group will behave in a given situation. The idea that there is such an animal as a "typical American" collapses under the weight of the enormous diversity of behavior exhibited by individual Americans. And what is true of Americans is equally true of Englishmen, Italians, Germans, Frenchmen, and members of any other nationality.

Not only is the question of the theoretical validity of the concept of national character excluded from this study. Also excluded are the many non-Americans who have written about the American character. De Tocqueville, Bryce, Dickens, Arnold, Siegfried, Brogan, and the many other foreign observers of the American scene will not be considered. (I have, I must admit, included some non-citizens in this study: George Santayana and the group of refugees from Nazi persecution who came to the United States in the 1930's. The refugees, however, subsequently became American citizens and apparently intended to do so from the time of their arrival, and Santayana was certainly a resident of the United States for a long enough period of time—he taught at Harvard for thirty years—to justify regarding him as a man who was acquainted with America from the inside.)

This study, then, is an attempt to determine what American intellectuals have said about the American character. It is confined to a consideration of those works which are directly concerned with determining what the national character is. It does not examine the many incidental references to national character that appear in almost all works on American history or American society, or the many attempts American historians have made to delineate the American character as it existed at some specified time in the past. The writers here considered come from a variety of backgrounds; they include academicians representing a variety of disciplines, journalists, novelists, indeed all intellectuals who have made extended attempts to express their views on the subject of the American character.

Chronologically, the study will be confined to the twentieth century, or, more precisely, to the period following the publication of Turner's essay on the frontier. Because of its simplicity, clarity, and cogency, Turner's essay has become the prototype of the national-character study. This inquiry begins with Turner and may be regarded as a survey of attempts to discover an alternative to the Frontier Thesis.

It is a commonplace that any scholarly work, even though it bears only one author's name, is actually the product of several individuals' labor. I wish here to repay in small measure the kind assistance I received in the preparation of this study by extending my thanks to the staffs of the following institutions: the University of Wisconsin Library, the Library of the Wisconsin State Historical Society, the Library of Case Western Reserve University, and the Cleveland Public Library. I wish also to extend special thanks and appreciation to Professor Merle Curti, whose criticism and guidance made this a far better work than it otherwise would have been. The dedication recognizes, although it cannot possibly discharge, another debt.

T. L. H.

Cleveland
May 1968

CONTENTS

THE DISTORTED IMAGE

INTRODUCTION

I

The concept of national character seems to be one of those ideas that people find it almost impossible to do without. How often we find ourselves saying or thinking or hearing, "That's just like a Swede," or, "What else would you expect from a German?" We have even arrived at a sort of informal folkloric consensus concerning dominant national traits: Englishmen are staid, Germans militaristic, Frenchmen avaricious and amorous, Italians volatile, Spaniards haughty, the Japanese inscrutable, and so on. And there are many who insist, "There's just something about an American; you can always spot one in a foreign country."

Stated in this crude fashion, such attitudes make most intellectuals wince. Intellectuals are more likely than the average man is to be aware of the dangers of overhasty generalization, and while they might agree that it is possible in many cases to pick out American tourists in a foreign country, they would also insist that this is because they are tourists and not necessarily because they are Americans.

But intellectuals, too, come under the spell of the idea of national character. We find references to the idea in the works of historians, social scientists, literary critics—in fact, all those who study human behavior in any of its forms. It would appear that the concept of national character is the intellectual's substitute for the cruder practice of racial stereotyping.

The tendency has been with us for a long time. It is at least as old as the first relatively systematic attempts to understand human behavior and personality. When the ancient Greeks turned to the problem of observing and analyzing human behavior, the concept of group character found a place in their speculations. Hippocrates, Herodotus, and Aristotle, having observed their neighbors in the culturally crowded eastern Mediterranean area, came to the conclusion that their distinctive behavioral patterns had been produced by the particular geographic and climatic conditions under which they lived.[1] Ever since these Greek thinkers turned to the analysis of people's behavior, countless others have followed their example; they have tried to isolate and describe distinctive behavioral uniformities among distinct groups of people and to determine what produced them.

All this despite the fact that warnings have been sounded against the practice. Boyd Shafer has argued that there is no such thing "as a constant or ever-present national character, unless it is invented by historians."[2] But the fact remains that historians have been assiduous in their inventiveness, and there is no reason to suppose they will not continue to be. Max Weber went even further in asserting that "the appeal to national character is generally a mere confession of ignorance."[3] He meant by this that the scholar who attempts to explain any individual's action on the basis of his nationality is not explaining anything at all. It may be perfectly true that individual X acted in a certain way because he was an inhabitant of country Y, and inhabitants of country Y always act that way, but there is more we need to know. It is a little like saying that the Green Bay Packers win championships because they win more football games than any other team in the National Football League; it tells us very little about the reasons for the Packers' success.

But the idea persists. Why? Because it is convenient. One of the jobs of the historian, or of any other analyst of human behavior, past or present, is to generalize on the basis of the available data, and the concept of national character may make his

[1] David M. Potter, *People of Plenty: Economic Abundance and the American Character* (Chicago, 1954), pp. 3–6.
[2] "Men Are More Alike," *American Historical Review*, 57 (1952), 606.
[3] *The Protestant Ethic and the Spirit of Capitalism*, trans. Talcott Parsons (New York, 1958), p. 88.

job easier. It is convenient to label large groups of people so they can be dealt with in a mass, ignoring for the moment their individual peculiarities. Such labels may facilitate thought and communication. But like all labels, the national-character label can be misused. People may forget that it is merely a label, a semantic convenience, that it ignores individual differences which may be significant in certain contexts; and they may begin to assume that it possesses some sort of intrinsic reality. At that point the label ceases to be an aid to thought and becomes a substitute for it.

II

Let us examine the assumptions implicit in the concept of national character.

Any collection of people which is not fortuitous and random is distinguished by certain characteristics that permit the ready identification of the group as a group. There is something about it that differentiates it from other groups; it is identifiable because it is distinctive in some way. Most of these distinctive characteristics consist of distinguishable patterns of behavior exhibited by members of the group. That is, groups are differentiated from one another because members of one act differently from members of another. And they act differently because they think or believe differently. Henry Pratt Fairchild points out that "it is the very essence of human association that persons who live together continuously in more or less intimate bonds of society should be characterized by many similarities of thought, feeling, and action."[4] Ultimately, therefore, group differences exist because there are characterological differences between members of the group and those who are not members.

Of course, this reasoning could apply equally well to any human group. The concept of national character is a special case in which the group considered is the politically organized state. The analyst of national character tends to assume that the nation is the most important group to which the individual belongs; that it is his nation rather than his church, his political party, his

[4] *Race and Nationality as Factors in American Life* (New York, 1947), p. 4.

3

occupational group, or his social class to which he owes his primary loyalty, which has the first claim on his services, and to which he will sacrifice his other loyalties in case there should be conflicts between them. In this view the nation is the primary locus of political, economic, and cultural influence upon the individual. It has, therefore, become the primary unit of interest for the historian and the social scientist.[5] Because of this, the problem of national character as a special case of the larger problem of group character assumes a special importance.[6]

These are the basic assumptions that lie behind the idea of national character. They are debatable at many points. To accept them wholeheartedly is to give assent to the proposition that in the ideal case there exists in any given group a personality type or a range of types so distinctive that it is possible to distinguish *each* member of the group from *all* non-members. This would appear to be impossible in practice. Even if we do not insist on full attainment of the ideal, we still find problems. Is it really possible to isolate for any particular group of people a set of "normal" behavior patterns that will serve to distinguish all members of the group from all non-members? It is always a distinct possibility that some members of the group may not exhibit the normal pattern and that some non-members may. In addition, the concept of "normality" itself implies some deviation. We are able to distinguish what is normal only because we are able to contrast it with the abnormal. Normality is essentially a statistical concept, an abstraction from many particular cases, and any particular case will probably only approximate the statistical norm. In other words, to speak of a range of normal

---

[5] Hans Kohn, *The Idea of Nationalism: A Study in Its Origins and Background* (New York, 1944), pp. 11–12, 23; C. Wright Mills, *The Sociological Imagination* (New York, 1959), pp. 135–136, 158.

[6] It will be seen that there is a relationship between national character and nationalism, but that they are not by any means identical. To the extent that nationalism may be defined as the perception of differences between one's own national group and others, it may be said that the concept of national character is one manifestation of nationalistic thinking. On the other hand, nationalism usually connotes not only the perception of differences between one's own group and others but also a fervent belief in the superiority of one's own group. This is not true of the national-character study, which may just as easily be critical as commendatory.

behavior does not mean that all members of the group for which the norm has been deduced will exhibit the same behavioral patterns. For instance, murder is not a "normal" act in the cultures of Western Europe, but it does occur. The neat conceptualizations of social scientists often attain their neatness only by overlooking the fact that there are and always will be differences between individuals and that these differences may in certain instances be more obvious, and more important, than the similarities between the members of the group under examination at the moment.

Even if it were possible to isolate behavioral patterns in a group so that one could with absolute precision distinguish between members and non-members, it is not at all certain that these patterns would be reflections of underlying psychological uniformities. Two people may act in the same way in the same situation, but we cannot conclude that they are acting in the same way for the same reasons or that their acts have the same meanings for them. Nor is it possible to say that people who act differently do so because of personality differences. The task of deducing character or personality from observed behavior belongs to the psychologist and the psychiatrist, and it is difficult enough to do it for individuals without attempting to extend the process to large groups of people.

The study of national character involves all these difficulties and a few new ones besides. It requires the assumption that political citizenship creates psychological similarity. This is certainly a shaky assumption when applied to modern, heterogeneous nations which include people of many different occupations, religious beliefs, political views, class positions, and in many cases racial and linguistic backgrounds. Attempting to discover one national character to describe all these disparate elements would seem to be an impossible task. It would certainly run the risk of being far too abstract and generalized to provide an accurate picture of the more unusual types of people in the nation, the people who, precisely because of their deviation from the average, lend much of the distinctive color to the nation's life and culture. Indeed, national-character studies have been criticized on precisely these grounds: that they ignore too many of the differences that actually exist within the nation studied and present a picture that does violence to reality by being too uniform.[7]

As if these theoretical difficulties implicit in the concept of national character were not enough, we also find at least one serious problem which is purely practical: no one seems to know precisely what the concept means. Or, if any author does have an idea, no one else agrees with him. Even the same author is likely to use the term in many different senses, and any two authors will probably have at least three different definitions— if they bother to define the phrase at all. Most do not, at least not explicitly, and many do not recognize that they are dealing with national character at all.

The phrase "American national character" may be used in two distinct senses: it may refer to the character of the individual American, or it may refer to the nation itself. The term "character" is interchangeably applicable to the nation and to the individual, and it may very well be used in both senses in the same work. It should be kept in mind, however, that this identity of usage is semantic only; the underlying realities are different. We may say, for instance, "Fluidity of class structure is an American characteristic." We may also say, "Aggressiveness is an American characteristic." The two statements refer to two different orders of phenomena, the first to America, the second to the American. The two conceptual models defined by Walter P. Metzger may be interpreted as special cases of these approaches. His "Freudian" model is a scheme for determining the personality of the individual; his "dramaturgical" model is a scheme for determining the cluster of social roles, norms, expectations, and values characteristic of a given society.[8] The phrase "national character," therefore, is not always used in a sense which makes it identical with or analogous to individual character, nor does it necessarily mean individual character

[7] Otto Klineberg, *Tensions Affecting International Understanding: A Survey of Research*, Social Science Research Council Bulletin, no. 62 (New York, 1950), 19; Ralph Linton, "What We Know and What We Don't," in *Aspects of Culture and Personality*, ed. Francis L. K. Hsu (New York, 1954), p. 209.

[8] "Generalizations About National Character: An Analytical Essay," in *Generalization in the Writing of History: A Report of the Committee on Historical Analysis of the Social Science Research Council*, ed. Louis Gottschalk (Chicago, 1963), pp. 84–94.

multiplied and writ large. It may have nothing whatever to do with individuals.

There are several other possible varieties of approach. The anthropologist Anthony F. C. Wallace has discussed some of the concepts which have been employed in the analysis of the relationship between the group and the personal characteristics of its members. He pointed out that this relationship could be described in the following ways: as the "genius" of a people, that is, the general frame of reference of the whole society; as the world view, the characteristic outlook of a people on the universe; as the "themes" of a particular culture, a list of propositions which describe the good life and the goals of human existence; as the "ethos," or usual style of emotional experience. To Wallace, national character was another concept of this kind, with its own unique features.

The description of the national character of a people is apt to include statements about genius, world view, and values. What distinguishes national character as a concept is, first, its usual restriction to the citizens of modern, politically organized states; and, second and more important, its emphasis upon the articulation of a large number of components into a structure or pattern.[9]

In addition, the personal background of the individual analyst of national character will affect his treatment. Anthropologists will tend to focus on kinship systems and child-rearing practices, psychologists on sibling rivalries and frustration-aggression complexes, sociologists on social structure, stratification patterns, and mobility, philosophers on dominant modes of thought and value systems. In short, the phrase "national character" has come to mean many different things, and the study of national character has come to involve the consideration of many different types of data with many different types of conceptual tools. To say that it is vague is a gross understatement. In practice the national-character study consists of a series of generalizations about a particular nation, designed to illustrate the ways in which it is distinctive.

Thus the difficulties in the way of the intelligent use of the

[9] *Culture and Personality* (New York, 1961), pp. 94–111.

concept of national character are serious, but they may be minimized if one clearly understands and constantly remembers that descriptions of national character are, and must be, descriptions of *tendencies* only. No conscientious student of national character would argue seriously that the inhabitants of any nation are uniform—psychologically or in any other respect. No one would attempt to prove that all Americans are alike. But a serious social scientist might argue that Americans tend to be more like each other than they are like the members of any other nation; that members of a given culture tend to respond in similar ways; that while there may be individual differences, the pressures of the culture will impose a more or less common direction on these individual differences and mitigate them to some extent; and that, since individuals are probably not that idiosyncratic inherently, there will emerge large areas of near uniformity. Kluckhohn and Murray have pointed out that every man is in some respects like all other men, in some respects like some other men, and in some respects like no other men.[10] The analyst of national character works in the broad field covered by the second of these three propositions. He is concerned with the precise ways in which the individual member of a particular national culture is like the other members of that culture. By assuming the existence of a national character he has given tacit assent to the proposition that the individual constitutions of the people within the same national culture are nearly uniform in certain areas. And he has imposed upon himself the task of delineating these areas of near uniformity as precisely as he can.

This, however, presents another problem. The concept of national character is inherently comparative. When the analyst of American society reports, for example, that Americans are "joiners," he does not mean that all Americans join one or more voluntary organizations and that members of other national groups join no such organizations at all. What he means is that a greater proportion of Americans join such groups than is true in any other nation, or at least most other nations. In order to demonstrate the validity of such a generalization, the student of the American character would have to consider data from other

[10] "Personality Formation: The Determinants," in *Personality in Nature, Society, and Culture*, eds. Clyde Kluckhohn and Henry A. Murray (2nd ed.; New York, 1953), pp. 53–54.

nations as well as from the United States, but the fact is that most students of the American character have confined themselves to a consideration of data from the United States alone.

III

John A. Kouwenhoven has said, "I have a shelfful of books purporting to define the American spirit or the American character and they offer as many different definitions as there are books."[11] In one sense this is quite an apt summary. Writers on the American character have adopted all the various approaches to the problem noted above and have devoted themselves to describing not only the American character but also the "typical American," "the American mind," the American value system, or any combination of these. But the variety in approach is more apparent than real. Most writers on the American character have approached their subject in ways that are substantially similar to those employed by others writing on it at the same time. Moreover, descriptions of the American character have tended to be monotonously similar. There has been a constant repetition of· certain themes, with little or no variation. David Potter has argued that most treatments of the American character may be regarded as belonging to either of two general categories: those which picture the American as a materialistic conformist and those which picture him as an idealistic individualist.[12] Even these differences are usually the result of differences in attitude rather than differences in the perception of actual substantive facts concerning the American character. Over the years, however, there have been changes of attitude that are of fundamental significance in a consideration of American interpretations of the American character.

Many descriptions of the American character have followed the line established by Turner. The Frontier Thesis can be seen in slightly modified forms in several subsequent treatments, largely because it is one of the clearest expressions of the agrarian

[11] *The Beer Can by the Highway: Essays on What's "American" About America* (Garden City, N. Y., 1961), p. 27.
[12] "The Quest for the National Character," in *The Reconstruction of American History,* ed. John Higham (New York, 1962), pp. 197–220.

9

philosophy which has exercised an almost hypnotic influence on many American thinkers. Henry Nash Smith has said:

> From the time of Franklin down to the end of the frontier period almost a century and a half later, the West had been a constant reminder of the importance of agriculture in American society. It had nourished an agrarian philosophy and an agrarian myth that purported to set forth the character and destinies of the nation. The philosophy and the myth affirmed an admirable set of values, but they ceased very early to be useful in interpreting American society as a whole because they offered no intellectual apparatus for taking account of the industrial revolution.[13]

But the myth has persisted, and persisted strongly. It could not take account of the industrial revolution, so it rejected it. Industrialism became anathema in America, at least in most intellectuals' formulations of an ideal vision of the American future. Nurtured as they were in the Jeffersonian tradition, they thought that to the extent the nation had been affected by the industrial revolution the nation had suffered. They assumed that agrarianism and democracy went hand in hand; conversely, they felt that industrialism and democracy were incompatible. This solid substratum of agrarian longing has resulted in a series of studies of the American character that are critical in temper and elegiac in mood. The disappearance of the frontier was a catastrophe; the national course has been, if not precisely downward, then certainly toward strange and probably undesirable horizons ever since; the future offers little or no hope for the realization of any kind of shining vision—these seem to be the deepest feelings of most native commentators on the American character. This was not always the case. Around the turn of the century, the dominant tone of most studies of the American character was quite optimistic, but this was because the full horror of the disappearance of the frontier had not yet been realized. When it was, a chorus of moans rose from the throats of American intellectuals who were convinced that their entire way of life, indeed their very national identity, was in danger of being extinguished.

[13] *Virgin Land: The American West as Symbol and Myth* (New York, 1957), p. 303.

Recently, however, there have been signs that agrarianism is losing its grip on some American intellectuals. There is a growing tendency to question the Jeffersonian assumption that there is an inevitable connection between an agrarian way of life and political democracy. Smith's book is one example. And A. Whitney Griswold has pointed out that the persistence of the Jeffersonian ideal in the United States is radically anachronistic, for by Jefferson's definition the nation would long since have ceased to be a working democracy.[14] Other writers have questioned the set of traditional ideas which we may call the "myth of mobility," the belief that the class structure of the United States is becoming progressively more rigid under industrial conditions and that the social mobility which was characteristic of America's fluid, open, agrarian past is dying out in the rigid, industrial present. Lipset and Bendix have argued that there never was as much real mobility in the United States, relative to other nations, as many people have tended to assume, and others have pointed out that there is reason to believe that social mobility in the United States has actually increased under industrial conditions.[15] At present, American intellectuals are more inclined than ever to regard industrialism as an inherent and necessary part of the American scene and to welcome it as a valuable contributor to the prosperity and well-being of the nation. Studies of the American character made during the 1950's seem quite optimistic in many respects, and the reason is that for the first time commentators on the American character freed themselves from their enslavement to the agrarian myth. They were not forced to labor under the handicap of trying to find something nice to say about an industrial society when all their presuppositions—conscious or unconscious—inclined them toward the belief that industrialism is synonymous with evil.

There has also been a change in the type of questions that students of the American character have tried to answer. The earliest studies were devoted to the problem of determining the

---

[14] *Farming and Democracy* (New York, 1948), pp. 177–178.

[15] Seymour Martin Lipset and Reinhard Bendix, *Social Mobility in Industrial Society* (Berkeley, 1959), pp. 11–75. See also W. Lloyd Warner and James C. Abegglen, *Big Business Leaders in America* (New York, 1955) and *Occupational Mobility in American Business and Industry* (Minneapolis, 1955), both of which provide some evidence that mobility and opportunity have increased rather than decreased in recent years.

characteristics of the typical American. This was true of those writers in the first years of the twentieth century who stressed the importance of racial inheritance as the primary determining factor, and it was just as true of those who paid increasing attention, beginning in the 1920's, to cultural and historical influences. At roughly this time, however, developments in the social sciences caused some writers to question the assumptions of the individual-centered approach. For instance, the interest in social class which was one of the hallmarks of the sociology of the 1930's resulted in an attempt to demonstrate that different character types existed in different classes, that different character patterns existed in different types of communities.

A new approach began to evolve in response to the growing awareness of the heterogeneity of the United States and the accompanying conviction that the attempt to define a typical individual was based upon an unwarranted assumption of uniformity throughout the whole social order. This new approach rested upon value analysis. Instead of trying to discover who the typical American was, students of the American character tried to discover what he thought and believed. They assumed the existence of a common value system, an assumption which made especially good sense after the advent of mass communications. Most recent studies, therefore, have ignored the individual-oriented approach and instead have concentrated on value analysis or some other type of approach that is admittedly social and supra-individual in its focus. The phrase "national character" has consequently come to mean the character of the nation rather than the character of the individual citizen.

Not only have approaches to the problem varied, but so has the degree of interest in it. In recent years there has been a great upsurge of interest. Why? One obvious answer would be that a period of profound crisis like the Cold War inevitably stimulates interest in American institutions and characteristics. It is reasonable to assume that people become more interested in understanding themselves and their way of life when that way of life appears to be threatened. But this has not happened invariably. The problem did not receive any particular attention during World War I except as the war contributed to a growing concern with immigration, which *was* reflected in concern with the American character. Nor was there any great interest in the problem during the Depression. But World War II saw an increase in interest, and so did the Cold War which followed it.

In other words, some crisis situations seem to call forth a concern with national character; others do not. The important consideration is the type of crisis. When it is one that consists largely of an ideological confrontation between the United States and an alternative social and cultural system, concern with the American character grows. World War I did not involve such a confrontation to nearly the same extent that World War II and the Cold War did. The Depression was a crisis that involved only American institutions. The controversy over immigration in the first two decades of the twentieth century created a situation that led inevitably to comparisons between the culture of the native Americans and the cultures of the immigrant peoples.

Comparisons between American institutions and those of other nations or peoples are not always made explicit in the American-character study. In fact, usually there is no reference whatever to nations other than the United States. But behind this apparently exclusive concern with American institutions lie the need and the desire to understand and explain America so that it may be compared rationally to what is known and understood of other nations. The American-character study is thus a symptom of cultural self-consciousness, a manifestation of a feeling of ideological and cultural competition. Accordingly, the recent interest in the American character is nothing more than a particularly intense manifestation of a feeling and a response that have existed previously in American history.

There is another factor involved, a factor having to do not with great movements in history but with developments within the American intellectual community itself. In the early decades of the century, national character was defined as racial inheritance at least partly because many American intellectuals, enchanted by recent discoveries in biology, especially genetics, were avid in their desire to apply this new knowledge to an understanding of social phenomena, just as they had been swept off their feet shortly before by the possibilities that Darwinism seemed to offer in the study of human relations. The development of the culture concept by anthropologists and the increasing stature of Freudian psychiatry called the assumptions of the racists into question, and in the 1920's there emerged an explanation of national character on cultural and psychological principles. This shift, therefore, reflected a growing sociological sophistication among writers on the national character. This, in turn, was largely because the problem of national character was coming more and more to be treated as a problem in social science. Up to roughly 1930 most of the writers on the American character were philosophers, novelists, journalists, and literary critics. Beginning in the 1930's, however, sociologists, anthropologists, psychiatrists, and historians with a knowledge of other social sciences began to concern themselves with the problem. Investigation of the American character became a legitimate field of inquiry for the social scientist.

It still is. One of the more important trends in current research in the social sciences is the widespread attempt to develop interdisciplinary cooperation. The study of national character lends itself admirably to the interdisciplinary approach; it is a difficult, if not impossible, undertaking if confined within the bounds of any single academic discipline. This is perhaps one of the reasons why academicians in general tended to shy away from the subject until recent times. With the current emphasis on interdisciplinary study the academician is not only permitted to indulge in the kind of broad generalization demanded by the subject of national character, but is even praised for doing it. Given the present state of development of the social sciences, analysis of the American character is precisely the kind of problem one would expect social scientists to investigate.

1

THE AMERICAN CHARACTER AT THE TURN OF THE CENTURY

THE YEARS OF OPTIMISM

I

In 1893 Frederick Jackson Turner read his paper on the frontier to the American Historical Association. In it he described the American character in the following fashion:

> That coarseness and strength combined with acuteness and inquisitiveness; that practical, inventive turn of mind, quick to find expedients; that masterful grasp of material things, lacking in the artistic but powerful to effect great ends; that restless, nervous energy; that dominant individualism, working for good and for evil, and withal that buoyancy and exuberance which comes with freedom—these are the traits of the frontier, or traits called out elsewhere because of the existence of the frontier.[1]

Almost immediately, Turner's hypothesis became one of the seminal ideas in American historiography, providing a stimulus for a whole series of books on various aspects of the history of the American West. Rarely has a theory which has proved to be of so much importance been accepted so rapidly and slipped into the mainstream of American historical thought with so little opposition. The great controversy which arose a few years later

[1] "The Significance of the Frontier in American History," in American Historical Association, *Annual Report* (Washington, D.C., 1894), pp. 226–227.

over the economic interpretation of history simply did not occur in regard to Turner's work, despite the fact that Turner himself was convinced of the validity of the economic approach and seems to have intended his work as a partial application of some of the ideas of those who argued for the economic interpretation of history.[2]

Much of the reason for the ready acceptance of the Frontier Thesis can be attributed to the fact that in many respects the ideas it contained were not fundamentally new. Turner's emphasis on the distinctive contributions of the West to American history can be seen as an instance of the general romantic attachment to the West which had been an integral part of the intellectual and emotional equipment of the nation from its very beginnings.

Thus it should not be surprising that most of the interpretations of the American character that were offered around the same time as Turner's were not appreciably different from his. It seems that Turner succeeded in saying clearly and succinctly something that many people in the United States had been thinking. Commentators who followed him found the American character to be essentially as he had described it. Their descriptions of its fundamental traits were not at all different from Turner's, if one corrects for slight differences in phraseology. Most of them also attributed, either explicitly or implicitly, a strong formative influence to the frontier.

Turner's interpretation did differ from those offered by his contemporaries in one important respect, however. His paper can be read as an announcement of the end of an era in American history. The Frontier Thesis was both a formulation of and a funeral eulogy for what Turner considered to be traditional Americanism. He felt that with the passing of the frontier the influence primarily responsible for making America distinctive and great had gone out of existence. Behind his celebration of the virtues of the frontier character, it is possible to detect a note of concern for what was to take its place. His paper announced that a profound change had occurred in the United States, and it is clear that the change disturbed him.

[2] On the ease with which the Frontier Thesis was accepted see Frederick L. Paxson, "A Generation of the Frontier Hypothesis: 1893-1932," *Pacific Historical Review*, 2 (1933), 36-37. The controversy over the Frontier Thesis did not arise until the 1920's.

Turner was almost alone in his concern. It is possible to argue that the Gay Nineties were not really very gay, but it does seem that the prevailing intellectual climate around the turn of the century was marked by a complacent optimism. There was discontent, to be sure, and it did create an intellectual ferment, but it was a ferment based on the assumption that correction of the existing abuses in American life was possible. The heated discussions on Populism, free silver, and the single tax, and the bitter feelings and fearful memories aroused by the labor troubles of previous years, resulted on the whole in a desire for reform, not in the kind of philosophical pessimism characteristic of the *fin de siècle* mentality in Europe and articulated most eloquently in the United States by Henry Adams. Thus if Turner's paper was a funeral eulogy for a distinctive way of life and a distinctive American character, he was one of the very few who were aware that the patient had died. Around the turn of the century most people seemed to feel that the frontiersman was still healthy and thriving.

II

The extent to which Turner articulated a consensus concerning the American character is revealed by comparing his views with those of the scholars who made up the Anglo-Saxon school of political scientists and historians, those who held the "germ theory" that American political institutions, practices, and ideas were inherited from the centuries-old political traditions of the Anglo-Saxon peoples of the world. Since one of Turner's purposes in writing his paper had been to offer an alternative to the germ theory, one might expect that the germ theorists would have interpreted the American character in a way that was substantially different from Turner's. In certain respects they did, preferring to call upon the Anglo-Saxon tradition and racial inheritance to explain the American character where Turner would have cited the influence of the frontier. But their descriptions of the American character were nearly identical.

John W. Burgess, perhaps the foremost American exponent of the germ theory, for instance, sounds almost like Turner when he describes the American. Though Burgess was not sympathetic to the Frontier Thesis, he shared Turner's high opinion of the capacity of the American people for democratic political life. He characterized the Teutonic peoples, among whom he included the Americans, as follows:

[They have] a high sense of individual worth and of individual rights. . . . Out of it has sprung their profound respect for individual life and liberty, for the chastity of women and the sacredness of the home, for freedom of thought and conscience, and for the security of private property—impulses which, as time and thought and experience have given them form in the understanding, have become elaborated into the so-called bills of rights, which are the chief glory of their political constitutions and the realization of which is the chief end of their governmental arrangements. It is not too much to say that the individual initiative in enterprise, the individual energy in research and the individual conscience in ethical development, which have thus been fostered, sustained and encouraged in these great states, have been the prime forces in the civilization of the modern world.[3]

Notice also the striking similarities to Turner's ideas in the following passage:

We are by no means a peaceably inclined people. The continuous conquest of a new country from the savage, the wild beast, and the jungle, through a period of three centuries, does not tend to produce a peaceably inclined people, but an adventurous, warlike, and vainglorious people. In fact, besides being belligerent and boastful, we are restless, nervous, and at times hysterical.[4]

Even the germ theorist saw the effects of frontier violence on the American character, and he too felt that nervousness and restlessness were important elements in it.

Of course, Burgess was not speaking of Americans alone. The germ theory rested on the assumption that there was a common Anglo-Saxon—or in Burgess' phrase "Teutonic"—heritage. The

[3] "Germany, Great Britain, and the United States," *Political Science Quarterly*, 19 (1904), 3.
[4] *The Reconciliation of Government with Liberty* (New York, 1915), p. 373.

proponents of this theory insisted that the American and the Briton (and Burgess would also have included the German) were brothers under the skin in their possession of superior political judgment and aptitude.

III

This raises the question of America's distinctiveness. A meaningful description of a national character should be confined to the traits that distinguish it from other national characters. If the British, or any other people, were believed to share the political genius which was the birthright of the Anglo-Saxon, Americans could not be considered the unique representatives of political wisdom and virtue; the writings of the germ theorists should then be considered as descriptions of the Anglo-Saxon character, not the specifically American variety of it. But in fact the similarities between Britain and America that the Anglo-Saxon theory pointed out usually received only lip service from American germ theorists. They spoke of Anglo-Saxons, but they were thinking of Americans. It would be inaccurate to imply that they were not ardent Anglophiles, for most of them were, but what really concerned them was not the Anglo-Saxon destiny but the American destiny; what filled them with a sense of exaltation was not the contemplation of the political superiority of the Anglo-Saxon in general but of the American in particular. The concept of a destiny to rule conferred upon the Anglo-Saxon because of his superiority was, at least in the American context, little more than a scholarly formulation of the dramatic sense of mission which had already taken firm root in the American mind.[5] It became, in fact, the basis of a vigorous

[5] On the question of Anglo-Saxon destiny see John R. Dos Passos, *The Anglo-Saxon Century and the Unification of the English-Speaking People* (New York, 1903); Charles A. Conant, "The Economic Basis of 'Imperialism,'" *North American Review*, 167 (1898), 326–340; George Burton Adams, "A Century of Anglo-Saxon Expansion," *Atlantic Monthly*, 79 (1897), 528–538; John P. Proctor, "Isolation or Imperialism," *Forum*, 26 (1898), 14–26; and A. Lawrence Lowell, "The Colonial Expansion of the United States," *Atlantic Monthly*, 83 (1899), 145–154. On the sense of destiny among Americans themselves see Edward McNall Burns, *The American Idea of Mission: Concepts of National Purpose and Destiny* (New Brunswick, N. J., 1957).

and distinctively American imperialism, most eloquently articulated by Albert J. Beveridge, Senator from Indiana.

Beveridge's impassioned imperialism was firmly rooted in good Anglo-Saxon doctrine. He asserted that the superior political capacity that Americans possessed because they were Anglo-Saxons provided a justification for their expansion at the expense of less favored peoples. But Beveridge was an American politician, and his field of reference was the United States. Though his vocabulary was reminiscent of the trans-Atlantic emphases of the scholars of Anglo-Saxondom, he paid little attention to the wider Anglo-Saxon group.

His most extensive journey into the discussion of the American character, Beveridge's book *Americans of To-Day and To-Morrow* was a product of his concern with imperial expansion. It was written because of his belief that Americans were fast becoming world leaders as God's chosen people. Beveridge felt that under these circumstances it was imperative for Americans to come to a surer understanding of themselves, their capacities and their limitations, and their ultimate destiny. He felt that America was moving into a new and strange world, and he wanted to assess the capacities of the American to make his way in it.

The results of his investigation reassured him. He discovered traits which he felt would enable the American to dominate his world. Adaptability, discretion, practicality, and energy were some of the traits he stressed. But the keynote of the American character to Beveridge was simplicity and moderation.

> With all our fervency of disposition, with all our intensity of purpose, with all our enthusiasm of manner, we are still in the great bulk a nation of plodders. And thank Heaven that this is so![6]

This is a rather curious description—a plodder is certainly not a very dashing figure. It may seem strange that a fervent imperialist like Beveridge should characterize the American in this way at a time when other advocates of imperial expansion were extolling the strenuous life, dash, daring, and the martial virtues.

[6] (Philadelphia, 1908), pp. 130–131. The summary of American traits appears in the chapter called "The American Type," pp. 115–133.

Indeed, Beveridge himself, when he spoke in his role as the high priest of the glorious imperial destiny of the United States, said that Americans were "more virile types of men." As he described it, the march of the American to a position of world dominance seemed to be a juggernaut propelled by determined, willful, hardy people. It does not seem that the men who were to carry "American law, American order, American civilization and the American flag" to "shores hitherto bloody and benighted" could accurately be described as "plodders."[7]

Why, then, did Beveridge choose to apply this rather surprising term to the American? His meaning can be understood best through an examination of the connotations he seemed to attach to it. It is clear that he was not suggesting any lack of personal dynamism or of intellectual and physical energy. In calling the American a plodder Beveridge was not saying that he lacked energy, but was instead saying something about the way in which he characteristically expended his energy. By "plodding" Beveridge meant steadiness as opposed to fire, dogged determination as opposed to quick adroitness, deep slow thought as opposed to cleverness. (One might say, to use the phrase that Beveridge himself would probably have found most congenial, "mere cleverness.") What emerges in Beveridge's picture of the American is the same sort of moral, determined, righteous, virtuously stubborn individual, conscious of having right on his side and of the fact that he is doing God's work, which had been held up throughout the American past as a contrast to the brilliant, sophisticated, cultured, clever European. Beveridge was extolling the homely virtues of simplicity and rectitude and, at least by implication, looking somewhat askance at the traits of intellectual quickness and subtlety. In this he was articulating a point of view which had run through many analyses of the American character in the past and was to be characteristic of still more in the future.

The composite portrait of the American presented by writers on the American character at this time is interesting not only for the qualities it includes but also for the qualities that are lacking. The picture of the typical American was certainly a

---

[7] These quotations are taken from a speech Beveridge made to the Middlesex Club of Boston on April 27, 1898. It is reprinted in Claude G. Bowers, *Beveridge and the Progressive Era* (Boston, 1932), pp. 68–69.

handsome one: he appeared to be a thoroughly admirable chap. To be sure, a closer examination reveals a few minor shortcomings. He seemed to be rather one-sided. Though he certainly had an outstanding aptitude for political life, outside the halls of government he tended to be a rather dull individual. His most obvious deficiency was that he was not concerned enough with or good enough at artistic endeavors. Analyses of the American character during this period were almost universally agreed that the typical old-stock American was somewhat deficient in the arts.

To most commentators this deficiency was relatively unimportant. If all of life was politics, as the germ theorists tended to assert and as others seemed to believe whether they said so or not, who needed artistic excellence? John W. Burgess said:

> Not all nations, however, are endowed with political capacity or great political impulse. Frequently the national genius expends itself in the production of language, art or religion; frequently it shows itself too feeble to bring even these to any degree of perfection.[8]

The condescension implicit in the use of the words "even these" reveals an attitude that was widely held. Even when the American's lack of artistic potential was explicitly recognized, it was done in such a way as to leave the impression that this was simply one of the defects of the American's characteristic virtues and that, in any case, the defect was really not very important. The lack of a strong cultural tradition was unfortunate, but it was not something that these writers on the American character could get excited about. Bliss Perry revealed the spirit of complacency on this question that was characteristic of most of his contemporaries. He admitted that it was fair to accuse the American of barbarism, but "it has been the barbarism of life and not of death. A rawboned baby sprawling on the mud floor of a Kentucky log cabin is a more hopeful spectacle than a wholly civilized funeral." We can see at work here the old and deeply

[8] *The Foundations of Political Science* (New York, 1933), pp. 5–6. This is a republication, unchanged, of those parts of Burgess' great work *Political Science and Comparative Constitutional Law* (2 vols.; Boston, 1890) that relate to the nation and the state.

ingrained American tendency to find cause for self-congratulation in the supposed contrast between a wholesome America and
an effete Europe.[9]

On all counts, there was a remarkable consensus on the temperament, character, values, and thoughts of *homo Americanus*.
Behind slight differences in vocabulary lies a basic agreement
concerning the most significant characteristics of the typical
American. He was idealistic, but practical; a political sophisticate
well versed in the arts of government and passionately devoted
to liberty; a thorough individualist whose individualism at times
had the unfortunate tendency to lead him slightly astray, in the
sense that it made it difficult for him to cooperate for the attainment of socially approved and necessary ends; energetic and
aggressive, both in the assertion of his claim to political suprem-
acy and in his quest for wealth, but also adaptable to changing
conditions and capable of high moral idealism and considerable
emotional warmth. The American of these treatments, in short,
was vital, materially and morally, and capable of dealing effectively with the problems he had to face in the world. Above
all, he was a man ready and equipped to meet any challenge.[10]

IV

Turner's American was thus the American who appeared in
the portraits drawn by most of his contemporaries. But Turner's
view was retrospective; he was taking a last nostalgic look at
something that either was already dead or was threatened with

[9] *The American Mind* (Boston, 1912), pp. 69–70. Mark Twain's *Innocents Abroad* (2 vols.; New York, 1869) is the most entertaining expression of this attitude. Of course, Twain was exaggerating his own lack
of sophistication and that of his fellow countrymen, but, although his
satirical sword had two edges and was used against America as well as
Europe, his criticism of the ways of the "cultured" Old World expressed a view held by many Americans at the time.

[10] In addition to the works already cited see John W. Burgess, "The
Ideal of the American Commonwealth," *Political Science Quarterly*,
10 (1895), 404–425, and *Recent Changes in American Constitutional
Theory* (New York, 1923), pp. 35–36; Robert Ellis Thompson, *The Hand
of God in American History: A Study of National Politics* (New York,
1902); Lyman Abbott, *America in the Making* (New Haven, 1911);
Nicholas Murray Butler, *The American as He Is* (New York, 1908).

imminent extinction. His contemporaries, however, felt no such threat. They believed that the frontiersman still lived, functioned, and flourished. They saw no cause for gloom.

Much of the reason for this difference in mood was that Turner's explanation of the genesis of the American character was radically different from that of others. The Frontier Thesis stated that the American character had been formed by a set of specific historical conditions. Because these conditions had ceased to exist, Turner feared that the American character was bound to change significantly. His contemporaries could not admit such a possibility. Since they insisted that the American character was the product of racial inheritance, they had to conclude that it was permanent and enduring. Their basic premise made it impossible for them to worry about the end of the frontier, for their whole approach rested on the belief that the frontier had not had anything to do with the formation of the American character.

Turner's essay broke new ground in the social science of his day precisely because he did not accept the racial explanation of the genesis of national character. He was not unique in this, but he was certainly unusual.[11] The germ theorists had asserted that the political superiority of the Anglo-Saxon was genetically determined, and those who wrote on the American character at the time, whether or not they were members of the germ-theory school, tended to follow their lead. The Anglo-Saxon peoples were conceived of as a racial group, and their political capacities, indeed their political institutions, were spoken of as if they were a part of the group's genetic equipment. Habit, tradition, and experience were all conceded some importance, but only as they modified slightly or developed more fully elements already present in the germ plasm of the Anglo-Saxon.

Nearly everyone who wrote on the American character at

[11] Edward Eggleston shared Turner's distrust of the racial explanation of national character. "What are loosely spoken of as national characteristics are probably a result not so much of heredity as of controlling traditions. Seminal ideas received in childhood, standards of feeling and thinking and living handed down from one overlapping generation to another, make the man English or French or German in the rudimentary outfit of his mind." (Edward Eggleston, *The Transit of Civilization from England to America in the Seventeenth Century* [New York, 1900], p. 1.)

the turn of the century spoke in racial terms. Beveridge referred to the American "race" over and over again. Nicholas Murray Butler asserted that American character and American institutions were firmly grounded in the "Anglo-Saxon impulse." The sociologists Gustave Michaud and Franklin H. Giddings argued that the cultural backwardness characteristic of America would be corrected by the racial changes taking place in the United States as a result of immigration. They maintained that the volatile Latin peoples would inject their artistic talents into the American bloodstream. As a result, the politically sagacious genes of the Anglo-Saxon would dominate in politics and the culturally adept genes of the immigrant would rule in the field of art and culture, and America would have the best of both worlds.[12]

This emphasis on race had some curious features. We may use the term "racism" for the tendency to ascribe to heredity the non-physical differences in members of physically differentiable human groups. The belief that the intellect, temperament, emotional make-up, and personality characteristics of an individual are determined by the hereditary characteristics he possesses as a member of a particular group that is physically distinguishable from other groups can be called "racist." By this definition, it would seem obvious that the germ theorists and those others who concerned themselves with elaborating the distinctive qualities of the Anglo-Saxon were racists. But an important qualification must be entered. Throughout most of American history, racism has been a fighting doctrine, a position adopted for the purpose of establishing and maintaining the relative superiority and inferiority of existing racial groups. It is a theory born of a desire, an attempt to provide an intellectual justification for a set of social attitudes. However, at the turn of the century racism was somewhat different. I am not implying that most of the scholars under discussion here were not firmly convinced of the relative superiority of the racial group to which they belonged, but rather that at this time they did not perceive any serious challenge to their superior position. Racism had become something

[12] Butler, *The American as He Is*, pp. 3–31; Gustave Michaud, "What Shall We Be: The Coming Race in America," *Century Magazine*, 65 (1903), 683–690; Franklin H. Giddings, "What Shall We Be: Comments on the Foregoing," *Century Magazine*, 65 (1903), 690–692, and "The American People," *International Quarterly*, 7 (1903), 281–299.

other than a fighting doctrine, if only because there was no one to fight with, and the hereditary explanation was accepted simply because there was no satisfactory alternative. People spoke in terms of race because genetic transmission was the only acceptable hypothesis to explain the existence of what appeared to be identifiable mental and emotional tendencies in certain groups. They used the word "race" where modern scholars would use "people" or "culture" or "nation." "Race" was frequently no more than a shorthand expression concealing the fact that the user really did not know what had caused the distinctiveness of the group he happened to be studying at the moment. Personality formation was not yet an item of great concern to academic psychology, Freud's work on the importance of early childhood experiences in the formation of character had not yet attracted wide attention in the United States, and the concept of "culture" as a mechanism for transferring beliefs, institutions, and values from one generation to another had not yet been well developed. So the scholar who wanted to explain the distinctive characteristics of any particular group merely said that they were due to its distinctive racial characteristics and let it go at that, because everyone "knew" that such characteristics existed.

Another reason why writings on the American character were heavily freighted with racism is that an individual who has adopted a racist viewpoint is predisposed to think in the terms required by the concept of national character. He has already solved to his own satisfaction and with a stout affirmative the question of whether it is valid to think in terms of group characteristics. It is possible, of course, to discuss national character without being a racist, but being a racist does make it easier, since one has a ready-made solution for some of the more complex theoretical difficulties implicit in the concept of national character.

It would not be strictly accurate, however, to maintain that race was the only available explanatory principle. One could also have resorted to the economic terminology offered by the socialists. But this course was not congenial to the majority of American social scientists, because the economic explanation of history and social institutions was too intimately associated with socialism for intellectual comfort. The racist explanation became the inevitable refuge of the conservative thinker who wanted to explain the origin of the phenomena he was describing but could not accept the economic approach—or indeed any kind of environmentalist approach—because it had apparently been appropriated by the socialists, with whom he wanted to have as little to do as possible.[13] The racist explanation of national character was, of course, an explanation that did not explain anything, reducible ultimately to the proposition that Americans behaved like Americans because they had the genetic equipment of Americans. The whole process of thought depended upon inferring an individual's genetic equipment from his behavior, then explaining his behavior by referring to his genetic equipment. A more perfect example of circular reasoning could hardly be contrived.

There was one other possibility for those who were not comfortable with either the economic or the racial interpretation. One could find an explanation for group characteristics in climatic influences. Bliss Perry, for instance, attributed many of the traits of the American mind to the operation of climate.[14] Climate was politically neutral in its connotations as economics was not. It also had the advantage of being quite vague, so that one could ascribe characteristics to the effects of climate without really concerning oneself with the precise mechanisms of causation. (One is reminded of Oscar Wilde's question whether the fogs caused the English mentality or the English mentality caused the fogs. One might reply that the thickest fog was generated by the initial assumption that any kind of mental characteristics could be explained by talking about fogs at all.) Fundamentally the climatic explanation was little different from the racial explanation. Both were based on the assumption that the national character was relatively permanent and enduring. Both permitted what appeared to be a discussion of the problem of genesis without requiring the discussant to bother with trying to define

---

[13] It is probable, for instance, that one of Butler's reasons for adhering to the racial explanation of American character was his unhappiness with the potential alternatives. He was one of the staunchest opponents of the current of thought typified by Charles Beard and others who were attempting to introduce the economic interpretation into American social science. There is an apocryphal story that when Butler was asked if he had read Beard's last book he replied, "I hope so."

[14] *The American Mind*, p. 4.

any precise causal mechanism. In many respects both were merely semantic habits which made it possible to avoid thinking.

For in practice, no matter how much commentators on the American character might have spoken of racial or climatic influences, when they attributed causative influences to specific forces these forces were nearly always historical in character. With all his talk of climate, Perry cast his explanation of the American character in terms of the frontier and the pioneer experience. He saw American adaptability, versatility, and curiosity as products of life on the frontier, where they were absolute necessities for survival and growth. American provincialism and lack of sophistication were brought about by the fact that Americans had lived out of contact with the rest of the world. Confidence, the gambling spirit, and a spirit of braggadocio were also typically American, rooted to a considerable extent in the American's experience of having unlimited space and resources at his disposal. Beveridge spoke of the traits necessary to the continued healthy existence of the nation as growing "out of the situation in which the nation finds itself." Michaud and Giddings included historical factors in their analysis of the genesis of the American character. Butler noted that "despite differences of climate as marked as those between Denmark and Greece, despite separation by distance greater than that between England and Siberia, despite variety of race origin greater than that of all Europe, the ninety millions of American people are at bottom a single and recognizable political type."[15] Since Butler had already excluded racial and climatic influences, the presumption would seem to be that the result had been produced by the American historical experience.

Thus racism was not a well-developed doctrine. It simply provided a convenient set of labels to explain phenomena which could not be explained on any other acceptable basis. It was, in fact, a substitute for thought. Both in their descriptions of the dominant traits of the typical American and in their tendency to pay lip service to the hereditary principle instead of searching for an alternative explanatory hypothesis, writers on the American character at the turn of the century displayed remarkable similarities.

[15] *Ibid.*, pp. 54–82, 243–245; Beveridge, *Americans of To-Day and To-Morrow*, p. 33; Michaud, "The Coming Race in America"; Giddings, "Comments on the Foregoing"; Butler, *The American as He Is*, p. 30.

V

The Promise of American Life by Herbert Croly stands out because his analysis differed in several important respects from those of his contemporaries—including Turner. Like Turner, he rejected the roseate view that was standard among other writers on the American character, but in other respects he was as different from Turner as Turner was from the rest of his contemporaries. His catalogue of the basic American traits was not appreciably different, nor was his explanation of the genesis of the American character, but his attitude toward these facts was unique.

He began conventionally enough, discussing American patriotism, especially its distinctive orientation toward the future. Americans loved their country, he said, not for what it had been but for what it was going to be. They regarded their nation as a land of promise, and they had an easy faith that the promise would be fulfilled. Up to this point Croly had not said anything that could not have been said equally well by any one of his contemporaries. Indeed, many of them had made almost exactly the same point; if allowances are made for slight stylistic differences the statement would have been in place in almost any discussion of the American character written at the time. The shock comes when Croly says of this attitude, "I am not a prophet in any sense of the word, and I entertain an active and intense dislike of the foregoing mixture of optimism, fatalism, and conservatism."[16] Croly's predecessors had chosen different words, but to say that the American character was distinguished by optimism, fatalism, and conservatism is a reasonably accurate summary of their views. Yet while they were content with it, Croly was not. Indeed, the whole point of his book was that the promise of American life would not be fulfilled unless the American people shook themselves out of their optimistic lethargy and began devoting their energy and their intelligence to that fulfillment.

He did maintain that the American people were justified in a certain degree of complacency. A prosperous country, with free institutions, had produced a distinctive type of individual,

[16] Herbert Croly, *The Promise of American Life* (New York, 1909), pp. 1–5.

not necessarily wiser or better than the European, but certainly more energetic, more hopeful, and more vital.[17] Unfortunately, Croly felt, that individual was one-sided. His mind was alert and flexible, but he was so devoted to the purely practical that he was incapable of disinterested intellectual effort.[18] This point of view is reminiscent of the frequent emphasis, in the national-character studies of the time, on the artistic and cultural short-comings of the Anglo-Saxon. However, earlier commentators had been speaking of a pleasant but largely unnecessary luxury. They had regarded the American's one-sidedness as unimportant, because the one area of life in which he did show special apti-tudes, politics, was of far greater significance than any other part of life. To Croly, on the other hand, this one-sidedness was disastrous because of the qualities it left undeveloped. In his view, they were not unimportant luxuries, but the very basis of a fully realized American promise. Indeed, Croly's remarks seem to indicate that he felt that even the American's political abilities could not be very highly regarded as long as he lacked these qualities.

Some of the qualities Croly admired were revealed in his com-parison of the character of the typical American with the char-acter of Abraham Lincoln. Croly felt that it was grossly inac-curate to regard Lincoln as a man of the people. Croly pointed out that Lincoln did accept contemporary patterns of behavior and belief that were useful and valid, but that he was far superior to the people around him in the reach of his mind:

> He had made himself intellectually candid, concentrated, and disinterested, and morally humane, magnanimous, and humble. All these qualities, which were the very flower of his personal life, were not possessed either by the average or the exceptional American of his day; and not only were they not possessed, but they were either wholly ignored or consciously under-valued.[19]

Croly was also unusual not because he differed on the question of what had formed the American character in the first place but

[17] *Ibid.*, pp. 13–14.
[18] *Ibid.*, pp. 90–91.
[19] *Ibid.*, pp. 98–99.

because he took a look into the future. He believed that the United States had undergone an economic revolution in the years immediately following the Civil War and that from the end of the war the primary fact of economic life in the United States was not free land and the frontier, but industry and the city. He felt that the day of the pioneer was over. So had Turner, of course, but Croly insisted that it had been over for some time, and he devoted more attention to an analysis of the new situation than Turner had. Turner had stopped at the end of the frontier; Croly looked into the future to see what new factors would shape the American character.

He insisted that the jack-of-all-trades no longer had a place as a significant economic figure. The day of the specialist and the expert had come. The pioneer ideal of a perfectly homogeneous society composed of independent and self-reliant individualists was becoming more and more divorced from reality. Americans were becoming members of groups, and the individualism upon which they prided themselves was disappearing. Croly maintained that this was not necessarily bad; the real difficulty was that Americans still looked at themselves and their country with a strong preconception in favor of the pioneer ideal of social and economic homogeneity, and this ideal no longer coincided with the reality. Actually, the new reality of specialization, organization, and group participation could be far more efficient in the long run, according to Croly. It created problems, yes, but only because the American ideal had not yet caught up to the American reality.[20]

The ultimate result of this unfortunate tension between the ideal and the reality was that, in adhering to one ideal, Americans were in danger of violating another. Specifically, economic individualism could destroy individuality: economic pressures could make it impossible for the individual to maintain his freedom of thought and action. This was true not only for those who were at the bottom of the economic ladder but also for those who had "succeeded." Croly felt that a pervasive sameness would be the final consequence of the American practice of measuring results in purely quantitative terms:

[20] *Ibid.*, pp. 100–140.

Different as American businessmen are from one another in temperament, circumstances, and habits, they have a way of becoming fundamentally very much alike. Their individualities are forced into a common mold, because the ultimate measure of the value of their work is the same, and it is nothing but its results in cash.[21]

Being able to do slightly better than someone else something that everyone else was trying to do was not a sign of individuality to Croly. In the American system, money-making had become a universal value, and to the extent that men pursued this value they could not be regarded as true individualists. Indeed, conformity and not individualism was the keynote of the American character:

The American intellectual habit has on the whole been just about as vigorous and independent as that of the domestic animals. The freedom of opinion of which we boast has consisted for the most part in uttering acceptable commonplaces with as much defiant conviction as if we were uttering the most daring and sublimest heresies. In making this parade of the uniform of intellectual independence, the American is not consciously insincere. He is prepared to do battle for his convictions, but his really fundamental convictions he shares with everybody else. His differences with his fellow-countrymen are those of interest and detail. When he breaks into a vehement proclamation of his faith, he is much like a bull, who has broken out of his stall, and goes snorting around the barnyard, tossing everybody within reach of his horns. A bull so employed might well consider that he was offering the world a fine display of aggressive individuality, whereas he had in truth been behaving after the manner of bulls from the dawn of domestication.[22]

Thus Croly departed from traditional descriptions of the American character in several ways—most important, he saw it in a completely new context of economic and social conditions.

[21] *Ibid.*, p. 410.
[22] *Ibid.*, pp. 420–421. This applies with particular relevance to studies of the American character contemporary with Croly's.

The frontier American was dying because the frontier as an effective social force no longer existed in the United States. A new American type would have to evolve in response to the new conditions of industrialism, large-scale economic organization, and corporate life in general. Croly believed firmly that such an evolution was possible, discussed the means by which it could be facilitated, and in effect became one of the leading evangelists of the new dispensation.[23] In the meantime, however, the American character seemed to him to be caught in a trap, formed as it was in conformity to an ideal that was no longer relevant to the actual conditions of life. The American ideal was an agrarian one; American life had become industrial and urban. The tension between an agrarian ideal and an industrial reality produced in the American character a sterile conformity instead of the creative adaptability necessary to deal effectively with the changed conditions.

Croly's approach was therefore unusual, most obviously in that he was contemptuous of the easy optimism of his contemporaries, most significantly in that he recognized the fact that American life had changed fundamentally and was continuing to change. Croly thus joined Turner and Adams as a prophet of a new way of life for America. He differed, however, in the attitude he took toward this new scheme of things. Turner had bemoaned the passing of the frontier; Adams was afraid of the dynamo. In contrast, Croly was willing, even eager, to welcome industrialism, organization, specialization, all the accompaniments of life in a highly developed society. If he was pessimistic, it was not because he feared what was coming but because he feared that the American people were unprepared to take advantage of the opportunities that the new way of life would offer them. He was unhappy to find Americans imprisoned in an outmoded and false set of beliefs about themselves, their nation, and its institutions. Change itself held no terrors for him; he was disturbed because the American people seemed to be incapable of seeing it. Croly could easily have found support for this contention in contemporary analyses of the American character, which expressed quite clearly the attitudes of mind he found disturbing.

[23] *Ibid.*, pp. 427–454.

One analysis which did not do this was Turner's. Turner and Croly were much closer than a superficial examination of their writings would lead one to believe. They were, of course, in fundamental disagreement on one important point: Turner feared industrialism, Croly welcomed it. But Turner had at least recognized that America would have to make its way as an industrial nation. Though he was not happy with the situation, he did perceive it and was therefore able to deal with it and to attempt to arrive at a workable adjustment of America's agrarian past to its industrial present and future. Thus for all the differences in their attitudes toward it Turner and Croly agreed in their analyses of the situation.

The vision of their contemporaries was not so clear. They shared Turner's preconceptions but not his clear perception. Given their preconceptions, they should have been as disturbed as Turner was. Their characteristic mood should have been one of unease, discomfort, and apprehension. The fact that this was not the mood of the period, the fact that they remained staunchly optimistic, resulted only from their unawareness that the United States was changing into something far different from the agrarian nation they had known and loved and whose virtues they celebrated.

2

THE AMERICAN CHARACTER IN DANGER

THE BATTLE AGAINST IMMIGRATION

I

Of the many social, political, and intellectual issues that were debated in the first years of the new century, the one most immediately relevant to a consideration of changing conceptions of the American character is the immigration controversy. Most discussions of the American character were absorbed in this debate, since the essential issue was the relationship between the immigrants and their adopted country and its inhabitants. Because of the furor that immigration had aroused, any person who was willing to assume that an American character existed almost inevitably presented at least some of his views on it in the form of an analysis of the way in which it was affected by immigration.

Of course, opposition to immigration was not a new phenomenon in the United States. Immigration had often been a burning social issue, from the time when Franklin had expressed his concern about the growing numbers of Germans in Pennsylvania, through the anti-radical fears which had driven the Federalists to pass the Alien Acts, and on to the fervent religious bigotry of the Know-Nothing crusade. But the nativist movement of the first years of the twentieth century was an intellectual movement to a far greater extent than these previous eruptions of anti-immigrant feeling had been, as nativists strove mightily to formulate a rationale and a "scientific" justification for their position. And, probably partly because of its greater intellectual respectability, the nativism of the twentieth century drew far more people into its orbit, attracting people of all social classes and sections, not remaining the exclusive property of any single social, political, or economic group. More important than its somewhat self-conscious intellectuality in attracting interest was the enormous wave of immigration that the nation was experiencing, the largest in its history. This fact seemed to augur a complete transformation of the American scene. There was a growing feeling among many American intellectuals that the American character was in imminent peril, that it was threatened by changes so profound as to result in its destruction and its replacement by something infinitely less desirable. The floods of immigrants were portrayed by many as a wave that would drown the type of American who had populated the country hitherto, and produce a polyglot amalgamation of generally undesirable elements.

Nativist fears that the American character was in danger of being substantially altered for the worse were not, of course, entirely new. Both Turner and Croly had expressed concern about the American character, but they were worried about the effects not of immigration but of the profound social upheaval they saw taking place in the change from agrarianism to industrialism, from a predominantly rural to a predominantly urban society. The vision of the nativists was not as clear. The changes that Turner and Croly had pointed out were the driving force in the mentality of the Progressive Era and provided the main impulse to its reforming spirit, but they were not widely recognized by those nativists who wrote on the American character. Though the nativists recognized that changes were occurring, they were guilty of a persistent misconception and misinterpretation of the sources from which those changes stemmed. They knew that something was wrong, and their writings on the American character reveal a mood of discomfort and distress. But their awareness of the source of the trouble was vague at best, and it seems at times that they were almost willful in their failure to sharpen it.

The most pervasive and influential of the social changes taking place in the period was the transition from agrarianism to industrialism. Industrialism was no longer the Jeffersonian bogeyman of some vaguely defined future; it was a present fact, and it made the many Americans who had a heavy emotional investment in the agrarian principles of the Jeffersonian tradition extremely uncomfortable. For to these people the transition from agrarian-ism to industrialism was not simply a social change; it was a revolution, a catastrophic alteration of traditional patterns which threatened to extinguish what they had become accustomed to thinking of as distinctively American. This horrible possibility provided much of the underlying emotional force of the nativist movement, but it received very little explicit attention. Apparently the nativists were so appalled that they could not bring themselves to face the problem squarely and so retreated into practicing a kind of verbal magic; apparently they hoped that by never mentioning the menace which confronted them they would somehow succeed in making it go away. But their uneasiness demanded an outlet. Since they could not face the real problem, they had to find a substitute, and they found one in immigration. Certainly opposition to immigration existed because people feared that immigrants would let loose a wave of radical political agitation, that they would be incapable of making American political institutions work properly, that they would adulterate American culture, and that they would lower the moral tone of American society. But behind these fears lay a more general fear that was largely unexpressed and was perhaps largely unconscious: a fear of fundamental social change of which the immigrant became the symbol and for which he was made the scapegoat.

The immigrant was a satisfying target for a number of reasons. For one thing he was a remarkably effective symbol of the problems created by social change. The presence of large numbers of unassimilated immigrants had produced severe social dislocations. Furthermore, the immigrant was unmistakably an urban creature who found his economic home in industry rather than in agriculture. Consequently it was not at all difficult for nativists to make him into a personification of the forces which were transforming America. An attack on him was a symbolic assault on everything they found distasteful in their America. Since the immigrant was a person, not a vague system or a dimly perceived combination of broad social forces, the nativists could dispense with complex and difficult analyses of the structure of society and the arduous thought necessary to construct programs for reform, and rest secure in the belief that all would be well if only someone would throw the rascals out. Attacking the immigrant also permitted nativists to place the blame for the transformation of their beloved system on an outsider. His presence relieved them of the necessity of asking themselves embarrassing questions about their own responsibility in bringing about the situation that confronted them, the kind of questions, for instance, that Croly had raised by insisting that America had brought industrialism upon itself in its obsessive drive for material wealth. The attack on the immigrant can be seen as a monumental attempt to shirk social responsibility, permitting people to have their material benefits and their moral self-esteem at the same time. In short, by setting up the immigrant as the symbol of the new, nativists were able to derive considerable emotional satisfaction from their self-appointed role as defenders of the traditional American way of life and the old-style American character.

II

Nativists seemed to feel that the most important single element in the American tradition was politics. Their main focus of attention was the political health of the United States. Their attacks on the immigrant and their commendation of the native American resulted from their fervent belief in the deficient political aptitude of the former as opposed to the political genius of the latter. They feared the immigrant because they feared he would have a deleterious effect on American political life. Even before the immigration controversy became heated in the first years of the twentieth century, there were those who had expressed such fears. John W. Burgess was apprehensive about the socialist ideas that immigrants might import. He was disturbed by the possibility that continuous immigration might ultimately destroy the political capacities of the American citizen by destroying his ability to resist the socialists' blandishments. Burgess was not attempting to prove that the socialist argument was especially seductive, nor was he convinced of its ability to attract converts because of its inherent charm, but he was deeply afraid that if immigration continued unchecked, traditional American democracy might simply be overwhelmed by sheer numbers.[1]

[1] "The Ideal of the American Commonwealth," *Political Science Quarterly*, 10 (1895), 404–425.

Such fears found occasional expression in the mid-1890's, but even the crisis that seemed to exist in these years was not sufficient to extinguish the faith of most commentators on the American character that the American was destined to play a master's role in the political history of the world. Expansion was his tradition, and it would be his future, and his virility and energy would ensure his success.[2] In any event, fear was overwhelmed by the upsurge of triumphant imperialism that occurred at the time of the Spanish-American War. Later, after the first flush of ardent jingoism had passed, domestic problems once more engaged the attention of commentators on the American character. One nativist after another pointed with horror to the malfunctions he saw in American politics and administration and insistently attributed them to the pernicious influence of the immigrant.

It is not surprising, therefore, that the nativists' descriptions of the American character were for all practical purposes identical to the formulations of previous commentators. The traits they attributed to the American were the same Anglo-Saxon virtues that had been lovingly catalogued over and over again. This set of traits defined an American who was almost exclusively a political animal; aspects of life other than politics received little if any attention. Henry Cabot Lodge felt that the primary American traits were self-discipline, self-control, will power, energy, initiative, independence, activity, religiosity, and sense of duty. Lydia Commander, a Congregational minister actively involved in the movements for peace and women's suffrage, enumerated the outstanding American traits as follows: opposition to oppression, energy, self-reliance, the instinct for improvement, race pride, equality of opportunity, equal rights, self-government, and forethought. The political bias is even more apparent in the latter list, for many of the "traits" Commander included were not traits of character at all, but political values. This would seem to indicate an implicit belief on her part that an individual's character was defined to a considerable

[2] Frederick Jackson Turner, "The Problem of the West," *Atlantic Monthly*, 78 (1896), 289–297, and Charles Francis Adams, *Imperialism and the Tracks of Our Forefathers* (n.p., n.d.), pp. 10–11. This is the text of an address delivered before the Lexington, Massachusetts, Historical Society, on December 20, 1898.

extent by his system of basic political views. Many of her nativist contemporaries shared this belief.[3]

The burden of the nativists' attack was that the immigrant, lacking the superior political sense of the native American, did not have the capacity to adjust to American political institutions. These institutions had been established by and were adjusted to regulate and be run by people with the inherent capacity to appreciate a political system whose ultimate guiding principle was individual liberty. Immigrants were not such people; they were simply not the right sort of men. (It will be seen that the whole line of nativist reasoning began from the premise that institutions are formed by and take their characteristics from people; its corollary is a rejection of the idea that men's beliefs and behavior can be significantly molded by the institutions under which they live. The human raw material was all-important, and the influences of the environment, either physical or social, were relegated to an inconsequential position.)

The most important specific charge against the immigrants in the nativist indictment was that they were men who did not know what freedom was, or how to use it. They were "beaten men from beaten races," not fit for self-government because they had been subjected to centuries of debasement and degradation. They had been dominated and downtrodden for so long that they had become incapable of understanding what democracy was. Americans were able to make democratic government work because they "never have a sense of inferiority; never a grudge against those who, by one chance or another, occupy a place above them. Every American born to the manner of his kind, feels the world to be open to him." The immigrants did not have this attitude; they lacked the self-confidence necessary in a democratic system. They were convinced of their own inferiority. They were creatures of habit and completely lacking in initiative. The underlying attitude was pungently summed up

[3] U. S., *Congressional Record*, 54th Cong., 1st Sess., 1896, XXVIII, Part 3, 2816–2820; Lydia Kingsmill Commander, *The American Idea* (New York, 1907), pp. 53–55. In *Race or Mongrel* (Boston, 1908), p. 181, Alfred P. Schultz, a German-born doctor of medicine, listed a series of basic American traits which was almost identical to the lists of Lodge and Commander. See also Gino Speranza, *Race or Nation: A Conflict of Divided Loyalties* (Indianapolis, 1923), pp. 14–16, 124–131.

by Dr. Charles E. Woodruff, a retired army doctor, who believed that his experiences with the "lower races" while serving in the tropics made him admirably qualified to comment on the current controversy over immigration. "After spending oceans of blood to wrest our sovereignty from kingly tyrants, we foolishly give it away to negroes, Slavs, Italians, peasants—none of whom ever owned it, do not want it, are damaged by it, and few of whom are able to use it."[4] Thus immigration was thought to threaten the continued existence of American political institutions by introducing into the American body politic large numbers of people who lacked the necessary qualifications of mind and character to understand, let alone operate, them.

Another reason for apprehension in nativist circles was the belief that the presence of the immigrant placed a considerable strain on American government even apart from his undesirable characteristics as an individual. Nativists saw all around them what they took to be the disastrous effects of immigration: bossism, machine politics, graft, corruption, the "shame of the cities" were some. They maintained that one of the major reasons for this dreadful state of affairs was that immigration had destroyed the national unity that was indispensable to the existence of efficient political institutions. Prescott F. Hall, the president of the Immigration Restriction League and one of the leading figures among upper-class Eastern intellectuals in the campaign against immigration, articulated this view:

So far as mere commercial and material progress is concerned a heterogeneous people may be as successful as any. But where depth and not breadth is concerned, that freedom from distinction and multiplicity which results from the prevalence of certain standards and ideals, seems almost essential to the development of extraordinary products in any line.[5]

[4] *The Expansion of Races* (New York, 1909), p. 400. The preceding quotations are taken from Francis A. Walker, "Restriction of Immigration," in *Discussions in Economics and Statistics* (2 vols.; New York, 1899), vol. 2, pp. 437–450, and N. S. Shaler, "European Peasants as Immigrants," *Atlantic Monthly*, 71 (1893), 646–655.

[5] *Immigration and Its Effects upon the United States* (New York, 1906), pp. 172–173.

Even if the nativists had had no other grievance against the immigrant, they could argue that diversity of people was a threat to political and social institutions that had been created by and for a uniform people.

Those who called for unity in American life assumed that disunity was the root of the specific evils they saw. They never proved this assumption; they never even tried to. They simply said, in effect, that since life in the United States had run smoothly when there was a homogeneous population, the new problems must have arisen because the population was no longer homogeneous. It was a perfect *post hoc, ergo propter hoc* argument. The nativists never bothered to show why diversity in itself should have had the specific pernicious effects they attributed to it.

Another threat the nativists saw arising from immigration depended upon the reaction of native Americans to the presence of the immigrant. Pride, sometimes called "race pride," was a trait frequently ascribed to the American. Because of it, according to the standard thinking of the day, he would refuse to submit to political control by people he considered inferior. So jealous was he of his political freedom that he would refuse to endanger it by allowing his political institutions to be tampered with by unworthy sorts of people. Thus John R. Commons maintained that the presence of the immigrant had induced Americans to "despotize" their political institutions in order to retain control in their own hands. Possibly because of his association with Turner at the University of Wisconsin, Commons saw the American as a frontiersman, and he felt that one of the consequences of the frontier heritage was an overeagerness to resort to lynch law as a method of keeping in their place those people whom the American was not willing to admit as equals. Lydia Commander also feared that one of the results of continued immigration might be that aliens would come to exist as dominated races under American control and that this would mean the gradual but inevitable sapping of democratic political life and thought.[6] Thus, ironically, American democracy seemed to be endangered by exactly the same traits in the American

[6] *The American Idea*, pp. 66–67, and John R. Commons, *Races and Immigrants in America* (2nd ed.; New York, 1920), pp. xviii, 5.

people which had been responsible for its original establishment and for its preservation in the face of considerable obstacles; both Commons and Commander were convinced that the American they had described was a thorough democrat, passionately devoted to the cause of liberty.

Note that in this case opposition to immigration was dictated by liberal, not conservative, political beliefs. Immigration was thought to constitute a threat to American democracy because of the traits of the American democrats themselves, and there was no indication that either Commons or Commander wanted these traits to be changed. Nativism in many respects appears to be an inherently conservative doctrine. It rests on the belief that specific groups are innately superior or inferior to other groups, on the corollary belief that certain groups of people may be endowed with the right or the duty to rule others, and on a strong adherence to a tradition and to a specific past. All these beliefs are profoundly conservative in their general implications. But in the political context of the early twentieth century, when Progressivism was beginning to flower, it is indisputable that many nativists were politically liberal, or rather that many liberals were nativists when they spoke on the subject of immigration. The apparent paradox is resolved by the realization that they were nativists precisely because of the profundity of their commitment to democracy and because of their reading of the American character.

Perhaps the most obvious exemplar of the connection between nativism and certain currents of liberal thought was the sociologist E. A. Ross. Ross was one of the best known of the many liberal scholars at the University of Wisconsin, and he was also one of the most vehement of the nativists. Generally speaking, academic proponents of nativism were less violent in their attacks on the immigrant and less extreme in extolling the virtues of the native American than non-academic proponents were, for reasons that are inherent in the nature of academic life. The typical academician would check the fervor of his presentation by considerations of professional propriety—he would probably wish to avoid laying himself open to charges of sensationalism from his colleagues. In addition, he would probably be in a better position than the non-academician to know both sides of the question, and fanaticism flourishes best on ignorance. But these considerations do not apply to Ross. The vehemence of some of his attacks on the immigrant was rarely equalled and never surpassed. He blamed immigration for increased illiteracy, lower intellectual standards, peonage in the economic system, bossism and corruption in the political system, and a striking and alarming growth in the spirit of class differences, and he predicted that such dislocations would become progressively more intense unless restrictions were enacted. The root of the trouble, he maintained, was that immigration was wiping out the original pioneering breed of the United States. The American character that had thrived on the frontier was being slowly destroyed, and as it deteriorated the pace of social progress became slower and slower. Immigration had to be restricted because the immigrants "must act as a drag on the social progress of the nation that incorporates them." Ross was saying in effect that immigration was an anti-democratic political force.[7]

The Progressives were interested above all in establishing— or re-establishing—American democracy, and anything that seemed to them to endanger it was to be opposed. It is interesting to examine the views of Jane Addams in this connection. Although she was not enlisted in the anti-immigrant crusade, she did note that the presence of the immigrant tended to inhibit political reform by providing political power for the anti-reform bosses of America's large cities.[8] Now, it is perfectly reasonable to point out, as Addams and many other Progressives did, that the bosses found their greatest source of electoral strength among immigrant groups. But most Progressives ignored the equally evident fact that immigrants lent their support to the bosses because they received fairly substantial favors in return. The big-city political machine was probably the most effective assimilative organization in American society. This reveals one of the underlying themes of the Progressive movement. The feeling that political behavior should not be dictated by sordid self-interest was fundamental to Progressive thought. Indeed, the transition from the Populism of the nineteenth century to the

[7] *The Old World in the New: The Significance of Past and Present Immigration to the American People* (New York, 1914). The quotation is on p. 230. See also Ross's book *What Is America?* (New York, 1919), pp. 3–20.

[8] Jane Addams, *Twenty Years at Hull House* (New York, 1910).

Progressivism of the twentieth involved not a change of program so much as a change of moral assumptions. Populist politics was a politics of interest; Progressive politics was a politics of morality. Populists fought primarily for the interests of a particular group in American society; Progressives strove for reforms which would root out corruption and evil wherever they existed and for the strengthening of the ideal of disinterested concern for the welfare of society as a whole. To the extent that immigration contributed to the corruption of American political life and rendered more difficult the realization of the goal that disinterested idealism should be the primary political motivation of all American citizens, Progressives were bound to be dismayed by it.

Of course, not all Progressives were nativists, and those who were differed substantially from other nativists. Generally speaking, they were much clearer-minded, because their concern with immigration was not obsessive. It was only one of many threats they perceived, while other nativists seemed to think that immigration restriction would solve all problems. The Progressives in the nativist movement were better able to recognize the other ways in which America was changing and did not exhibit the single-minded obtuseness that was one of the main features of nativist thought in general.

III

In the midst of this concern with immigration and the apprehension about the future of the American character that accompanied it, there appeared a curious tendency to exalt the American to even greater heights than he had held before. At the same time that nativists were contending that he was being overwhelmed by immigrant hordes, they began to insist that he was a paragon of all the virtues. Previously it had been generally conceded that the American had certain deficiencies in his character, but the deficiencies began to disappear when the attack on immigration began. Since it was the purpose of the nativists to restrict immigration, they naturally showed the immigrant in a very poor light and steadfastly refused to grant that he had any significant redeeming features. As the nativists put increasing stress on the inherent viciousness and depravity of the immigrant, the native American, by contrast, appeared to be more and more virtuous and intelligent, and nativist commentators on the American character were less and less inclined to admit the existence of *any* limitations in it.[9]

There is an interesting paradox in the nativist position here. One might reasonably inquire just how an individual with such admirable qualities could possibly be threatened seriously by a group of people as vastly inferior to him as the immigrants were supposed to be. The nativists appreciated the difficulty. They found a way out of it by following the general lines of an argument put forward by some of the anti-imperialists during the debate over the retention of the Philippines. Christopher Lasch has shown that the anti-imperialists were tinged with racism, that in fact some of their most insistent arguments rested on racist premises. They argued that Filipinos were incapable of self-government because of their racial deficiencies and that it was therefore impossible to incorporate the Philippines within the American body politic as another state in the Union. On the other hand, it would prove to be impossible for Americans to govern the Philippines effectively because even the superior racial endowments of the American governors of the islands would decay under the impact of the unfavorable geographic and climatic influences of the tropics.[10] The nativists were able to find in this anti-imperialist argument an example of how it might be possible to maintain a belief in racial superiority while issuing dire warnings about the destiny of the racially superior group. The idea of the degenerative influence of the tropics was

[9] For evidence of this attitude see Woodruff, *The Expansion of Races*, in which he argued that northern Europe was the world's "brain factory" and that people who came from this area were necessarily superior to all others. Madison Grant also believed that the "Nordic" was *generally* superior to all other peoples. See *The Passing of the Great Race, or the Racial Basis of European History* (4th ed.; New York, 1921) and *The Conquest of a Continent, or the Expansion of Races in America* (New York, 1933).

[10] "The Anti-Imperialists, the Philippines, and the Inequality of Man," *Journal of Southern History*, 24 (1958), 319–331. For two particularly strong statements of the unwholesome effects of life in the tropics see David Starr Jordan, *Imperial Democracy* (New York, 1899), pp. 44–45, and George S. Boutwell, *Problems Raised by the War* (Washington, D. C., 1898), p. 17.

useless to them, of course, but they found an equivalent in certain statistics concerning immigration.

It was not simply that immigrants were coming to the United States in huge numbers, for after all the native Americans still outnumbered them overwhelmingly. What worried the nativists was that the immigrants were multiplying much faster than the native Americans, so that it seemed inevitable that those who shared the immigrant heritage of viciousness and depravity would eventually outnumber those who were the products of the old American tradition. This argument necessitated an implicit revision of some basic attitudes about the American character. If the typical old American was a frontiersman, or the product of the frontier heritage, then, according to the standard picture of the frontiersman, one of his outstanding qualities was his ruggedness and his talent for survival under adverse conditions. But the nativist position required that the American be threatened by the immigrant, and so frontier ruggedness had to be temporarily forgotten. This indicates, for one thing, that the nativists' descriptions of the American character were to a considerable extent dictated by the tactical requirements of the nativist movement.

It also reveals some interesting things about the Progressive movement. Articulate nativism was largely the property of a more or less self-consciously aristocratic class, as is revealed by the concern that a superior minority would be overwhelmed by an inferior majority. But those Progressives who also happened to be nativists surely found it difficult to live with the anti-democratic implications of the nativist argument. Committed to making democratic government work more effectively, they could hardly be comfortable with the anti-majoritarian implications of nativism. This probably explains why Commons, for instance, took a nativist position not because he feared that native Americans would be overwhelmed by an immigrant majority but rather because he feared that Americans might institute a despotic majority rule to keep the immigrant minority in its place. He was worried about majority tyranny, but it would be a tyranny established and imposed by Americans to protect, at least for themselves, what they believed to be the essence of their political system. He apparently found it difficult to concede that a majority could be as depraved as the nativists insisted that an immigrant majority would be. To grant the validity of such an argument was entirely too dangerous to the general theory of democracy. Not all Progressives were as disturbed as Commons apparently was, though. There was in Progressivism an inner conflict between the avowed interest in democracy and the tendency on the part of many individual Progressives to think in terms of elite leadership. It would be untrue to say that they were not sincere democrats, but many of them thought of a democracy guided and led by a morally and intellectually superior elite; their nativism may well have been at least partly a product of this feeling.

The disposition to regard the American as universally superior and the immigrant as universally inferior was not characteristic of all nativists. There were some who maintained that immigration was contributing to national social dislocations because immigrants were *different* from native Americans and not necessarily because they were inferior to them. This attitude was rooted in the belief that homogeneity was necessary to the political and cultural health of the nation, and it was not incompatible with a willingness to be moderately charitable to the immigrant and to admit that he had many admirable qualities. "Almost any race is superior to others in some particular," said Charlotte Perkins Gilman, an ardent Progressive who was also deeply involved in the feminist movement. "Each has not only a right but a duty to develop its own special powers."[11] The implication was that continued immigration would have the unfortunate effect of destroying valuable elements in the cultures of the immigrants, since they would not be able to compete with the dominant American culture. Such concern for the cultural welfare of immigrants would be touching if one could manage to dispel the suspicion that the concern was dictated not by any real appreciation of the worthiness of the immigrant cultures and their possible contributions to American culture and character but rather by the need for a tactical position from which it would be possible to attack unrestricted immigration without appearing to be inhumane. It was a thoroughly specious argument. Morally analogous to the separate-but-equal doctrine, it

[11] "Is America Too Hospitable," *Forum*, 70 (1923), 1988. Charles W. Gould made the same point in *America, a Family Matter* (New York, 1922).

48

served the same function for the advocates of immigration restriction that the latter argument serves for advocates of segrega-
tion. The most that can be said of it is that it was probably not
consciously deprecatory; it was largely a product of the tactical
requirements of the nativist crusade.

IV

Tactical considerations also played an important part in the
nativists' insistence that national character in general and the
American character in particular were determined primarily
if not solely by racial factors. In itself the racist argument was
already somewhat old-fashioned; it had been the main stock in
trade of the Anglo-Saxonists who wrote on the American character. To support the nativist point of view, however, the argument was significantly altered. John Higham maintains that the
three main themes of American nativism have been racism, anti-
radicalism, and anti-Catholicism.[12] It is important to understand
how these nativist orientations differ: anti-Catholicism and anti-
radicalism are *reasons* for opposing immigration while racism
is a *weapon* for attacking it. To adopt a racist position on the
immigration question makes no sense unless one assumes that
racial intermixture would predispose the American people to
some kind of undesirable belief or behavior. Its usefulness to the
nativist cause is readily apparent. By insisting that the determinants of human thought and behavior were racial, that they
were carried in the germ plasm and were essentially unchange-
able, nativists could go on to argue that the problems which
immigration introduced were insoluble, since they were created
by the immigrants' hereditary characteristics. The problem was
not simply that the immigrants *were not* assimilated; it was that
they *could not be* assimilated, at least not until the American
character itself had been radically transformed by the racial
amalgamation of the immigrants and the native Americans. The
defects which the immigrants brought with them in their genetic
baggage were permanent and ineradicable. They would persist
even after racial intermixture had taken place, and this would

[12] *Strangers in the Land: Patterns of American Nativism, 1860–1925*
(New Brunswick, N. J., 1955), pp. 5–11.

mean the diminution and possibly even the complete extinction of the admirable qualities of the native American. The only possible course of action, therefore, was to minimize the extent of this potential disaster by preventing further immigration as quickly as possible.

For racism to be a truly effective weapon in the nativists' fight it had to be honed to a sharper intellectual edge. It had to be transformed from an attitude into a coherent philosophy. It was no longer sufficient to let it stand as the unstated major premise of interpretations of the American character; it had to be stated clearly and refined so that it could be openly defended and justified. As racism acquired a specific purpose, it also had to acquire a rationale and an intellectual apparatus. It had to become "scientific."

The source which the nativists pursued most eagerly in their quest for the required aura of scientific objectivity was the new science of genetics and the attempts that were being made to apply genetic knowledge to the study of human problems. Mendel's work and its further extension by men like Morgan, DeVries, and Weissman appeared to open the way to providing a detailed explanation of the precise way in which character traits were transmitted from one generation to the next. The nativists pounced on the opportunity thus offered. They argued that "recent discoveries in biology show that heredity is far more important than environment or education; for though the latter can develop, it cannot create."[13] The recent discoveries did not in fact show any such thing, but nativists were quite willing to believe that they did. Doctors with nativist leanings suddenly discovered that their medical training endowed them with a special wisdom on the social problem of immigration, and they presented their nativist views as if they were based on unimpeachable medical knowledge. Nativists eagerly appropriated the work of the eugenists, too. The eugenists, for their part, were usually quite willing to see their arguments thus appropriated, for most of them were sympathetic to the cause of immigration restriction. But they did manage to maintain some degree of scientific detachment. The eugenics movement did not become a prisoner of the nativist crusade, because it was a serious in-

[13] Hall, *Immigration*, p. 99.

tellectual movement in its own right and because the eugenists were for the most part members of the academic community and thus somewhat cautious in their pronouncements.[14] But if some of the eugenists were less ardent than the full-blooded nativists might have wished, the nativists contrived to ignore with the utmost cheerfulness this evidence of scientific caution and used the work of the eugenists whenever it came in handy.

The fact that racism was largely an *ad hoc* response, chosen because of its usefulness in a specific situation, is also revealed by the nativists' willingness to disregard their racist theories whenever they interfered with nativist purposes. One of the primary grounds for the rejection of the immigrant was that he was supposed to have been *made* unfit for democracy by his long experience with the political institutions of despotism. This implies that his characteristics as a political animal had been determined by particular historical experiences repeated over several generations, not by any genetic mechanism. These characteristics were spoken of as having been "bred into" the immigrant, of having become, in fact, part of his racial heritage. Yet one of the main principles of racist theory was that acquired characteristics could not be inherited. The nativists were concerned with securing the passage of legislation restricting immigration, not with presenting a perfectly consistent theory of racism.

The tactical importance of racism to the nativist cause is perhaps most strikingly revealed when one considers that it turned the nativists' basic arguments into nearly perfect examples of self-confirming hypotheses. Nativists contended that the racial differences between the American and the immigrant would make true assimilation impossible, that attempts to promote it through anything short of complete biological amalgamation of the native American and the immigrant would be futile. It is quite probable that the progress of assimilation was considerably slowed because many people assumed that conscious efforts to promote it were wastes of time and effort. (It is interesting to speculate how much faster assimilation might have occurred if more people had just assumed that it would occur swiftly, easily,

[14] Mark Haller, *Eugenics: Hereditarian Attitudes in American Thought* (New Brunswick, N. J., 1963), is a good secondary account of the eugenics movement.

and painlessly.) Since the nativists drummed away at the theme of genetic inferiority, the immigrants were treated like inferiors and thus were denied the opportunity to prove that they were *not* inferior. In other words, the assumption that the immigrant was inferior and could not change became one of the primary causes of his remaining for some time in an inferior position. The hypothesis confirmed itself. Again, there are obvious analogies between the arguments that nativists employed against immigrants and the current arguments that segregationists employ against Negroes.

V

The impact of nativism also produced a change in the time orientation of writings on the American character. Nativists portrayed the typical American as an admirable figure, but increasingly their strident warnings of the dangers of immigration forced them to set him against a background taken from the American past, not the present. They emphasized the original immigration to the American colonies and the "magnificent racial treasures"[15] which existed there, the process of rigorous selection by which the originally admirable qualities of the colonists had been even more fully developed, the love of political freedom expressed in and intensified by the American Revolution, the individualism, self-reliance, and adaptability that had been the products of life on the frontier. But this American character had been formed in the past and brought to a high state of development by forces that no longer existed. The colonial experience had ended long ago, and the frontier was now gone, too. The racial heritage was the last refuge of the true American character, and even this was in danger of being swamped by the immigrant influx. Therefore, the nativists had to discuss the American character as it had existed in the past, for immigration had already begun to work its vile influence on it in the present and would wreak even more appalling havoc in the future.

Behind this overt concern about immigration it is possible to

[15] Lothrop Stoddard, *The Rising Tide of Color Against White World-Supremacy* (New York, 1920), p. 261. The phrase was Stoddard's, but it expressed an idea which was the common property of almost every nativist.

detect a more profound disquiet for which immigration was but the symbol. Consider the following quotation from the political analyst and journalist Alleyne Ireland:

> The average voter in a large town brings into politics a mentality utterly different from that of the country voter. It is the mind of the propertyless wage-earner, of the clerk, of the shop assistant, of the day laborer, of a man herded with other men and profoundly affected by the herd instinct, of a man of weak individuality, of a man who spends his working hours doing things for other people and his leisure hours in having things done for him by other people, of a man whose life is passed in surroundings entirely created by machinery and in circumstances where his freewill is perpetually constrained by the contagion of an artificial environment, of a man who knows (or at least of whom it is known) that if he drops dead while at his work he can, in normal times, be replaced in an hour by another man who will do just as well.[16]

Ireland dressed this individual in American clothes, but he bore an uncanny resemblance to the generalized immigrant against whom the nativists had been turning their wrath. The lack of individuality, the "herd instinct," the tendency to want to have things done for one by someone else, the implied disposition toward socialism, all these qualities had been found in the immigrant by the nativists, and it was because of these qualities that they attacked him. One of the most frequent charges against him was that he tended to congregate in cities. This tendency toward urbanism was held up again and again as an unfavorable contrast with the healthy preference for agricultural life exhibited by the native American and the immigrants who had come to the United States in the earlier part of the nineteenth century. The virtues of the native American were agrarian virtues and were reinforced by his agrarian way of life; the vices of the immigrant were the vices of men brought up in an urban and industrial culture.

Nativists often spoke as if they felt that immigration was the

[16] *Democracy and the Human Equation* (New York, 1921), p. 190.

major, indeed the sole, threat to American life, but an examination of the roots of their anti-immigrant attitudes reveals their deeper fears. In an early article, Ross discussed the factors involved in "race superiority." He constructed a scale of five elements which he used to determine the relative standing of the various races. These elements were climatic adaptability, energy, self-reliance, foresight, and "value sense," roughly synonymous with economic ability. Except for the first and last items, this was the old list of the primary Anglo-Saxon virtues. It is therefore no surprise to find that Ross rated the American high on all of them. But he did not insist that the American was universally superior to men of other races. He felt that the colored races were more adaptable to a variety of climatic conditions than whites were. Further, he maintained that the American, except possibly for the sub-variety known as the "Yankee," had to take second place to the Jews and Chinese in economic and commercial aptitude. He felt that the virtues which had sustained the American in the past were becoming progressively less valuable in the modern world. The American was above all else a pioneer. This was fine in times of dynamic change, but in periods of relative stability the qualities of patience and frugality were more to be desired. The American, said Ross, "has been chiefly farmer and is only beginning to expose himself to the deteriorating influences of city and factory."[17]

In this early article, Ross did not express any serious fears concerning these "deteriorating influences." Later, however, after he had become acutely worried about the way in which America was being transformed, he expressed his fears in a full-scale assault on immigration. He felt that immigration was dangerous because it would create conditions that would place a premium upon those very qualities in which the American character was deficient. Again and again, Ross and other nativists asserted that the distinctive qualities of the American, produced by racial inheritance and the selective influences of colonization and the frontier, were not well suited to industrial and urban life.

An interesting perspective on the underlying sources of anti-immigrant feeling in this period is provided by the work of

[17] "The Causes of Race Superiority," *Annals of the American Academy of Political and Social Science*, 18 (1901), 67–89.

Monroe Royce, a Protestant minister and missionary who recorded his impressions on his native land after his return from a long stay abroad. He felt that immigration was a threat to American ideals, institutions, and character, but his view differed significantly from that of most nativists. Royce said of the typical American:

> He is perhaps, or has been, the quickest-witted, most fearless, most inventive, and the most adventurous person the world has ever known. But he is not, and never was, a plodder; and doesn't like continuous hard work. But the time has now come for these things, and he is found wanting, and is giving place to the dull-witted, heavy-handed foreigner, who is willing to work, and who knows how to work.[18]

Now, Beveridge had said quite emphatically that the American was a plodder; here Royce denied it, just as emphatically. Actually, in many ways they were in very close agreement; they simply used the word "plodder" in different ways. Beveridge's plodder was a man who stuck resolutely to the job at hand because of his confidence that determined effort would result in substantial future rewards; Royce's plodder was a man who continued in a distasteful and uninspiring job largely because he was incapable of doing, or even imagining, anything better. Beveridge's American plodded straight ahead in a dogged drive toward personal advancement; Royce's plodder shuffled along in a dreary rut. Beveridge would certainly have agreed with Royce that the American was definitely not a "plodder," at least as Royce used the term.

The difference in usage was due largely to the different contexts in which Beveridge and Royce were considering the American character. Beveridge saw the American pursuing an imperial destiny of considerable grandeur while Royce was worried about the way in which Americans were going to adapt themselves to a new economic situation. To Royce, the jack-of-all-trades, the typical American economic figure of the past, had become an anachronism in a modern society that demanded specialization, attention to detail, and an aptitude for the dull,

18 *The Passing of the American* (New York, 1911), p. 17.

repetitive tasks of modern industry. Like Croly, Royce was not opposed to industrialism in itself but was concerned because the new social and economic conditions in the United States required the development of a whole new set of characteristics in the American people. From this concern came his opposition to immigration: he felt that the Americans were likely to be hindered in the development of the necessary characteristics because they had fallen into the habit of letting the immigrants do their hard work for them.[19] Thus Royce and the other nativists arrived at the same position, but from opposite directions: nativists opposed immigration because they feared it would change the American character; Royce opposed it because he believed that it prevented necessary changes from taking place.

Royce did agree with other nativists that the American character was not suited to an urban and industrial society. Though he clearly saw industrialism in the American future and seemed to be pleased with the vision, below the surface one can detect a mood not of enthusiasm but of resignation. He pointed out the need for a change in the American character, but there is reason to believe that he did not like the kind of change it would have to be. After all, he felt that the immigrant—"the dull-witted, heavy-handed foreigner"—was ideally suited to industrial work. If the American character changed to adapt to industrial conditions, would it be any less unattractive? Royce gives no indication of thinking so.

Thus, the nativists were most deeply disturbed by the prospects of an industrial future for the United States. They made an identification—largely unconscious—between the immigrant and the urban and industrial society coming into being, and they were fighting to keep the agrarian society of the past from disappearing. Throughout their writings on the American character they portrayed the American as a person who lacked artistic ability and was somewhat deficient in economic and commercial aptitudes—the classic virtues of the city—while possessing in abundance individualism, self-reliance, and independence —the virtues of the country, born in the forests of Germany and polished to a fine edge on the frontier. Similarly, their repeated attacks on American materialism in contrast to the high idealism

[19] *Ibid.*, pp. 53–60, 118.

of the early years of the nation reflect their concern for a changing America. They blamed the immigrant for these changes, but were they not due instead to a fundamental change in the economic situation of the nation, a change which they saw but were not willing to admit? In opposing immigration, the nativists adopted a racist philosophy to belabor the immigrant, but their real concern was with the basic change in the economic and social foundations of their own civilization.

3

THE AMERICAN
CHARACTER IN NEED

THE ANTI-NATIVIST POSITION

I

Since a part of the nativist case depended upon an analysis of
the American character and the way in which it was likely to
be affected by immigration, those who opposed the restriction of
immigration found it necessary to present an alternative view of
the national character to refute nativist claims. As a result, the
whole discussion of the American character became firmly imprisoned in the controversy over immigration. It was largely
incidental to the main problem. The contending factions described the American character only because they could press
such descriptions into service in their arguments on the immigration question.

One would expect, therefore, that the anti-nativists would
present a picture of the American character that differed substantially from the nativist portrait. But this was not the case.
There were some differences of shading, tone, and emphasis, to
be sure, but on the whole the most striking feature of the anti-
nativist position on the American character was that on many
points it was in basic agreement with the nativist view. Many
anti-nativists even seemed to share the nativists' general ideas
about the immigrant.

The preceding remarks might be taken to imply that there was
a unified anti-nativist argument. No such implication is intended.
The opponents of restriction were not as united in the defense
of existing policy as the nativists were in their attack on it.
Nativism was, to a certain extent at least, a definite movement
toward a clearly defined goal, possessing an articulate and con-

59

sistent—although not always perfectly logical—doctrinal base. The nativists had the advantage of knowing exactly what they wanted and being able to state it simply. Their opponents, however, were a random collection of individuals who, for a wide variety of reasons, did not find nativism appealing. They searched frantically for an appropriate and telling response to the nativist challenge, but there was little or no coordination of their individual efforts. They suddenly found themselves required to provide a reasoned defense for policies whose validity they had hitherto taken for granted, and they were not prepared for the effort, at least not to the point of being able to present a united front. It is often very difficult to justify one's basic assumptions, because one of the important features of such assumptions is that they are usually accepted as a matter of course, without question, and without conscious thought. Suddenly forced to make their assumptions articulate and to defend them, the anti-nativists, not surprisingly, went off in many different directions in their analyses of the American character, the character of the immigrants, the forces which had molded them, how they would probably interact, and what was likely to happen to the American character in the future.

II

On one proposition, however, the anti-nativists were forced to unite in order to present even a remotely effective response to the nativist attack. The essence of their position was that the United States had benefited from immigration in the past and would continue to benefit from it in the future. Previously, even those who were generally sympathetic to the immigrant had not gone that far. Consider, for instance, the position of Charles W. Eliot:

Thus every capable American, from youth to age, is bent on bettering himself and his condition. Nothing can be more striking than the contrast between the mental condition of an average American belonging to the laborious classes, but conscious that he can rise to the top of the social scale, and that of a European mechanic, peasant, or tradesman, who knows that he cannot rise out of his class, and is content with his hereditary classification. The state of mind of the American prompts to constant struggle for self-improvement and the acquisition of all sorts of property and power.[1]

Now, this is not at all different from what many nativists had said about the American and the immigrant. But Eliot was not a nativist. Later in the same essay he said:

> In two respects the absorption of large numbers of immigrants from many nations into the American commonwealth has been of great service to mankind. In the first place, it has demonstrated that people who at home have been subject to every sort of aristocratic or despotic or military oppression become within less than a generation serviceable citizens of a republic; and, in the second place, the United States have thus educated to freedom many millions of men.[2]

He felt that immigration should be continued, but it is important to realize that he felt this way because of the benefits that would accrue to the immigrant, not to the American. Unlike the nativists, Eliot felt that the immigrants could and would change when exposed to the beneficent influences of the free air of America. We can see in Eliot a proponent of the old idea that it was America's mission to set an example to the rest of the world, to show that men could live under a libertarian system and make political democracy work. But such arguments did not adequately counter the nativist case. It was not enough to show that immigration had done no harm, or even to maintain that it had benefited the immigrants. Such arguments could not be expected to generate much enthusiasm in the general public. It was necessary to show that immigration was a positive benefit to the United States, and the anti-nativists accordingly presented a set of propositions which may be collectively called the idea of immigrant gifts.

It had long been fairly generally agreed that the native American was lacking in artistic sensibility and that this deficiency might be corrected, or at least balanced, by adding to the nation's

[1] "Five American Contributions to Civilization," reprinted in *American Contributions to Civilization and Other Essays and Addresses* (New York, 1907), pp. 22–23. This address was originally delivered in 1896.
[2] *Ibid.*, p. 31.

population a stock of peoples with a strong artistic heritage. This idea, too, was quite old and had in fact become commonplace. Consequently it was no longer capable of attracting much attention. In addition, it had become almost completely irrelevant, for the nativists had made the primary issue not the perfection of the American but his preservation in the face of what they insisted were substantial threats to his continued existence. In such a situation an interest in art and culture might well have seemed to be frivolous.

To meet this fear that the American way of life was in peril, the anti-nativists enlarged the idea of immigrant gifts to argue that the immigrant, far from being a threat, was in fact the nation's best hope. It was the immigrant, according to the new argument, who was primarily responsible for preserving the original ideals of America in their pure form. These ideals *were* in danger of dying out, but only because native Americans, more interested in material comforts than in liberty, had begun to take them for granted. The very presence of the immigrant served to remind Americans that there were areas in the world where these ideals were not realized in practice. Thus the immigrant helped the native American to recognize and appreciate the unique virtues of America.[3] More important, the immigrant rekindled the idealistic spark of devotion to freedom. In short, the immigrant could save the American character from the twin dangers of commercialism and materialism. Mary Antin, herself an immigrant, believed that the basis of the American character was the Puritan ethic: idealism, courage, a sense of political and civic conviction, respect for education, culture, and the arts, constructiveness, and determination, and she insisted that these virtues were more highly developed in the immigrant than in the native American. She looked to the immigrant to spark a revival of those virtues in native Americans by giving them a living example of an individual motivated by idealism, not by the materialism that had infected most Americans and caused most of the evils plaguing the nation.[4]

[3] Oscar Straus, *The American Spirit* (New York, 1913), pp. 82–86.
[4] *They Who Knock at Our Gates: A Complete Gospel of Immigration* (Boston, 1914).

III

It is interesting that the anti-nativists, like the nativists, seemed to feel that most of the traditional American principles, at least the most significant ones, pertained to political life. Both groups tended to define Americanism as adherence to a set of political beliefs, practices, and institutions. The anti-nativists, of course, were almost forced to adopt this position, because the most prominent single charge in the nativist assault on the immigrant was that he lacked political acumen. They accepted the nativist challenge willingly, quite prepared, at least in this case, to do battle on a field chosen by their opponents. They made the point that native Americans did not seem to know what Americanism was, or, if they did, that they did not act on the basis of their knowledge. Many people agreed with Frances Kellor "that we shall have to Americanize our native Americans first."[5] They argued that the attachment of the immigrants to the basic principles of Americanism was much firmer than that of many native Americans, because immigrants did not take liberty for granted. In their search for a new way of life, they had found the courage to give up their homes and travel long distances. "This spirit was that which brought this nation into being," said Edward Hale Bierstadt, "and it is one to be encouraged."[6]

Another interesting feature of the debate between the nativists and the anti-nativists is that neither group bothered to define with any precision just what America's distinctive political principles were, beyond a general devotion to liberty and political democracy. Shailer Mathews, the dean of the divinity school of the University of Chicago, was much more specific than most when he outlined the major American ideals:

First, a society composed of free and equal individuals; second, democracy as an actual way of free individuals living together in equality and peace; third, a written constitution embodying the principles of such democracy; fourth, cooperative sovereignty.[7]

[5] *Straight America: A Call to National Service* (New York, 1916), p. 44.
[6] *Aspects of Americanization* (Cincinnati, 1922), p. 158.
[7] *The Validity of American Ideals* (New York, 1922), p. 41.

63

But even this is distressingly inexact. It is possible, for instance, to get involved in endless discussions of exactly what is meant, or should be meant, by the statement "All men are created equal," and Mathews' propositions present the same sort of difficulty.

Peter Roberts, the head of the Y.M.C.A., also offered a definition of the characteristic ideals of America:

> When a typical American town is visited we come face to face with what America means to civilization. The streets are clean, the homes are well kept, the yards and lawns are cared for, the gardens are full of flowers. The church and school are centers of light, the public library is well patronized, literature comes to the homes, and the children are trained in the ways of virtue and decency. That is the character of towns which are true to the American type.[8]

From this picture, one might conclude that the American heritage consisted most significantly of legislation on public sanitation, that America's chief contribution to civilization was the street cleaner, and that an individual's loyalty to American ideals was to be measured by the size of the morning glories in his garden or the number of books he took out of the library. But insofar as these ideals implied an underlying respect for orderliness and decency and for the qualities of mind and heart necessary to build and maintain towns of "the American type," they are approximately comparable to those cited by Mathews.

For the most part, the nativists and the anti-nativists simply seemed to assume that everyone knew, or should know, what Americanism was. Part of this unconcern with precise definition was undoubtedly due to the fact that they were not really interested in formulating a coherent conception of the American character but were instead using "Americanism" as a slogan with a powerful emotional appeal in the debate over immigration. Such slogans need not be precise; in fact, they are probably more effective if they are not, for then each individual to whom the appeal is addressed can invest it with his own meanings and thus become more likely to respond to it. But we can also see here one of the inherent difficulties in the concept of national

[8] *The New Immigration: A Study of the Industrial and Social Life of Southeastern Europeans in America* (New York, 1912), p. 306.

character. One can either choose to describe it in terms which are so general as to be almost meaningless or one can choose to make his description specific and detailed, thus laying himself open to the charge that there are many people to whom his description does not apply. In the majority of instances, analysts of the American character have preferred the first approach.

The discussion of American political ideals reveals still another point of contact between the nativists and their opponents. Given the anti-nativist contention that America would benefit from immigration, one might have expected them to argue that the American character would be made into something new and better. They did, of course, insist that the American character would be improved, but the improvement they foresaw was not to be accomplished by the creation of something new, but by the return to something old. Their eyes were fixed just as firmly on the past as the nativists' were. Like the nativists, they insisted that the highest and best type of American character had existed when the nation was young. Whatever improvement was to occur as a result of immigration would consist of a revival of the old patterns. They agreed with the nativists that any change in the American character as it had existed in the past was likely to be a change for the worse.

IV

There was some disagreement among the anti-nativists on just what the immigrant was going to do for the American character and just how he was going to improve it. Not all of them gazed only into the past. Some of them also looked into the future, to an American character significantly modified by the addition of some of the traits of the immigrants in such a way as to correct some of its long-standing deficiencies. Friends of the immigrant had long contended that he had benefited the economic life of the nation with his labor, especially valuable in a nation which needed manpower. They now extended the argument to include quality of labor as well as quantity. Edward A. Steiner, Czech-born professor of applied Christianity at Grinnell College, argued that

the native-born American is apt to lack the sense of thoroughness, the genius for application and devotion to detail, necessary in some of the more skilled trades. It is therefore not unreasonable to say that without the particular types of labour furnished by the immigrants, industrial activities in the United States would have been greatly hampered. Foreign labour manifests a certain work courage, a ready facing of the full day's task, and honesty in the performance of duty.[9]

The views of Frances Kellor on this point are similar. There is little doubt that she felt that the immigrant's primary contribution to American life was economic. What he possessed above all was a capacity to labor in industrial situations, for which he was better suited than the native American. She pointed out that he had "a capacity for faithful operation and a natural instinct for perfection," discipline in working with others, patience which allowed him to put up with monotonous and drudging work, and a sense of frugality which would help to eliminate waste. She felt that such characteristics were extremely valuable and would take on a much greater value in the future. "The American producer who must compete in the markets of the world, including America, with the products which these races will make in their native lands, may well consider whether the encouragement of immigration of races possessing these qualities in a high degree is not a matter of considerable importance to American commerce."[10]

Mixed in with their praise of the immigrant as an industrial worker, however, there is an unmistakable note of condescension. What Steiner and Kellor were saying, in effect, was that there were certain types of work for which immigrants were better fitted because such tasks were too dull, repetitive, and unchallenging to stimulate the native American worker. Neither of them saw the immigrant in any sort of a managerial position.

[9] *The Making of a Great Race: Racial and Religious Cross-Currents in the United States* (New York, 1929), p. 22. Steiner had made the same point about the American character fourteen years earlier in *Introducing the American Spirit* (New York, 1915), p. 108. At that time, however, this deficiency concerned him because he was apprehensive about the possibility of American involvement in the World War and the capacity of the American to sustain a major war effort with these deficiencies in his character.

[10] *Immigration and the Future* (New York, 1920), p. 261.

And Steiner implied that the presence of the immigrant who was suited to industrial labor would have unfortunate side effects on American society:

As in agriculture, so in industry, the American does hard labor with skill, and efficiently, but he does not accept it as his permanent lot either for himself or his children. Moreover, our machine-driven industrial life has increased certain monotonous drudgeries, which are distasteful to the quicker-witted American. There is little or no chance for self-expression or for adventure, in handling a punching-machine, or turning the same lever the same way all the time.[11]

The individual adapted to this kind of labor emerges from Steiner's portrayal as a slow-witted drudge, a sort of mindless machine. Indeed, Steiner felt that it was distinctly possible that "too much of the peasant strain may lower the present level of our intelligence."[12] The implication contained in Steiner's work, and in Kellor's, was that such labor as the immigrants could perform well, valuable though it might be in an increasingly industrialized world, was somewhat beneath the native American, and that an American character adapted to life in an industrial economy would necessarily lose something of its original nobility and fineness.

The immigrant, therefore, would improve the American character only in the sense that he would help to make the best of a bad situation. The immigrant would be the source of several necessary—but rather crude and vulgar—traits which would enable the American character to survive and prosper in an unfamiliar world of industrialism and urbanism. The anti-nativists, it turns out, were just as committed to a pro-agrarian, anti-industrial view of the ideal American society as the nativists were. The difference was that the nativists seemed to feel that the ideal was still attainable, and the anti-nativists did not. But they agreed on a definition of the ideal.

The distrust of industrialism and urbanism that was character-

11 *Making of a Great Race*, p. 21.
12 *Ibid.*, p. 63.

istic of many anti-nativists can be seen in the writings of Jane Addams. Her biography, *Twenty Years at Hull House*,[13] begins with an idyllic account of her early life in a small town in northern Illinois. Later she left the country and went to Chicago, not from any preference for the city, but rather because her social conscience led her there; she wanted to be where the problems were. Obviously, she would not have gone to work in the city in the first place unless she believed that something could be done to improve conditions there, but one still gets the feeling that she regarded herself as a missionary, carrying civilization and light to less fortunate people, and that she felt that the problems would not have arisen in the first place if everyone had stayed in the country. In her mind and heart, the city appears to be necessarily dirty and evil and inherently inferior to the country. Her nostalgic reverence for handicrafts and for the folk arts of rural communities, foreign and American, is also revealing.

Anti-nativists agreed with the nativists and with the Progressives who were attacking the greed of the political bosses, the cupidity of the robber barons, and the coarseness of the *nouveaux riches* that the American soul was endangered, if it had not already been overcome, by materialism, that the typical American of the past had been a staunch idealist but was in these decadent latter days becoming increasingly crass and greedy. Sometimes these critics seemed almost to equate materialism with the mere possession of material riches. At the very least, they were highly suspicious of the industrial machine, which was producing wealth in increasing amounts. They, nativists and anti-nativists alike, unconsciously regarded materialism and industrialism as nearly synonymous and felt that if America was becoming industrialized it was necessarily becoming materialistic. To embrace industrialism was to violate the basic traditions of the nation and to be untrue to the American character. The anti-nativists differed with the nativists only in their feeling that this violation was necessary and inevitable. They did not believe that it was possible to turn the clock back to the purer, happier days of the pre-industrial past. They felt nostalgia for what had been, but, with an attitude which suggests they were taking some vile-

[13] (New York, 1910).

tasting medicine, they resolutely turned their attention to a consideration of what had to be.

V

Since nativists had based their attack on the immigrant on a set of racist doctrines, anti-nativists responded by arguing that group characteristics were not determined by heredity.[14] Steiner said: " 'Blood is thicker than water,' but culture is thicker than blood." In other words, group characteristics could be transmitted by non-genetic means and racial characteristics were malleable under environmental pressures.[15] One significant reflection of this repudiation of the hereditary principle in social analysis was that the anti-nativists, far more than the nativists, couched their discussions of the American character in terms of the distinctive values and ideals of American civilization and devoted correspondingly less attention to the description of the character traits of a supposedly typical American. They tended to describe the American by considering what he thought and believed rather than what he was genetically.

This difference between the nativists and the anti-nativists was relative, not absolute. Nativists often concerned themselves with American ideals, and anti-nativists just as frequently spoke as if they believed that there was such a thing as a "typical" American or even an "American race." Much as the anti-nativists may have rejected racist theory, racist notions had a way of creeping into the thoughts and writings of the most vigorous opponents of immigration restriction. Despite the fact that there was an increasingly wide appreciation of the theoretical shortcomings of racism, it was apparently so deeply ingrained in the thinking of many commentators on the social scene that they resorted to it unconsciously when they wanted to explain the persistence of group traits through several generations.

[14] It is significant that the major figure in the attack on racist theory in the United States in the early twentieth century was himself an immigrant. Franz Boas devoted much of his work to an investigation of and attack upon the theories of the racists. His major work, *The Mind of Primitive Man* (New York, 1921), was an imposing assault upon the assumption that heredity was the primary factor in determining human characteristics.

[15] *Making of a Great Race*, pp. 45–53.

Frank Hankins, a professor of sociology at Smith College, illustrates this ambivalence. He was extremely critical of the race theorists of Europe and the United States. When he began to describe the American character, however, he did it in terms that were heavily freighted with the theories he had just rejected. He said, for instance, that the American colonists were a superior group of people because of their excellent racial inheritance. Though it is not fair to Hankins to call him a racist, at least not in the fullest sense of the word, he was deeply influenced by the eugenics movement and did believe that important mental and emotional traits were determined primarily by heredity. The result was that there were affinities between his views and those of the racists, despite his scathing comments. His example is quite obvious, but he was by no means alone in his inability to free himself completely from the habit of thinking in racist terms, or at least of expressing himself in a racist vocabulary.[16]

The sociologists Robert E. Park and Herbert A. Miller recognized that many of those who were sympathetic to the immigrant suffered from the same inconsistency. They met the problem forthrightly by insisting that the whole concept of immigrant gifts was sociologically absurd. They were not unsympathetic toward the immigrant—far from it—but they were deeply disturbed by the view that the immigrant would show particular racial aptitudes for particular fields of endeavor. To them, this appeared to be nothing more than a slight variation on the racists' belief in the hereditary specialization of function among human groups, and they wanted to have nothing at all to do with it.[17]

---

[16] *The Racial Basis of Civilization: A Critique of the Nordic Doctrine* (New York, 1926). Frances Kellor referred to "racial powers, instincts, and susceptibilities" in *Straight America*, p. 64, and Steiner stated his belief in the potentially beneficial effects of "the infusion of peasant blood into our new racial body" in *Making of a Great Race*, p. 63. Perhaps this racism was purely semantic, but so was the racism of many avowed racists.

[17] *Old World Traits Transplanted* (New York, 1921), pp. 299–302. Another sociologist, Peter Speek, reversed the normal pattern by defending racism in theory but giving a non-racist interpretation of the American character, in which the primary influence was the frontier. (Peter A. Speek, "The Meaning of Nationality and Americanization," *American Journal of Sociology*, 32 [1926], 237–249.)

VI

Although there were significant areas of agreement between the nativists and the anti-nativists on many points in their discussions of the American character, many anti-nativists took a radically different view on the question of the desirability of national unity. Nativists maintained that national unity, by which they usually meant racial homogeneity, was essential to the effective functioning of American political institutions and possibly to the flowering of a truly worthwhile American culture as well. Some anti-nativists tended to agree. Both Roberts and Kellor argued that the benefits to be derived from the incorporation into American life of some of the desirable cultural traits of the immigrants were outweighed by the paramount necessity of assimilating the immigrant as quickly as possible in order to achieve the higher goal of national unity.[18] But others put forward the idea that homogeneity was not intrinsically better than heterogeneity and that, indeed, there was an inherent value in diversity.

Josiah Royce expressed this idea quite clearly. He upheld the value of "provincialism"—loyalty to a particular locality and its customs, traditions, and ideals. He maintained that the cultivation of provincialism would help to establish a sense of community spirit in America, a sense which was all too likely to be lacking because of the great mobility of the American population; that it would provide a necessary balance to the effects produced by the nearly uniform exposure of the American people to modern mass communications, a strong tendency toward the virtual extinguishing of individuality and creativity, and the reduction of the American people to "a dead level of harassed mediocrity"; and that it would help to solve the most serious problem of popular government in the United States, the unfortunate tendency to surrender to mob spirit, to resign individual judgments in favor of the current opinions of the crowd. This is a tendency to be feared in any popular government, but he felt that it was

[18] Peter Roberts, *The Problem of Americanization* (New York, 1920), and Kellor, *Straight America*, exemplify this attitude in that in both books the authors consciously and explicitly subordinate the idea of immigrant gifts to the necessity of assimilating the immigrant to achieve national unity.

especially acute in the United States, where organs of mass communication made it possible to spread the contagion of popular hysteria far beyond the limits of the immediate locality. Royce argued that it was thus imperative to encourage the development of small groups and small-group loyalties:

> Freedom, I should say, dwells now in the small social group, and has its securest home in the provincial life. The nation by itself, apart from the influence of the province, is in danger of becoming an incomprehensible monster, in whose presence the individual loses his right, his self-consciousness, and his dignity. The province must save the individual.[19]

He saw national unity as a real danger to the continued existence of much that was valuable in American life and the American character.

Royce's fears of the growing tendency toward conformity and uniformity exemplified an idea which was later to become important. De Tocqueville had noted this tendency in American civilization, but it was not widely emphasized by Americans themselves in his day. Yet in time it was to become an almost constant theme in analyses of the American character, and the pressures toward conformity exerted by mass communications were to be widely discussed. Royce was among the first native commentators to express concern over this phenomenon. It can be interpreted as evidence of Royce's distrust of the effects of modern industrial civilization, for mass communications, of course, were a product of that civilization.

Later the arrogant insistence of the leaders of the campaign for "Americanization" that the immigrant be immediately molded to preconceived notions of Americanism called forth more defenses of the proposition that there was an inherent value to be derived from the diversification of American life. It was argued that diversity had both cultural and political benefits. Julius Drachsler formulated the concept of a "synthetic" culture in which the immigrants were to be encouraged to contribute to the intellectual development of the United States not by retaining their old cultural forms but by expressing their distinctive ideas as individuals, rather than as

[19] *Race Questions, Provincialism, and Other American Problems* (New York, 1908), pp. 57–108.

THE ANTI-NATIVIST POSITION

representatives of any particular ethnic or cultural group.[20]
Constantine Panunzio, a naturalized immigrant, questioned the
political effects of an overemphasis on unity:

> Recent events of world-wide magnitude are too vivid in
> our memories to need specific mention of what may over-
> take nations which follow the god of intensified national-
> ity. If the history of civilization has been at all correctly
> written it would seem to point to the conclusion that a
> self-centered culture is capable of driving a people head-
> long toward the precipices of destruction and of setting
> a whole civilization into flames.[21]

Of all those who upheld the value of diversity in American
life the most important single figure was the philosopher
Horace Kallen. Strangely, Kallen, a student and disciple of
the pragmatist William James, came to conclusions which
were remarkably similar to those of the idealist Josiah Royce,
James's colleague, friend, and opponent. Beginning from the
Jamesian doctrine of pluralism, Kallen defined an ideal of
American life and institutions which he called "cultural pluralism"—an ideal of cultural diversity and richness, a "federal state"
not only in political and administrative matters but in cultural
affairs as well. Though this ideal closely resembled Royce's ideal
of provincialism, there were differences. While Royce defined
provincialism as a manifestation of geographical sectionalism,
Kallen's pluralism consisted in encouraging cultural diversity
throughout all sections and classes of the population. In broad
outline, however, the two ideals were nearly identical in that
they upheld the value, indeed the necessity, of diversity in the
face of increasing pressures toward deadly uniformity.

Kallen maintained that the presence of the immigrant had
done much to implement this ideal and had helped improve the
situation that had existed at the end of the Civil War:

> The prevailing emotional tone of the American of this
> period was one of self-assurance rising swiftly to self-glorifi-
> cation. Contagion from the prosperous economic enterprise

[20] *Democracy and Assimilation: The Blending of Immigrant Heritages
in America* (New York, 1920).
[21] *Immigration Crossroads* (New York, 1927), p. 207.

of the nation was not without a large influence on this feeling. There went with it a vast resilient faith, a confidence in the excellence of the American being and the happy outcome of American undertakings. . . . A naive pride of race and cult, attested socially in the rise of numerous social and religious historical societies and an identification of personal success with national progress, went with it. Optimistic emotion engendered by the urgent adventure of the winning of the continent absorbed all the contradictions in the American scene and projected an image of the "typical American," puritan and pioneer, sentimental and ruthless, snob and democrat, cock of the roost with Fortunatus' cap on his head, sitting pretty on the top of the world and whistling "Yankee Doodle."[22]

Heartily thankful that this was not the American character of the present, Kallen insisted that the change had been wrought by the influence of the immigrant. For the native American was not an especially admirable figure in his eyes:

. . . the contemporary representative "average" American of British stock—an individualist speaking an English dialect, interested in getting on, kind, neighborly, not too scrupulous in business, rather elemental in his pleasures, indulgent to his women, unthinkingly devoted to "laissez-faire" in economics and politics, very respectable in private life, tending to liberalism and mysticism in religion, naively credulous of the black arts and the sciences; moved, where his economic interests are unaffected, by formulas rather than ideas, in all matters by preference a "booster" rather than a "knocker." He typifies the aristocracy of America.[23]

In a note, Kallen mentioned that Sinclair Lewis' novel *Babbitt* "is a close, if somewhat external study of the type."[24] To the extent that America had freed itself from Babbittry, the immigrant was responsible.

[22] *Culture and Democracy in the United States: Studies in the Group Psychology of the American Peoples* (New York, 1924), pp. 20–21.
[23] *Ibid.*, p. 83.
[24] *Ibid.*

Kallen's conception of what the immigrant could do for American life was predicated upon a long historical discussion of American culture and character. In this historical reconstruction, he seemed to be reviving the Frontier Thesis, but he modified it by giving it a strong pessimistic twist. In Kallen's treatment there was none of the sense of exaltation produced by the wide availability of land and resources that appeared in other hymns to the American West; instead, there was a profound terror in the face of a completely empty and therefore completely inhuman continent. Man was not uplifted by this experience; he was overwhelmed by it—and the result was fear, withdrawal, and a kind of cultural agoraphobia. As the land was settled, the fear was allayed, but it was never completely erased. The pioneer was affected by it, and his character was shaped primarily by the fact that he was a civilized man forced into a primitive mold by the necessities of life in a primitive country. He was a man with a dual personality, at once civilized and primitive, and the victim of constant strain and tension between these opposed forces. The tension was summed up in the conflict between the two stock figures of the American past, the Puritan and the pioneer: "The pioneer is thus a Puritan compelled to live in the primitive present; the Puritan is the pioneer, remembering the civilized past."

These two facets of the American character still persisted, according to Kallen, but they had been transformed by fundamental changes in the conditions of economic life in the United States. The white-collar worker, who was a proletarian despite his bourgeois appearance, was subject to precisely the same kind of strains and tensions between opposed facets of his personality as the pioneer had been forced to endure. This time the dualism was a conflict between the requirements imposed upon employees by new patterns of highly mechanized industry and political doctrines which suited an older, bygone state of social and industrial development. The individualistic doctrines of the American past were radically out of harmony with the pressures toward uniformity in the American present. It was in this context that the immigrant emerged as the savior of America, because the various ethnic groups in the United States constituted "reservoirs of individuality" against the forces of science and the machine that were tending to reduce the nation to uniformity:

If then cultural history and the American present are any index, the cultural prospect has been enriched, not depleted by the immigration, settlement, and self-maintenance in communities of the peoples of all Europe upon the North American continent. The pioneer Puritan and the puritan Pioneer have thereby received their foils. Color and import have been added to life in the United States, and if the spirit of a co-operative liberty can be poured into the folkways of the British stock and insured in continuance among the others, the national fellowship of cultural diversities should eventually come to fulfillment in a truly "transnational America," a new and happy form of associative harmony.[25]

In certain respects, Kallen's treatment was in basic agreement with other analyses of the American character made at roughly the same time. He saw the American character as a combination of the Puritan and the pioneer, and so did most other people when they considered the problem in historical perspective. He perceived a tension between agrarian and industrial life in the United States, and this tension was at the bottom of many other treatments. He felt that the immigrant would compensate for certain deficiencies in the American character, and he was echoed in this belief by all who believed that immigration should not be restricted.

In certain significant respects, however, Kallen's analysis was divergent from the mainstream of contemporary opinion. His low regard for the qualities and capabilities of the Puritan-pioneer was not widely shared by his contemporaries whether they were racists or non-racists, nativists or anti-nativists. Like Turner, most analysts of the American character looked into the past and considered what they found there to be superior in most ways to what existed in the present and was likely to exist in the future. They felt that the Puritan was admirable, that the pioneer was admirable, and that the combination of

[25] *Ibid.*, pp. 203–232.

the two increased the good qualities of each geometrically. Kallen was not enchanted by the American character as it had existed in the past. He insisted that its deficiencies were becoming increasingly apparent and increasingly dangerous because of the transformations that were taking place in American society. It was the presence of the immigrant that would rescue the American character from the impasse into which it had been led, would relieve the sapping tension between ideal and reality, between belief and actuality, between an agrarian past and an industrial present, and would thereby create an American character that was not only new but better than what had existed before.

4

THE AMERICAN
CHARACTER IN THE 1920's

REBELS AND CRITICS

I

The intellectual atmosphere of the 1920's was marked by a conscious rejection of the mood and attitudes that had been characteristic of the pre-war era. In large sections of the American intellectual community there was a general loss of optimism, a repudiation of the fundamental assumptions of American intellectual life up to that time. According to Henry F. May, World War I marked the end of American innocence.[1] The high-flown moral idealism and the complacent belief in progress that had been the primary articles of faith among most American intellectuals in the late nineteenth and early twentieth centuries were crushed by the war, and the post-war era saw the prominence of a group of American intellectuals who felt that these beliefs were old-fashioned, naive, and even stupid.

These new attitudes were reflected in the discussion of the American character during the decade. Many American artists and thinkers seemed to suffer from a pervasive feeling of discontent, almost of disgust. Whereas previous commentators had emphasized the excellence of American civilization and character, these critics vigorously assailed their deficiencies. The qualities that the self-confident analysts at the turn of the century had regarded as a matter for self-congratulation, that the nativists had thought of as something to be defended and protected, that the anti-nativists had seen as capable of adapting, through the

[1] *The End of American Innocence: A Study of the First Years of Our Own Time, 1912–1917* (New York, 1959).

79

healthy influence of immigration, to a rapidly changing social and economic order, were to the intellectuals of the 1920's a matter for contempt. Some of them seemed to believe that the deficiencies could be corrected, others felt only that they afforded opportunities for cynically amused observation. But in any case the American character was to be despised.

When they looked at the American character they did not see the vigorous Anglo-Saxon individualist that the early racists had portrayed. They did not see the noble defender of racial purity and white man's civilization, struggling manfully against immigrant hordes, that the nativists had extolled. They did not see the anti-nativists' American, a man deficient in certain respects being brought into closer harmony with the realities of a new society through the beneficial effects of immigration. They saw instead a grasping materialist, harassed and harried by a driving compulsion to accumulate, and a determined conformist, slavishly adhering to public opinion. They saw in him nothing of nobility or refinement. They saw only pettiness, vulgarity, and, above all, fear. They contended that fear was the driving component behind most of the characteristic behavior patterns of the American. He was, as they saw him, a man afraid: of himself, of other people, of his whole environment. Fear governed all his relationships, all his reactions to the world around him.

II

The most pungent expression of this point of view came from H. L. Mencken. Perhaps the least profound of all the self-consciously critical writers of the 1920's, Mencken was also the most entertaining, the most widely read, and the best known. He labeled the typical American a "boob"—but not so much of a boob as to be unaware that in free competition with more generously endowed people he would come off second-best. This awareness caused Americans to "lack the ease and tolerance, the fine adventurousness and love of hazard which go with a sense of firm security—in other words with a sense of genuine superiority."[2] The American was terrified by the realization of his inferiority: "The normal American of the 'pure-blooded'

2 *Prejudices, Fourth Series* (New York, 1924), p. 40.

majority goes to rest every night with an uneasy feeling that there is a burglar under the bed, and he gets up every morning with a sickening fear that his underwear has been stolen."[3] He did not allow this fear to show, but his characteristic stance of bravado and boldness was nothing more than a protective mechanism designed to disguise, from himself and others, his actual inferiority:

> What lies beneath the boldness is not really an independent spirit, but merely a talent for crying with the pack. When the American is most dashingly assertive it is a sure sign that he feels the pack behind him, and hears its comforting braying, and is well aware that his doctrine is approved. He is not a joiner for nothing. He joins something, whether it be a political party, a church, a fraternal order or one of the idiotic movements that incessantly ravage the land, because joining gives him a feeling of security, because it makes him a part of something larger and safer than he is himself, because it gives him a chance to work off steam without running any risk. The whole thinking of the country thus runs down the channel of mob emotion; there is no actual conflict of ideas, but only a succession of crazes. It is inconvenient to stand aloof from these crazes, and it is dangerous to oppose them. In no other country in the world is there so ferocious a short way with dissenters; in none other is it socially so costly to heed the inner voice and to be one's own man.[4]

Most of Mencken's associates accepted the broad outline of the picture he painted. This highly uncomplimentary view of the American character was one part of a general assault on the basic premises of American thought up to that time, of an attempt to undermine what had come to be widely regarded as an intellectual Old Guard—the "official" custodians of American culture, the defenders of an old-fashioned, desiccated literature and philosophy, men like William Dean Howells, Paul Elmer

[3] *Ibid.*, p. 39.
[4] George Jean Nathan and H. L. Mencken, *The American Credo: A Contribution Toward the Interpretation of the National Mind* (New York, 1920), pp. 41–42.

More, and Irving Babbitt. These men were condemned not because they differed so widely from the rebels in their analysis of America and the American character; Babbitt, at least, held a view of the American character that was quite similar to Mencken's. Babbitt, too, was deeply disturbed by the materialism and commercialism of the American and by his increasing tendency toward conformity. He felt there was a danger that the United States would become "a huge mass of standardized mediocrity" and that this conformity was beginning to take on the marks of fanaticism: " It is becoming the dangerous privilege of the United States to display more of the crusading temper than any other country in both its domestic and foreign policies."[5] But if Babbitt's conclusions may have seemed congenial to the iconoclastic vision of Mencken, his approach was not. The rebels of the 1920's objected hotly to his insistence on adherence to firm, pre-established standards of culture and morality. The kind of classicism in art and morals which he preached seemed to them to be rigid, dogmatic, and stultifying.

The grounds for their objections can be seen even more clearly in the work of Babbitt's student and disciple, Stuart Sherman. Henry F. May says of Sherman that he was "less intelligent and more amiable, more democratic in intention and more snobbish in practice" than his mentor.[6] It was this very amiability and democracy in the defense of classical standards that made him a target for the ridicule that Mencken and others lavished upon him. In his essay "Towards an American Type," Sherman defined true Americanism as "athletic asceticism."[7] In "The Genius of America," after quoting Theodore Dreiser to the effect that there was no nation in the world so devoted to making the Ten Commandments work as the United States, he gave his enthusiastic approval to "a national genius animated by an incomparably profound moral idealism."[8] In a review of Wilbur Abbott's The New Barbarians (Boston, 1925), Sherman listed with approval the traits that Abbott had found to be

[5] Democracy and Leadership (Boston, 1924), pp. 239–243, 287. See also Randolph Bourne, "The Heart of the People," New Republic, July 3, 1915, p. 233, where he points out the danger of the creation of a standardized mass culture.

[6] American Innocence, p. 74.

[7] In Points of View (New York, 1924), pp. 1–28.

[8] In The Genius of America: Studies in Behalf of the Younger Generation (New York, 1923), pp. 23–24.

characteristic of the "American personality"—"love of liberty, opportunity, individualism, patriotism, democracy, honesty, cleanliness, sanitation, a passion for bathrooms, physical and moral prophylaxis, freedom for women, toleration, independence, gregariousness, nomadism, energy, organization, 'pep,' system, efficiency and a cheerful sentimentalism." Sherman called this "a 'bully' national type—as 'bully' a national type as any now going," and concluded his remarks by saying: "To speak of nothing else, a nation that loves bath tubs as ours does must be dear to God, and, like Greece and Rome and Israel, have a distinctive function in human history."[9]

It is entirely possible—even likely—that the whimsy of the last statement escaped Mencken entirely, making it much easier for him to set Sherman up as a butt for his jokes. It is certain that in the essays which he addressed to the "younger generation" Sherman adopted a pose which was a thoroughly ridiculous combination of Theodore Roosevelt's athleticism and Babbitt's classicism. The result of this mixture, and of his painfully self-conscious use of the latest slang at the most inappropriate points, was that he appeared to be either a high school football coach extolling the virtues of clean living or an old-maid schoolteacher selling culture—in effect, therefore, a sort of schoolmarm with muscles.

In fairness to Sherman, it must be said that his essays addressed to the younger generation were by far the least successful of his writings. In other essays, specifically those which he directed against Mencken and his associates, he gave every indication of being able to trade quips and vituperation on fairly equal terms. Perhaps this is no reason to regard him especially highly, but it shows that he was a worthy opponent for Mencken, even when fighting with Mencken's own weapons.[10] In any case, he pointed out that the critics of American civilization in the 1920's had overlooked some essential features of the American character:

> When we grow dull and inadventurous and slothfully content with our present conditions and our old habits, it is not because we are "traditionalists"; it is, on the contrary,

[9] "Middle-Class Strategy, or a Call to the Converted," in *The Main Stream* (New York, 1927), pp. 126–127.

[10] "Mr. Mencken, the *Jeune Fille*, and the New Spirit in Letters" and "Tradition," in *Americans* (New York, 1922), pp. 1–12, 13–27.

because we have ceased to feel the formative spirit of our own traditions. It is not much in the American vein, to be sure, to construct private little anarchies in the haze of a smoking-room; but practical revolt, on a large scale and sagaciously conducted, is an American tradition, which we should continue to view with courage and the tranquillity which is related to courage.[11]

Granted that the rebelliousness which Sherman extolled was safely ensconced in the past and that it was redeemed by practicality and sagaciousness, his remarks nevertheless illustrate something that is perhaps obvious but needs to be called to mind: that the Menckenian view of the American tradition was unashamedly polemical and unmistakably one-sided.

In attacking the moralism of the Old Guard, critics of American society in the 1920's were rejecting a principle of artistic judgment that they felt was outworn and irrelevant and that rendered its adherents incapable of recognizing and appreciating true artistic merit. But their attack was not confined to this particular target, for they regarded the Old Guard as representatives of America as a whole: the obsession with moral standards which robbed their artistic judgments of validity was simply an intellectualized version of the strident self-righteousness of the typical American "boob" and was the root cause of his grievous lack of artistic sensibility and cultural inventiveness. It was, in other words, a symbol of a basic defect in the American character. The emphasis on the artistic deficiencies of the American character had of course been a truism among previous commentators. But the rebel intellectuals of the 1920's took this deficiency seriously. Previous writers had noted it and had displayed proper contrition, but their concern was not really very profound; they gave the impression that they thought that an artistic soul was a superfluous piece of intellectual equipment. To Mencken and his associates, however, artistic sensibility was not at all superfluous, and its absence was a serious matter. It was symptomatic of a general inferiority of the American mind, of a lack of basic intelligence. To the American the world of ideas was as foreign as the world of art.[12] It was not possible

11 "Tradition," p. 26.
12 Mencken, *Prejudices, Second Series* (New York, 1920), p. 18.

to be an artistic moron and a political genius. The lack of cultural sensitivity was an expression—one might almost say a cause—of an underlying intellectual deficiency that extended to all areas of life and thought.

The rebel critics usually applied the label "Puritanism" to this intellectually debilitating tendency toward moralism, arguing that the American was intellectually, spiritually, and culturally inferior because he was a Puritan. Puritanism choked off cultural and intellectual life for two reasons: because, according to the Puritan conception—or the version of it presented by the intellectuals of the decade—all questions were fundamentally moral questions, which meant that judgments of artistic or intellectual validity were determined by the dictates of a rigidly defined morality; and because the Puritan assumed that morality was regulated by public opinion, which meant ultimately that standards of intellectual excellence were to be decided by a kind of mass referendum. Puritanism, therefore, was the bane of culture and intellectual life, and the cultural desert which existed in the United States was a direct result of the Puritan heritage: "Philistinism is no more than another name for Puritanism."[13] Puritanism, in fact, was frequently used as a general label for everything that was wrong with American life.

III

Puritanism was not the only component of the American character that received attention in the 1920's. The frontier was the source of another American tradition, and the pioneer was another stock figure from the American past who was held up as a model of the "typical" American. Kallen's thesis that there was in the American character a division between the Puritan and the pioneer was echoed in slightly different forms by many others who wrote on the subject at about the same time. As early as 1915, Van Wyck Brooks had put forward the idea that the American mind was divided into two separate and opposed parts: the high-brow and the low-brow. Jonathan Edwards and

[13] Mencken, *A Book of Prefaces* (2nd ed.; New York, 1918), p. 203. See the essay "Puritanism as a Literary Force," pp. 197–283, for a general treatment of the effect of "Puritanism" upon the American tradition.

Benjamin Franklin distributed dominion over the American mind between them, and the result was that "desiccated culture on one end and stark utility on the other have created a deadlock in the American mind, and all our life drifts chaotically between the two extremes." Brooks felt that the simplest expression of this division was the tendency of Americans to live in two separate compartments, labeled "theory" and "practice," with little or no possibility of communication between them.[14]

George Santayana also saw a radical division in American life and described it in terms very similar to those Brooks used. He pointed out that there existed "a curious alternation and irrelevance as between weekdays and Sabbaths, between American ways and American opinions." He provided concrete examples in his analysis of his colleagues William James and Josiah Royce. They were, said Santayana, "men of intense feeling, religious and romantic, but attentive to the facts of nature and the currents of worldly opinion; and each of them felt himself bound by two different responsibilities, that of describing things as they are, and that of finding them propitious to certain preconceived human desires."[15] They were in this respect perfectly representative of a well-established trait in the American character.

Although Kallen, Brooks, and Santayana agreed that there was a division in the American character, each defined it in his own way. To Kallen the American mind was the scene of a battle between the Puritan and the pioneer, between representatives of an intellectual and a radically non-intellectual tradition. Brooks, at least in this early essay, maintained that the differences between the high-brow and the low-brow were manifestations of two different types of Puritanism, the Puritanism of the intellect as opposed to the Puritanism of everyday life and conduct. Santayana felt that the dichotomy in the American mind was the product of a divergence between two separate intellectual traditions: Puritanism and the British heritage.

These differences were relatively minor. In practice, Santayana devoted most of his attention to the conflict between the original Puritan tradition and that tradition as it had been modified to

[14] "America's Coming of Age," reprinted in *Three Essays on America* (New York, 1934), pp. 20–30.

[15] *Character and Opinion in the United States* (Garden City, N. Y., 1956), pp. 5, 38. This book was first published in 1920.

meet American conditions. While Puritanism was originally an intellectual tradition, it had been transformed by the conditions of American life, which were not favorable to the survival of intellectual traditions, into a set of mental and emotional habits. The Puritan had turned into the pioneer, a man who rejected the past, looked optimistically toward the future, was concerned with his personal freedom, and was overwhelmingly devoted to practicality. He was not unimaginative, but his imagination was directed toward purely practical ends. Santayana called him "an idealist working on matter," intellectually flexible, interested in experimentation, and addicted to the quantitative as the primary standard of measurement and value.[16] Brooks, too, later turned his attention to the pioneer and indicted him for a whole series of crimes against American civilization. They consisted primarily of the materialization of American life, the externalization of all phenomena and all experience, the rejection of introspection, and the submission to the external environment because of a lack of inner resources. Even the richness of the American environment had proved to be unfortunate, since it had caused a virtual obsession with material riches. The only effective tradition in American life was the materialistic tradition. In surrendering to the demands of their environment, the American people had destroyed their creative spirit, which could not survive in the midst of frontier conditions or in the competitive bustle of practical life.[17] Thus Brooks and Santayana, like Kallen, saw the American as a mixture of Puritan and pioneer traits and saw essentially the same traits in the mixture.

They differed in that each of them was concerned with a different level of analysis. The tension between Puritan and pioneer noted by Kallen was a tension which existed primarily within the individual. Puritan and pioneer waged their struggle in the mind of each American. Brooks and Santayana dealt with a division in the whole culture. High-brows and low-brows, Puritans and pioneers, intellectuals and non-intellectuals were separate groups of people; they represented divergent tendencies

[16] *Ibid.*, pp. 107–115.
[17] "Letters and Leadership," reprinted in *Three Essays*, pp. 144–151. This essay was first published in 1918. See also Van Wyck Brooks, "The Literary Life," in *Civilization in the United States: An Inquiry by Thirty Americans*, ed. Harold Stearns (New York, 1922), pp. 179–197.

in the intellectual life of American society. In other words, Brooks and Santayana tended to describe American character in terms of the characteristics of American culture; Kallen's description concentrated on the typical American.[18]

They also adopted different attitudes toward the American character. Kallen was dismayed by it, but he thought it was redeemable. Brooks was dismayed, too, but he gave no indication at this time that he felt the situation could be improved. Santayana was also critical, but his criticisms were qualified. He felt that although the American was a conspicuous failure in art, high culture, academic life, and the whole area of "polite ideas," he was nevertheless a rousing success in politics.[19]

These differences in attitude and approach were intimately related to the differences in the general intellectual orientations of these men. Kallen's view of the American character must be evaluated in the context of his advocacy of unrestricted immigration, his plea for cultural pluralism, and his insistence that the immigrant was a necessary and valuable addition to American life. His emphasis on the character of the individual American probably owed a great deal to his studies with William James, whose pragmatic, pluralistic philosophy was concerned primarily with the concrete and the individual rather than with the abstract and the supra-individual. Brooks was a self-conscious rebel against what he regarded as an entrenched intellectual and artistic oligarchy whose ideas were responsible for a monstrous perversion of American life. He defined the American character in terms of the characteristics of American culture because he was attacking the premises upon which that culture was based. Santayana adopted the cultural rather than the individual approach because his whole mode of attack on philosophical problems emphasized the cultural and the aesthetic. His tone of judicious urbanity was probably the result of his conscious cultivation of the stance and the approach of a friendly but clear-eyed outsider. It seems obvious that he did not regard himself

[18] An exception must be noted here in regard to Brooks. In his study of Mark Twain, he placed the conflict between Puritanism and the frontier spirit within the mind of his subject and explained Twain's "failure" as an artist in terms of this irreconcilable tension. See *The Ordeal of Mark Twain* (New York, 1920). This is another illustration of the fact that differences between commentators on the American character are frequently—even usually—relative differences only.

[19] *Character and Opinion*, pp. 118–144.

as an American, in spite of his thirty years of residence in the United States.

Despite their differences of attitude and approach, however, these writers agreed that the American character was to be understood as a combination of Puritanism and the pioneer spirit. They also agreed that the distinction between the Puritan and the pioneer was drawn for purposes of analysis only. The Puritan and the pioneer were not by any means identical, but neither were they radically different. They were instead two distinct manifestations of the same basic character type, variations in the American character produced by subjection to different historical experiences. "The pioneer," said Kallen, "is thus a Puritan compelled to live in the primitive present; the Puritan is the pioneer, remembering the civilized past."[20] Deficiencies for which Brooks had blamed the Puritan in "America's Coming of Age" he attributed to the pioneer in "Letters and Leadership" and in his essay in Stearns's *Civilization in the United States*, indicating that he did not make much of a distinction between them except in terms of the historical context he happened to be concerned with at the time. And much of Santayana's discussion of the American character was devoted to a study of the way in which the Puritan heritage had been Americanized by the frontier experience.

The clearest expression of the idea that the Puritan and the pioneer were nearly identical, that the Puritan heritage and the frontier experience emphasized the same values and norms, came from Waldo Frank. He began by arguing that idealism in America had been extinguished on the frontier, where it was completely impractical and unworkable as a philosophy of life. The pioneer, however, had been strongly predisposed to a system of values suitable to life on the frontier, because the pioneer mentality had been pre-forged in the Puritan crucible. Puritanism had found a congenial home in America because its philosophy of self-denial had been tremendously useful in meeting the rigors of life in a frontier community. Frank wrote that the Puritan denial of the flesh

conserves energy: it sharpens wits: it quickens all the machinery of action. In other words, it prepares the Pioneer....

[20] *Culture and Democracy*, p. 217.

Pioneer and Puritan met on a base of psychological and temperamental unity. They merged and became one. The Puritan's nature fitted him superbly to be a pioneer. The Pioneer existence made permanent the Puritan's nature.[21]

IV

The vigor with which the Puritan and the pioneer were denounced tends to obscure the fact that these terms were usually only labels, convenient symbols which had been used for so long that they had become the accepted terms of discourse. Neither the Puritan nor the pioneer was viewed as a concrete historical figure functioning in a specific historical situation.

This was especially true of the way in which the critics of American civilization in the 1920's used the terms "Puritan" and "Puritanism." Richard Schlatter maintains that the discussion of Puritanism in American historical works has revolved around five or six major themes which may be taken as the essence of Puritanism: an emphasis on morality and religion, an emphasis on education and literature, the Protestant ethic in business, a belief in democracy and limited government, and utopianism (sometimes frustrated when American ideals are not realized in practice).[22] In the 1920's, however, Puritanism usually denoted moral compulsiveness, conformity, submission to the tyranny of public opinion, and the sheep-like following of the crowd. The discussion of Puritanism that took place in that decade was not intended to contribute to an understanding of the American past but to provide a starting point for criticism of the American present. It did not escape notice that the "Puritan" who was so widely excoriated bore little resemblance to the inhabitant of seventeenth-century Massachusetts. It was suspected and asserted that Mencken and his fellow intellectual rebels had created the Puritan, or their version of him, as a myth for polemical purposes.[23]

[21] *Our America* (New York, 1919), p. 63.
[22] "The Puritan Strain," in *The Reconstruction of American History*, ed. John Higham, pp. 25–45.
[23] Kenneth B. Murdock, "The Puritan Tradition in American Literature," in *The Reinterpretation of American Literature: Some Contributions Toward the Understanding of Its Historical Development*, ed. Norman Foerster (New York, 1928), pp. 83–113.

What many critics chose to call Puritanism could just as easily, and probably more accurately, have been called by some other name. The defects attributed to Puritanism could easily be found to have their roots in other causes. It was argued, for instance, that the American character was deficient in artistic aptitude not because of the Puritan morality but only because the American was young, because he suffered from the defects of his youth, because his material environment was so rich that it fascinated or obsessed him, because he lacked a past, a common tradition on which a vital culture could be based.[24] John Erskine, the critic and novelist, noted that the tendency toward moral interference in the lives of others that Mencken and his followers called Puritanism would be more accurately called "Prussianism": "If we used our memory, we should recall that our chief grievance against Prussia, a while ago, was a certain arrogance of manner, a certain indifference to the sensibilities of others, a certain disposition to have one's own way."[25] But Erskine left an important question unanswered: he did not explain how the American character had been Prussianized; he said it was not the Puritan's fault, but he did not say whose fault it was. He let the Puritan off the hook, but he did not provide a substitute fish.

The intellectual rebels paid a little more attention to history in their analyses of the effects of the frontier heritage on the American character. Most of them agreed with Turner that the American character had been formed largely by the frontier experience. Mencken occasionally employed a racist vocabulary, but his glib references to "racial strains" were not part of a coherent racist philosophy—they were simply another manifestation of his propensity to choose words for their polemic value. In his use of racial terms Mencken was different from most of his colleagues, who rejected even superficial verbal racism and gave their adherence to the Frontier Thesis.

But they gave it a pessimistic twist. In their view, the primary product of the frontier was not a sense of freedom produced by a consciousness of magnificent opportunities, but rather a feeling of insecurity and terror produced by a confrontation with an

[24] John Bunker, "Nationality and the Case of American Literature," *Sewanee Review*, 27 (1919), 82–91; John Erskine, *Democracy and Ideals: A Definition* (New York, 1920), pp. 41–63.

[25] *Prohibition and Christianity and Other Paradoxes of the American Spirit* (Indianapolis, 1927), p. 144.

empty and hostile continent. Puritanism itself was a consequence of this terror in that it was rooted in a fierce resistance to nature arising out of a profound fear of it. Restraint of natural passions and feelings therefore became the keynote of the American character. People were afraid to let themselves go, fearing that if they did they would be conquered by their environment. Rigid self-control was a basic survival mechanism. So was materialism. Americans tried to protect themselves against nature by accumulating material possessions. They repudiated art and ideas as unnecessary luxuries and felt that only those who were productive in the most immediate, concrete fashion had a valid reason for existence on the frontier. The frontier community had to stick together to function effectively, and this hard necessity precluded the toleration of divergent opinions. Americans subjected themselves to the tyranny of public opinion because they had learned from their past that only with such a surrender could they survive in an empty and therefore inhuman continent.

This outward conformity, however, disguised a fear of real human contact. In a frantic effort to conceal his true personality, the American walled himself in with material possessions to force other people to evaluate him by what he had accumulated and not by what he was. He conformed not only to protect himself from criticism for being "different" but also to enable himself to hide behind a pose which had little meaning on the deeper levels of his mind and emotions; by appearing to be like other people, he prevented them from discovering what he was really like. This fear of human involvement was another manifestation of the underlying assumptions produced by life on the frontier: that self-control, rigid morality, emotional isolation, and self-containment were necessary for survival in a hostile world.[26]

This analysis of the effects of the frontier experience, like the analysis of Puritanism, was intended only to provide an introduction to a critical treatment of contemporary America. The real target for the barbs of the intellectuals of the 1920's

[26] These ideas were implicit in many of the works on the American character in the 1920's. They are most clearly expressed in the following works: William Carlos Williams, *In the American Grain* (New York, 1925); Harold Stearns, "The Literary Life," in *Civilization in the United States*, ed. Stearns, pp. 135–150; and Harold Stearns, *America and the Young Intellectual* (New York, 1921), p. 18.

was neither the Puritan nor the pioneer, but the inhabitant of the industrialized city. The defects they attributed to the Puritan and the pioneer, conformity and materialism, had been ascribed to or predicted of industrial man in the United States since the time of Jefferson. Waldo Frank, for instance, maintained that although the frontier was gone and Puritanism lived on only in a figurative guise, their effect had been reinforced and intensified by industrialism. He held up the machine as a new scapegoat, responsible not only for fixing materialism even more firmly in the American character but also for creating an undesirably high degree of uniformity in American life. He saw the skyscraper as a perfect symbol of the American character dominated by the machine:

> We are a mass rigidly compressed into a simple structure; our rank is equalitarian, our aim is eminence, our dynamics is addition, our clearest value is the power of the bulk of ourselves. So the house that stands for us has immensity for its aim, and for its method the monstrous piling of sameness upon sameness.[27]

Frank's treatment of the effects of the machine upon the American character is another early and lucid presentation of the idea that a highly complex technological civilization exerts pressure for uniformity by feeding everyone the same stimuli in the form of standardized products, both material and intellectual.

While the critics of the 1920's felt that the American character had been formed in the American past, they were primarily concerned with the ugly way in which it manifested itself in the present. They denounced the religious narrowness of the seventeenth-century New Englander and the fear-ridden huddling of the pioneer, but they were far more incensed by the sanctimonious hypocrisy and abject conformity demonstrated by the inhabitants of industrial America. Most of their historical references were to the Gilded Age. It was in the massive scramble for wealth following the Civil War that they found the historical evidence to substantiate their criticisms. The 1920's seemed to many commentators to be a reincarnation of the

[27] *The Re-Discovery of America: An Introduction to a Philosophy of American Life* (New York, 1929), p. 90.

excesses of the Gilded Age: "Both periods were distinguished by an outrageous materialism; both saw a vulgar boom society in full flower, a tawdry popular culture, dismal and selfish statesmanship."[28] Matthew Josephson summed up the feelings of most of his colleagues when he said, "There is the same optimism about progress, the same exclusive interest in the merely exploitable, the same economic confidence gripping the entire human mass at the crest of each 'bull market.' "[29]

The tradition under attack was not Puritanism, but Puritanism in an industrial setting, that is, the Protestant Ethic. Henry Seidel Canby pointed out the applicability of the Protestant Ethic to the American experience when he argued that the real radicals in America were the businessmen who were driven by a practical idealism and strove to put into effect theoretical conceptions of a better world, conceptions which were defined in material terms but were also animated by the moral fervor of America's Puritan heritage. He believed that the traits of the typical American were those of the bourgeois:

> Our traits are not the fine exclusiveness, the discrimination, the selfishness of an aristocracy. Nor are they the social solidarity, the intellectual democracy, the intolerance of a proletariat. One finds rather individualism in opinion and unity in thought. One finds conservatism in institutions and radicalism in personal ambitions. One finds a solid, though dull morality, a distrust of ideas, a plentiful lack of taste, an abundance of the homely virtues of industry, truth telling, optimism, idealism, and charity. . . .[30]

Though Canby took a rather more charitable view of the American character than most of his contemporaries, he too was desperately worried that America was becoming "a vast corporate machine in which the individual man becomes a particle lost in the mass."[31]

[28] Alfred Kazin, *On Native Grounds: An Interpretation of Modern American Prose Literature* (Garden City, N. Y., 1956), pp. 213–214.
[29] *Portrait of the Artist as American* (New York, 1930), pp. 298–299.
[30] *Everyday Americans* (New York, 1920), p. 179.
[31] *Ibid.*, p. 76.

That industrialism was the real villain in the minds of the intellectuals of the 1920's is revealed by an analysis of the ideas of Lewis Mumford. In *The Golden Day*, he found the deficiencies of the American character to be fundamentally the same as those which had been noted again and again: materialism, conformity, and the lack of spiritual and intellectual concern and aptitude. These deficiencies existed because a group of people with no intellectual traditions to fall back on (to Mumford, the original colonists were traditionless) found themselves face to face with an empty land. Though they had succeeded in overcoming these deficiencies during the "Golden Day" of American literature, the period of what Van Wyck Brooks was to call "the flowering of New England," this excellent start came to nothing. The potentialities for great creative growth which had been revealed in the pre-Civil War era had been submerged under the rampantly acquisitive pressures and drives of the Gilded Age. Industrialism had sealed the doom of both American culture and the American character, imprisoning them within the bounds of a crass materialism which deadened all sensibilities, artistic and human.[32]

V

The attack on industrialism that was launched by the intellectual rebels of the 1920's, similar though it might seem to the attitudes underlying the earlier fear and rejection of industrialism, was different in that it did not involve a corresponding allegiance to the agrarian myth—at least not explicitly. The small town, after all, was one of their primary targets. Although most of them would have agreed with Louis Raymond Reid that the small town was the focus of the deepest emotional and sentimental allegiance of most Americans,[33] few of them would have painted as pleasant a picture of small-town life as he did. There is a picture of the traditional small town in American folklore. It is a picture in which elm-shaded streets, wide porches,

[32] *The Golden Day: A Study in American Experience and Culture* (New York, 1926).
[33] "The Small Town," in *Civilization in the United States*, ed. Stearns, pp. 285–296.

apple trees, peace, and harmony have prominent places.[34] But a new folklore was in the making in the 1920's, and in that folklore the small town was not an elm-shaded paradise but a collection of psychological malformations. Winesburg, Ohio, Spoon River, and Gopher Prairie, Minnesota, were not pleasant places to live, and almost all American intellectuals of the 1920's felt that American small towns were cut from this new pattern. Van Wyck Brooks summed up their feelings in his review of Edgar Lee Masters' *Spoon River Anthology*:

> But I know that he conveys an extraordinarily just and logical impression. He pictures a community of some thousands of souls every one of whom lives in a spiritual isolation as absolute as that of any lone farmer on the barren prairie, a community that has been utterly unable to spin any sort of spiritual fabric common to all, which has for so many generations cherished and cultivated its animosity towards all those non-utilitarian elements in the human heart that retard the successful pursuit of the main chance that it has reduced itself to a spiritual desert in which nothing humane is able to take root and grow at all. And yet all the types that shed glory on humankind have existed in that, as in every community! . . . Poets, painters, philosophers, men of science and religion are all to be found, stunted, starved, thwarted, embittered, prevented from taking even the first step in self-development, in this amazing microcosm of our society.[35]

Stearns also contended that the primary reason for the decadence of the United States was the prevalence of the small-town mentality:

> In these "dismal" places there is no art, no music, no drama, no intellectual life, no festivals and gala days that are not

[34] Expressions of this view of the small town are almost literally innumerable. The most moving and evocative one I know of is James Agee's "Knoxville: Summer 1915," which appears as a prologue to his novel *A Death in the Family* (New York, 1957). Equally effective, in an entirely different way, is Meredith Willson's musical comedy *The Music Man*.

[35] Quoted in *After the Genteel Tradition: American Writers Since 1910*, ed. Malcolm Cowley (New York, 1937), p. 220.

a mockery of gaiety, no religion that can summon and cleanse emotion, no concept of morality except a rancid, superficial Puritanism combined, as is usually the case—with an inward sordidness and hypocrisy, no sense of the joy of life, no graciousness, no urbanity. These home-towns are rural in a bad sense, through and through, self-complacent, envious and intolerant of what they do not understand, successful enough materially, but living a life that is wholly dominated by a conventional fear of the worst kind—a fear of what people will say.[36]

Thus, if these writers of the 1920's detested industrialism and what it had done to the United States, they were apparently no happier with the agrarian society that had existed in the past and continued to exist in its present manifestation as the small town, crawling with hypocrisy and provinciality, suppressing natural desires by the dictates of a crabbed Puritanical morality, constituting a monstrous graveyard for all that was fine and noble in the human spirit. It is significant that whatever hopes these critics had for the future development of civilization in the United States were to be realized in a society that was primarily industrial. Stearns, Brooks, Frank, in fact the entire nucleus of the group of the "young intellectuals," made it a point not to reject industrialism itself, but only the way in which it was currently manifesting itself in the United States. When they permitted themselves to be hopeful, their hopes were revealed in visions of an American future in which industrialism was the dominant economic fact.

Yet one cannot help feeling that the young intellectuals, too, were prisoners of the agrarian myth. Most of their critical comments were directed not against the civilization of the farms but against the civilization of the cities. Mencken enjoyed making fun of the farmers of Iowa, but the most pointed attacks were leveled against the small town or the big city, not against the farm itself. To these critics the Gilded Age represented everything that was reprehensible in American life, and they despised it precisely because it was the era in which American industrialism had come to flower. They looked to an industrial future not because they preferred it to any other sort of society, but because

[36] *America and the Young Intellectual,* p. 163.

they thought it was inevitable. Industrialism was a fact of life to them, and the best they could hope for was that American civilization would pull itself together on an industrial basis and that the American character would work out a kind of compromise salvation within an industrial economy. Industrialism was the only workable alternative, not their ideal choice.

What happened to conceptions of the American character, therefore, seems to be something like this: In the early years of the twentieth century, writers on the American character emphasized frontier individualism. But in the 1920's, when it was no longer possible to pretend that the frontier was a living force in America and it seemed implausible that frontier individualism was the dominant trait in the highly industrialized society that had come to exist in the United States, the emphasis shifted. The conformist tendencies of a machine civilization—tendencies which had been predicted by agrarian philosophers long before and had become one of the cardinal tenets of the American faith—were not only discovered in the American character of the present but were even projected back into the past and found to have roots in the frontier experience itself. The critics of American society in the 1920's accepted the main outlines of the agrarian philosophy in that they agreed that industrialism had had undesirable effects on the nation and its people. They merely found earlier evidences of such effects in America's preindustrial society. At least they *said* that these effects had been apparent before the advent of the machine, but, for all their talk of Puritanism and the frontier, their real historical target was the industrial society of the Gilded Age.

Thus, many of the differences between the intellectuals of the 1920's and previous writers on the American character were not so much differences in ideas as differences in focus, emphasis, and attitude. In their view, the dominant traits of the American character were lack of artistic ability, materialism, and conformity. All these traits had neen noted previously. But while the lack of artistic aptitude had not seemed especially important to writers at the turn of the century, it was of fundamental importance to the intellectuals of the 1920's, a symptom of more basic deficiencies in the American mind and character. Previously, tendencies toward materialism had been discussed in conjunction with a much stronger emphasis on idealism, so that materialism emerged only as the "practical" component of the "practical idealism" which was believed to be the distinguishing characteristic of the American. Conformist tendencies and the strength of public opinion had received attention, too, but they were either regarded as proper or submerged in a general torrent of praise for American individualism.

Of course, these differences in emphasis and attitude are important. But they must not be allowed to obscure the very real indebtedness of the young intellectuals to ideas formulated by previous thinkers and their subjection to many of the ideas against which they thought they were rebelling. Jay B. Hubbell said of them: "Even those who rebel against the tyrannous uniformity of American life and thought seem to rebel *en masse*, as it were, and merely substitute the conventions of the *American Mercury* for those of the *Saturday Evening Post*."[37] This kind of criticism is rather cheap because it is so easy; comparable judgments have probably been leveled against dissident groups attacking conformity in all times and places. The "conformity" of the rebel intellectuals of the 1920's went deeper than this. It was not merely that they were conforming to their own set of standards—that much is inevitable in any case—but they were far more enmeshed than they suspected in the toils of the system they attacked.

[37] "The Frontier," in *Reinterpretation of American Literature*, ed. Foerster, p. 57.

5

THE AMERICAN CHARACTER IN THE 1930's

TRANSITIONS

I

In Our Business Civilization, *James Truslow Adams* expressed the view of the American character that had become standard in the 1920's among a certain group of American intellectuals. As the title implies, his thesis was that American life was dominated by business to the extent that it had become a virtual obsession with the American people. As a consequence, Americans were thoroughly materialistic, devoted to the narrowest kind of "practicality," and completely submissive to the pressures toward standardization inherent in a society whose real religion was the worship of mass production. The frontier, which had originally implanted these traits in the American character, had disappeared, but its work was carried on by a substitute: the economic frontier of the eternal pursuit of a higher standard of living.[1]

But Adams' book was published in 1929, and the events of that year were to make his analysis seem almost wholly irrelevant. Economic and social conditions went through a wholesale transformation. Many people began to wonder whether any amount of pursuit would ever bring a higher standard of living within reach again. Catastrophic social change upset many old assumptions and called into question many of the old certainties. It created pervasive feelings of bewilderment and confusion among many American intellectuals; they simply did not know what

[1] (New York, 1929).

to make of the situation that confronted them. Sherwood Anderson said that America was "puzzled" by the Depression. It had knocked the intellectual props out from under the American people and had destroyed their confidence. They wanted to have faith, but they did not know where to find it. Instead of faith, they were filled with profound feelings of humility and guilt, since they regarded the Depression as a personal disaster and were inclined to interpret it as punishment for their sins. The trouble was that they did not know what those sins were.[2] In all of this Anderson was describing the feelings of the "common man." But he might well have been talking about American intellectuals, for a great number of them were just as bewildered and just as confused as the ordinary "puzzled" American.

This feeling of confusion among American intellectuals led to a re-examination of many of the premises of American thought. There was a general shifting of intellectual gears, reflected in certain changes, all interrelated, in treatments of the national character. There was a tendency to question the glib generalizations made by previous writers. Growing sophistication in the social sciences and growing awareness of the complexity and heterogeneity of the United States made students of the American character conscious of the difficulties in constructing generalizations that would apply to the nation as a whole. Consequently, they tended to move away from defining the national character in terms of the traits of a "typical" American and toward an analysis of the American value system. The social dislocations created by the Depression caused many writers to question the applicability of American values to the economic, social, and political system in which they had to function and to which they were supposed to relate; they contended that American values were fundamentally incompatible with the actualities of American life. There was also a willingness to extend intellectual horizons beyond the borders of the United States. Because of developments in international politics, and because the Depression had raised serious questions about the viability of the American way of life, intellectuals in the 1930's showed a far greater disposition than their predecessors had shown to examine the American character by making explicit

[2] *Puzzled America* (New York, 1935), p. 164.

comparisons and contrasts with the traits of other peoples. And the spectacular failure of the American economy brought home to many American intellectuals the fact that America was, for better or worse, an industrial nation, that the American people would have to live in an industrial society, and that the agricultural frontier was no longer a part of American life. This led to a search for substitutes for the frontier, for new frontiers within an industrial economy to perpetuate those traits in the American character that had originally been formed by the old frontier.

Now, the degree to which treatments of the American character changed in the 1930's should not be overemphasized. In certain respects they were perfectly consistent with those of earlier decades. There was in no sense a revolution in the ways in which people thought and wrote about the national character. Many of the themes and approaches of the 1920's were just as prevalent in the 1930's. It was simply that there appeared in the writings of many analysts the beginnings of certain trends which were over the course of time to develop into new doctrines and ideas.

II

In the early years of the decade it would have been difficult to determine whether or not conceptions of the American character had changed, for the simple reason that they had almost disappeared. The whole idea of national character seemed to make American intellectuals uncomfortable. There were an enormous number of books on the United States, from the semi-official *Recent Social Trends*, and all the monographs written in conjunction with the main volume, to the books on the states sponsored by the W.P.A. Writers' Project; from the many discussions of regionalism to the books recounting investigatory trips through the land made by novelists, journalists, and interested citizens in general. But the concept of national character found little or no place in the wholesale and rather desperate attempt to discover what was going on in the country and what the people of the United States were thinking and doing.

One explanation for this avoidance of the concept of national character is that it was too closely akin to the racist orientation of Nazism. Since the idea of national character had become thoroughly tarred with the racist brush during the immigration controversy, it is reasonable to assume that many American intellectuals would be very reluctant to give any appearance of assenting to an idea which could be interpreted as compatible with the claim by Nazis and other racists that large groups of people could be discovered to possess definite distinguishing characteristics. All concepts of group character were suspect, as Jacques Barzun revealed.

Groups exist, to be sure, and when they act as groups must be judged as such. But the failure to recognize the endless variety of human character under the national, social, economic, and racial label is the key-fallacy in all so-called racial-prejudices.[3]

There is, however, reason to doubt that the association with racism was the major factor in the tendency to shy away from the national-character concept. Even before Hitler had attracted wide attention in the United States, a general decline in the popularity of the concept among American intellectuals could be detected. The increased awareness of Nazism and its implied threat to American ways and ideals would, if anything, have stimulated an interest in analyzing the national character. It would have been perfectly possible, after all, to defend the validity of the concept in terms which had nothing whatever to do with racism. Those who were suspicious of its racist overtones were perhaps unduly sensitive, tending to see fascists behind every bush as other people saw and were to see communists.[4]

There were other, more substantial reasons for the relative dearth of studies of the American character. The American people at the time were confronted with a problem which was

[3] "Race-Prejudice," in *America Now: An Inquiry into Civilization in the United States*, ed. Harold Stearns (New York, 1938), p. 483. See also Barzun's *Race: A Study in Modern Superstition* (New York, 1937).

[4] In this connection, it is interesting to note that Barzun later apparently overcame his misgivings about generalizations concerning national character. There are several such generalizations in his book *God's Country and Mine: A Declaration of Love Spiced with a Few Harsh Words* (Boston, 1954).

primarily economic, and economics, of all forms of social analysis, is probably the least dependent upon the distinctive characteristics of a particular culture. Economic relationships are
less susceptible to national variations than are other aspects
of life. The national-character approach, therefore, was simply
not relevant to the current problem. To the extent that American
social analysts were concerned with a fundamentally economic
problem—and they could not very well avoid it—they were
almost forced to reject or ignore the national-character approach
to the study of society.

The upsurge of Marxism that occurred in the 1930's also
worked very strongly against the acceptance of the assumptions
upon which the concept of national character was based. The
Marxists' sensitivity to fascism made them even more militant
than most against racism and whatever seemed to resemble it.
If a liberal scholar like Barzun was suspicious of the concept
of national character because of its supposed analogies to fascist
thinking, American Marxists were much more likely to reject
it. In addition, Marxism was—and still is—a doctrine which
claimed to have universal applicability, in the sense that Marxian
analyses were independent of national frontiers and Marxian
laws knew no boundaries. Its emphasis was international; it
stressed class allegiances that transcended national boundaries.
National peculiarities, the very basis of the national-character
concept, were of little importance to the Marxist scholar—assuming that he recognized their existence at all. At the same time
he emphasized the divisions between classes within nations. If
he admitted the existence of group character, it was class character and not national character. To the extent that Marxism
had an impact on American intellectual life, the concept of
national character was rejected, or at least avoided.

But perhaps the most important reason for the disposition to
avoid the subject of national character was the general uncertainty of the intellectual climate. Before 1929, people believed
that they knew what the nation was and where it was going,
what the typical American was and where he was going. After
1929, no such certainty existed. It was as if America had suddenly
become incomprehensible to American intellectuals. The events
of the months and years after October 1929 had taught them
that they did not know as much about their country as they

thought they did. In their shock they began to wonder if they knew anything about it at all:

For seven months I drove an automobile over this land-scape, and now I have to justify some fifteen thousand miles of travel. People ask me: What did you see? What did you learn? What is happening to America, and what is going to happen? I tend to balk at these questions. The landscape is so huge; the forces so complex. How should I know, or venture to speak with much greater assurance than any other of those bewildered ants I passed on the road?[5]

American intellectuals, like the Americans in Carl Sandburg's poem "The People, Yes," were asking, "Where to? What next?" As a result, they became wary in their statements. Because they had seen too many broad generalizations proved conclusively wrong in recent years, their analyses were usually confined to small segments of the total reality. They resorted most frequently to the "documentary" or "objective" approach: the study of the particular community, the small region, a certain class, the special event. Their underlying assumption was that society was to be understood through a meticulous study of the individual and the particular. Explicit generalization was largely avoided. When social analysts did generalize, they tended to form their generalizations on the Marxist model. This meant that their generalizations transcended national boundaries and applied to the whole world and to all history. Between the two poles of the immediate, the individual, and the particular on the one hand and the general, the universal, and the timeless on the other, there was only a very restricted middle ground, and it is in this middle ground that the concept of national character lies.[6]

[5] James Rorty, *Where Life Is Better: An Unsentimental American Journey* (New York, 1936), pp. 16-17.

[6] The Beards noted several reasons for the general lack of interest in what they called the "idea of civilization" in the 1930's. (Charles A. Beard and Mary R. Beard, *The American Spirit: A Study of the Idea of Civilization in the United States* [New York, 1942], pp. 534-548.) The idea of civilization is not the same thing as the national character, but it is a generalization of the same order, and intellectuals who felt uncomfortable with one would probably also feel uncomfortable with the other, and for approximately the same reasons.

III

In the later years of the decade of the 1930's, American intellectuals began to show some signs of having recovered from the most immediate effects of the Depression. The sense of bewilderment and confusion began to disappear, and a degree of confidence and certainty returned. One evidence that American intellectual life was beginning to get back to its "normal," pre-Depression condition was that American intellectuals showed a revived interest in the national character. Despite the fact that the Depression was far from conquered, their view was quite rosy, especially compared with the attitudes they had expressed in the 1920's. Harold Stearns provides the clearest example of this change. In the 1920's he had been one of the most vehement critics of American civilization, but in the 1930's he re-examined some of his conclusions and, although he did not say so in so many words, he found that most of his pessimistic conclusions were in need of drastic revision. Puritanism was still characteristic of the American, but it was no longer a matter for serious concern. Indeed, Stearns felt that a certain amount of it was very desirable. The materialism of the pioneer still existed, but it had been transformed, by a mysterious process that Stearns never described, into a fiercely experimental attitude directed toward the solution of the economic problem. The American was still a conformist, but only in a restricted sense. In politics, for instance, Stearns was as impressed by American individualism in the 1930's as he had been by its lack in the 1920's. He summed up the American temper by saying that it was almost

> too easy-going; it bridles at political extremism, as indeed, at all forms of extremism, except as jokes. It is Yankee, terre à terre, non-apocalyptic, and refuses to be bulldozed into believing in miracles, manifest destinies, or the Perfect State.[7]

In the 1920's, Stearns had believed that the American was all too ready to be bulldozed into believing just about anything and into relinquishing whatever rights of private judgment he may have had regarding the various fanaticisms of the day.

[7] *America: A Re-Appraisal* (New York, 1937), pp. 111–112.

Stearns himself explained part of the reason for the renewed confidence of the intellectuals: "It was impossible to keep up the despairing mood of the 1930–31 blackness much longer than we did; there had to be an optimistic reaction just in the nature of things."[8] This optimistic reaction may well have occurred simply because American intellectuals had become accustomed to the Depression. The Depression had affected American intellectual life not only because it had demonstrated that there were fundamental maladjustments in the American social and economic order but even more because this demonstration had occurred so suddenly and so drastically as to produce a considerable shock. The lack of confidence and the uncertainty characteristic of the early years of the Depression resulted from the fact that the complacent assumptions of the 1920's had been proved so conclusively wrong in such a short time. (It should be pointed out that even the critics of the 1920's, whatever defects they may have seen in the United States, had not predicted any kind of economic disaster. They disliked many features of Coolidge prosperity, but they seemed to feel that it would continue more or less indefinitely.) After a few years, however, the sense of shock abated. People got used to the fact that their economic system was not functioning properly. Any social condition which continues for a long period begins to seem almost normal. At least, it begins to seem intelligible, and people are able to readjust their thinking to take account of it.

In some cases, however, this optimism did not go very deep. There was more than a little whistling in the dark; many people were firmly convinced that they could not allow themselves to be afraid and tried to prove that they were not. There appeared a kind of "enforced" optimism: people made hopeful statements at the conclusion of discussions which had given only reasons for despair. James Rorty said:

Indeed, I accumulated enough pessimism so that I began to wonder if my melancholy wasn't after all a kind of sentimental defeatism. But before I finished I had also discovered ground for a certain stoic optimism. . . . The present is tragic enough; the years ahead will be even more tragic in

[8] *Ibid.*, pp. 193–194.

all probability. But they will be less silly, less futile on the whole.

They will be *worthier*—at least I find myself able to hope this—in the sight of God and man.[9]

He seems to have been looking frantically for *something* to say that was not completely hopeless. It was this same desire that made Nathan Asch say that "there is hope, there is a chance, there is a future," when all the evidence he presented led to the conclusion that there were no grounds whatever for such hope.[10]

This resurgence of optimism, limited and somewhat pathetic though it may have been in certain cases, bore a close relation to current political developments. The Depression had not been conquered, but efforts were being made and those who were sympathetic to these efforts were emotionally, if not intellectually, committed to a hopeful outlook. No matter how unpleasant a situation may be, the liberal and the radical cannot allow themselves to believe that it is irretrievable; if they did, they would destroy the effectiveness of their plea for solutions. In political debate it is usually very bad tactics to give any hint that one believes that he is fighting in a lost cause.

Perhaps the most important single reason for the relatively favorable view of the American character that appeared in the latter half of the thirties is that American intellectuals began to consider it in comparison with the national characters of other nations. The growing awareness of the challenges and threats posed by fascism and communism called forth a spirited defense of American ways and institutions. Many features of the American character that had previously been criticized and ridiculed did not now seem to be quite so bad:

It is well enough in the quiet, Arcadian days of 1922 to show up Babbitt for the purpose of shaming him into taking steps for his own spiritual amendment. But today Babbitt is an angel of culture by comparison with the bitter fanatics

[9] *Where Life Is Better,* p. 50.
[10] *The Road: In Search of America* (New York, 1937), p. 11. See also Rollo Walter Brown, *I Travel by Train* (New York, 1939), pp. 302–317.

who have set their iron heel on the free human soul, who have harnessed learning and art and thought to the program of a political party. It is not in Zenith, U.S.A., that the new barbarian threat to the heritage of civilization has arisen. . . . Babbitt against his original background of 1922 is a pathetic figure. Babbitt fifteen years later is a man to cherish.[11]

Or, as Stearns said, "If what we have seen during the last four years in Italy, Spain, France, and Germany is a true expression of European civilization, then I prefer to take my chances in backward and hidebound, capitalistic America, for all our abuses."[12] In a paradoxical way, therefore, fascism restored American faith in American institutions and the American character. Other nations had succumbed to pressures toward fanaticism, and although fanaticism also existed in the United States, although there was a widespread tendency to think in apocalyptic terms and to offer radical or crackpot solutions to current problems, the American people had managed to resist. The individual who could remember the Palmer raids, the Scopes trial, and the Ku Klux Klan's career in the 1920's might reasonably have concluded that the 1930's were a substantial improvement, despite Dr. Townsend, Huey Long, and Father Coughlin. American intellectuals felt a new sense of pride in their nation, a new sense of commitment to it. They felt at home in their country. Richard Hofstadter suggests that this was partly because it now seemed that they were wanted, appreciated, and needed;[13] perhaps even more, it was because they realized that for all its defects the United States was a much more pleasant place to live than many other countries.

IV

Usually, analyses of the American character have been influenced profoundly by the problems that existed in American

[11] Simeon Strunsky, *The Living Tradition: Change and America* (New York, 1939), p. 400.
[12] *America: A Re-Appraisal*, p. 17–18.
[13] *Anti-Intellectualism in American Life* (New York, 1963), p. 413.

society at the time they were written. They are tracts for the times, sometimes disguised as "impartial" investigations of the nature of the American and his culture, but more often obviously intended as an introduction or background to a criticism or defense of contemporary conditions and policies. In the 1930's the Depression was the obvious problem, and there was a furious debate on the policies which should be adopted to end it. At least one writer, however, Marcus Hansen, managed to avoid describing the American character as it was revealed or affected by the economic crisis that the nation faced.

In 1936 Hansen published the essay "Immigration and Puritanism," one of his many contributions to the general subject of the history of immigration in America which made him the foremost author in the field. In this essay he concerned himself explicitly with the relationship between immigration and the American character. He argued that Puritanism had been a natural, practical response to the problems of colonization and frontier life. The life of the community was precarious at best, and the lack of individual discipline made its existence even more precarious. Discipline was made a matter of legislative concern from a motive of simple self-preservation. Because individual morality was thought to be so important to the survival of the community that it could not be left to the individual, Puritanism in the sense of legislative regulation of moral standards had become an inherent part of the American scene. Hansen believed that immigration had perpetuated Puritanism. Puritanical standards of behavior were forced upon the immigrants because the dominant forces in the community felt that only in such a way could the relations between the immigrants and the general community be effectively regulated.[14]

While Hansen's analysis of the American character was not directly related to the Depression, it is not true that what he had to say bore no relation to current social problems. The great debate on immigration had not ceased with the passage of the various restrictive acts of the 1920's. Though the focus had shifted from the question of the desirability of legislative re-

[14] Reprinted in *The Immigrant in American History* (Cambridge, 1940), pp. 97–129. Ernest Sutherland Bates also pointed out the Puritanical effects of the frontier experience in *American Faith: Its Religious, Political, and Economic Foundations* (New York, 1940), p. 329.

striction to the proper place of those immigrants already here in the life of the nation, immigration was still an issue, and Hansen was sympathetic to the immigrant. He was no more enamored of Puritanism than Mencken or Brooks had been, even if his disapproval was not expressed as vehemently, but it is important to note that his treatment implied that the immigrants could not really be held responsible for its perpetuation, since they had been forced into the Puritan mold by the dominant groups in American society. Louis Adamic's *From Many Lands* is another example of the continuing concern with the effects of immigration. Adamic emphasized the arguments of the cultural pluralists of the era of the great debate on immigration restriction, asserted the inherent value of diversity, implied that heterogeneity was the real basis of the American idea, and stressed the strong idealistic component which existed in the American character because of the infusion of immigrant peoples. This book was representative of a current of thought which was well marked in the late 1930's in discussions of immigration: the "we-must-all-pull-together-to-lick-the-Depression" school of thought. Later, this was easily transformed into the "we-must-all-pull-together-to-win-the-war" school.[15] In any event, the opponents of restriction did not seem to feel that the issue had been finally settled. Apparently they hoped to keep the question open.

The journalist Simeon Strunsky was another who continued to argue for the beneficial effects of immigration on American life. He maintained that immigration could constitute a new American frontier. The important thing about the old frontier was not that it was the source of free land, but that it was the source of opportunity, that it provided for freedom of movement: "The decisive influence was not the character of the frontier, but the mere fact that there was a frontier. There was something beyond the horizon." The adventure of immigration was spiritually analogous to the westward movement and pro-

[15] Louis Adamic, *From Many Lands* (New York, 1940). For expressions of the view that the war effort required the wholehearted cooperation and acceptance of ethnic minorities see *One America: The History, Contributions, and Present Problems of Our Racial and National Minorities*, eds. Francis J. Brown and Joseph Slabey Roucek (New York, 1937), and *Foreign Influences in American Life*, ed. David F. Bowers (Princeton, 1944).

duced the same kind of character, for it was another source of the mobility and opportunity that had been the prime determining factor in the shaping of the American character.

Strunsky's concern with immigration was only one part of a broader idea—that there were alternatives to the geographical frontier and that the American people had only to make use of them: "All Americans for more than three hundred years have been moving forward to the conquest of new frontiers of many kinds."[16] Strunsky was not alone in this belief. The journalist and novelist R. L. Duffus felt that the romantic hopefulness of the American people that had been born on the frontier still existed and was being reborn and renewed in other fields: "We have followed those hopeful trails in invention, in industry, perhaps we shall some day follow them in the arts."[17] The growing awareness of the existence of non-agricultural frontiers was, of course, another instance of the optimistic reaction against the despair of the Depression. It also challenged the implicit pessimism of the Frontier Thesis. It began to appear that the American people might, after all, learn to live with industrialism without sacrificing their distinctiveness or their greatness.

V

Not everyone adopted this hopeful view. There were still many who questioned the worth of frontier ideals and character in a predominantly industrial society. Gilbert Seldes, for instance, pointed out that Americans had found a substitute for the frontier in increased buying power but that this discovery had not protected them from the Depression. Indeed, this new frontier, by perpetuating the optimistic preconceptions of the old frontier, had rendered them incapable of taking prompt, decisive action against the Depression.[18]

This analysis reveals a point of view which became widely prevalent in the 1930's: that tensions were produced in society by the tendency of different aspects of social life to change at

[16] *Living Tradition*, pp. 22–29, 123–124.

[17] "The Open Spaces and the American Myth," in *America as Americans See It*, ed. Fred J. Ringel (New York, 1932), p. 3.

[18] Gilbert Seldes, *The Years of the Locust: (America, 1929–1932)* (Boston, 1933).

varying rates. In other words, America was suffering from cultural lag; American ideals were not in harmony with American reality, and the result was a paralysis of will. This idea was expressed in many different ways by many different writers. Gerald Wendt argued that science could become a new American frontier but that scientific thinking had not yet become characteristic of the American people, despite the fact that science was perhaps the dominant force in American society. Roger Burlingame maintained that while American technology had transformed the United States into a mechanical civilization characterized by concentration and collectivism, American thought persisted in an individualist orientation. American civilization suffered, so to speak, from a split personality.[19]

The clearest and most thorough presentation of the theme of cultural lag and the conflict between ideal and reality, between values and actualities, was made by the Lynds. Their studies of Middletown revealed to them that differential rates of change in various aspects of Middletown's culture had produced tension and conflict. There is little doubt that they regarded Middletown as a microcosm of American society in general.[20]

Now, it is eminently reasonable to argue that results obtained from the study of a single community, no matter how "representative" the community or how thorough and imaginative the study, cannot be extended to the whole nation. But in effect Robert Lynd did make this extension. The broad generalizations of his *Knowledge for What?* are based on the specific formulations of *Middletown in Transition,* the second book of the Middletown series, in which the Lynds had attempted to construct a central value pattern and intellectual orientation for the community.[21] In the later book, Lynd found exactly the same fundamental social forces operating to produce the same kind of value system and character structure. The only difference was one of scale.

In *Knowledge for What?* Lynd presented a statement of the basic value system of the United States. He found that nearly

[19] Gerald Wendt, "Science," and Roger Burlingame, "Invention," in *America Now,* ed. Stearns, pp. 185–201 and 222–236 respectively.
[20] Robert S. Lynd and Helen Merrell Lynd, *Middletown: A Study in American Culture* (New York, 1929), pp. 3, 7.
[21] *Middletown in Transition* (New York, 1937), pp. 402–510.

every one of the important values of the American people had a substantial qualification that was often directly contradictory to the general proposition. For example, Americans valued individualism, believed that individualism had made America what it was, and insisted that restrictions on individual freedom were to be deplored as un-American; but they also put a strong emphasis on cooperative endeavor. Americans believed that everyone should try to succeed; but they also insisted that personal traits were far more important than material success. They extolled the family as the core of national life; but there was no question that business was the most important American institution and that other institutions of American culture were required to conform to its dictates. Lynd found the entire American value system riddled with such contradictions. The inevitable consequence was a feeling of confusion among the people of America, for they had no clear guide to what they should do in any given situation.[22]

Lynd maintained that this conflict of values was produced by a fundamental conflict in the American mind between two opposed definitions of the good. On the one hand were the values of generosity, kindliness, hospitality, and cooperation. On the other were the aggressive values of the successful businessman. Lynd felt that the latter set of values had triumphed in everyday life but that the other values persisted in the minds and hearts of the American people. The tension between these contradictory values had produced guilt and confusion. Americans tried to solve the contradiction by striving for success, which they defined in purely monetary terms. Material advancement became the means by which all men's values were to be achieved. Community welfare was accordingly conceived of as an automatic by-product of money-making.[23]

These contradictions existed, said Lynd, because American culture lacked techniques for coping effectively with social change. The situation in which Americans lived had changed, but their culture, their values, and their attitudes had not. There was consequently a debilitating tension between past ideals and values and present reality; between a culture formed primarily

22 *Knowledge for What?: The Place of Social Science in American Culture* (Princeton, 1939), pp. 60–62.
23 *Ibid.*, pp. 70–100.

by the frontier experience and replete with institutions designed to further the quest for individual liberty, and a social situation which demanded institutions capable of providing the American people with a sense of organized community purpose; between a culture which looked resolutely toward the future and required an unquestioning belief in the inevitability of continuous progress, and a social situation which was likely to produce frustration when people reached the age of fifty, looked around, and found that they had not achieved all the glorious goals they were supposed to achieve through a program of hard work, self-denial, thrift, and discipline.[24]

The Lynds' emphasis on value analysis in the attempt to describe the American character was not entirely new. Croly, too, had insisted that the American system of values needed adjusting so that it would conform more closely to the requirements of a complex industrial civilization. In certain respects the Lynds were even more old-fashioned than Croly had been. If there were any villains in Middletown—and, by extension, in the United States—they were the businessmen. They were the people upon whom the Lynds fixed the ultimate responsibility for the disharmonies and disjunctions that existed in the life of Middletown and the nation. This "devil theory" of business dominance of political affairs was very well developed in all kinds of social analysis in the 1930's, but it receives particular emphasis in the Middletown books.[25] Of course, to attack the business community is not necessarily to attack the system that that community represents, but it does seem that the Lynds' distrust of the businessmen was at least partly the product of a lingering, unconscious dislike of industrialism. Although they did not feel that Middletown had changed very much between 1920 and 1930 under the impact of the Depression, they did feel that it had changed substantially between 1890 and 1920 under the impact of industrialism. The Middletown of 1890 was seen in a warm light of nostalgia that was entirely missing from the treatments of the later Middletowns: pre-industrial Middletown

[24] *Ibid.*, pp. 87–95.
[25] Nelson W. Polsby has argued that the Lynds tended to exaggerate the degree to which the businessmen of Middletown controlled their town. See "Power in Middletown: Fact and Value in Community Research," *Canadian Journal of Economics and Political Science,* 26 (1960), 592–603.

was a more pleasant place to live than post-industrial Middletown. This degeneration could have been attributed to the men
who ran the industrial system rather than to the system itself,
except that the Lynds thought characteristically in terms of the
influence of social forces on human actions; they felt that men
did not mold the system but were molded by it. If something
was out of joint, they blamed the system, not the men. They
were not comfortable with industrialism and felt a strong nostalgic bias toward the simpler agrarian society of the American
past, when American values and American realities were more
in harmony.

The Lynds' interpretation was nevertheless an example of the
fact that new ground was being broken in the study of the
national character. The emphasis on the sociological concept of
cultural lag and the transition from analysis in terms of the
typical individual to analysis in terms of values both pointed
up the fact that the study of the national character was becoming more and more a problem in social science. Previously, most
of the commentators on the national character had been journalists, philosophers, or literary figures. Though this was still true
in the 1930's, the social-science approach was becoming more
widely adopted. As students of American society began to question the concept of a "typical" individual in a heterogeneous
society, they turned to value analysis as a means of generalizing
on a society-wide scale, for this approach was explicitly supra-
individual and thus avoided the obvious deficiencies of the former
method.

It was not assumed, however, that a value consensus existed
in the United States. To be sure, the society was bound together
by mass communications, but concern with the effects of mass
communications had not yet become general among sociologists.
The 1930's, consequently, saw the beginnings of a transition in
studies of the American character. Sociological awareness had
reached the point where the deficiencies of the individual approach were obvious while at the same time the possibilities of
the value approach were only imperfectly realized. Still, a beginning had been made. American culture, not the American
individual, was becoming the primary focus of interest, and the
national character was becoming more and more the province
of the social scientist, to be investigated with the concepts and
methods of the social sciences.

6

THE AMERICAN CHARACTER AND THE SOCIAL SCIENCES

CULTURE AND PERSONALITY THEORY

I

In their introduction to Middletown in Transition *the Lynds* included a brief statement of an important theoretical principle. They said:

> Middletown tends to regard human nature as "rational," "free," and "responsible," and there is large precedent for so doing. On the other hand, the emphasis of recent psychology is that actions of human beings are only to a limited extent rational, while to a far greater extent they are colored by individual emotional needs and responsive to previous cultural conditioning.
>
> People tend, therefore, to act as cultural agents, and society shares responsibility with the individual for his actions. A given culture tends to select out and to emphasize personality types that are viable in it.[1]

This is a good brief statement of the basic principles of the "culture and personality" approach to the study of society. Culture and personality theorists assert that the individual is molded by the culture he lives in, that many of the characteristics of human personalities are strongly influenced by cultural forces, that many individual character traits are at least partly cultural products, and that, since all members of a given cultural group are subject to roughly the same cultural experiences, their per-

[1] Pp. xv–xvi.

sonalities will exhibit substantial degrees of congruence or similarity. Reduced to its simplest terms, the basic argument of the culture and personality theorist is that people who live in the same culture tend to be similar to one another *because* they live in the same culture. This theory is obviously applicable to the study of national character, for if one chooses to regard any given nation as a meaningful cultural unit he can find in this theory a ready-made validation of the assumption that a national character exists.

Originally the theory was conceived not as a device for the study of national character but rather as a tool that would make the work of cultural anthropologists more significant by freeing them from mere ethnographic description and permitting a wider range of generalization than had been possible previously. The chief figure in the early years of its development was the anthropologist and linguist Edward Sapir, who rejected the idea that what he called the "genius" of a people could be explained by heredity and advocated instead the analysis of cultural and historical factors.[2]

In itself this was not new. The idea that the individual was "molded" by his environment and that a distinctive set of historical experiences could give rise to a distinctive type of personality was a truism. In many ways Sapir's formulation seemed only to involve a substitution of the word "culture" for the word "tradition" in the analysis of group traits. Turner, among many others, had already shown what could be done in the analysis of the effects of distinctive historical experiences upon the people of the United States.

Yet the culture and personality theory went somewhat deeper than this. It offered a more precise and systematic description of the mechanisms by which tradition or historical experiences or social environment actually affected the individual; it made clearer the ways in which cultural influences operated or the ways in which historical experiences were transformed into personality traits. It turned a widely held assumption into a systematic doctrine. It spelled out the connection between ex-

[2] David G. Mandlebaum (ed.), *Selected Writings of Edward Sapir in Language, Culture, and Personality* (Berkeley, 1949), and Edward Sapir, "Personality," in *Encyclopedia of the Social Sciences*, ed. E. R. A. Seligman (15 vols.; New York, 1930–1934), vol. 12, pp. 85–88.

perience and character and, by focusing attention on the concept of socialization, paved the way for an attack on the problem of how the connection was effected.

The interest in socialization, in the series of processes by which the human infant was made ready to function in his culture—or, phrased another way, to take his place in society—was directly related to the Freudian emphasis on the experiences of early infancy as the source of the fundamental psychological characteristics of the individual. The culture and personality movement was essentially an attempt to apply Freudian concepts to anthropological materials. Freud's view of the role of the unconscious was especially stimulating, because it enabled anthropologists to justify and explain their assumption that much of the patterning of behavior that occurred in society occurred unconsciously. It also gave them insights which they could use in the task of determining precisely how this unconscious cultural conditioning took place. Anthropologists began to believe that with the aid of psychiatric concepts they could not only describe cultural patterns but also make significant progress toward understanding their origin and their impact upon individual members of the cultural community.

The way in which this might be accomplished was described most thoroughly by the psychiatrist Abram Kardiner. His concept of the "basic personality structure" was perhaps the clearest single theoretical expression of the way in which psychiatric insights could be employed in the study of cultures. He maintained that the institutions with which an individual came into contact in infancy exercised an influence on him throughout his whole life. Because individuals who lived in the same culture would come into contact with the same institutions, the chances were good that they would have fundamentally similar character structures. The basic personality structure was the expression of this similarity. As the embodiment of the similarities that existed between one individual's character and another's, it was an abstraction from the actual personality structures of specific individuals in a given culture. Conversely, the individual's character could be regarded as an idiosyncratic variant of the basic personality structure.[3]

[3] See the following works by Kardiner: *The Individual and His Society: The Psychodynamics of Primitive Social Organization* (New

This concept is a tool that would appear to be extremely useful in the investigation of national character. Indeed, if one is willing to assume that a nation constitutes a cultural unit, one may choose to regard the basic personality structure and the national character as identical. But not everyone was willing to make the necessary assumptions. Ralph Linton, Kardiner's consulting anthropologist in the formulation and application of the concept, insisted that it was not a synonym for national character. It was applicable only to small, homogeneous societies, and modern nations were neither small nor homogeneous.[4] Moreover, Kardiner's theory raised serious methodological questions. In practice, the basic personality structure was developed by inference from the cultural milieu, not by the examination of individual personalities. The theory begins by postulating a link between cultural institutions and individual character traits, asserts that it is possible to discover through an analysis of the institutions the type of personality which will be produced in any given culture, and then blithely contends that this personality type *must* be the norm within that culture, without providing any method for checking the accuracy of the predictions. It is significant that sociologists, on the whole, have not been comfortable with the culture and personality approach. Because they usually deal with societies that are more heterogeneous and complex than those with which anthropologists are concerned, they are more prone to question the possibility of finding a typical personality. Instead, they tend to approach the problem of national character through an examination of value systems.[5] The practitioners in the field of culture and personality studies have, for the most part, been anthropologists and psychiatrists.

York, 1939) and "The Concept of Basic Personality Structure as an Operational Tool in the Social Sciences," in *The Science of Man in the World Crisis*, ed. Ralph Linton (New York, 1945), pp. 107–122.

[4] "What We Know and What We Don't," in *Aspects of Culture and Personality*, ed. Hsu, pp. 207–209.

[5] Talcott Parsons is probably the leading theoretician of the sociological school that stresses the importance of value analysis. See *The Structure of Social Action* (New York, 1937) and *The Social System* (Glencoe, Ill., 1951).

II

The trend toward the employment of psychiatric concepts in studies of the American character began in the 1920's. Alfred B. Kuttner considered American civilization in terms of the characteristic mental disturbances which existed in it and the sources from which they had sprung.[6] He said nothing that was appreciably different from what other critics of American civilization were saying at the time; he simply used a slightly different vocabulary. This was a reflection of the fact that Freudian ideas were not very well understood in the United States in the 1920's outside of the professional circles of psychology. Freudianism was something of a fad and, like most fads, it attracted shallow and superficial interest. Many people who talked glibly of "repression" and "inhibition" had only the vaguest notion of the meaning of these terms. It is a tribute to the viability of Freud's ideas that they were able to survive even the good intentions of many of his early converts.

By the 1930's the relevance of Freud's ideas to other fields of inquiry had been fairly well accepted. The alliance between anthropology and psychiatry had been firmly established by Sapir and others. The stage was set for the wholesale adoption of psychiatric concepts by social scientists and the application of these concepts to their fields of study.

Another strong impetus to the growth of interest in psychiatric ideas in the United States came from outside the country. In the 1930's the United States suddenly found itself the psychiatric center of the world as German and Austrian scholars fled there to find refuge from Nazi persecution. Karen Horney, Erich Fromm, Franz Alexander, Bruno Bettelheim, and many others came to America and took up permanent residence. This sudden influx of many of the leading lights in psychiatry not only stimulated greater interest in psychiatric concepts among American thinkers but also led to a new interpretation of the American scene. The refugees were immigrants and felt the desire common to all immigrants to arrive at an understanding of the new and unfamiliar situation in which they found themselves.

[6] "Nerves," in *Civilization in the United States*, ed. Stearns, pp. 427–442.

They were probably more sensitive and certainly more articulate than most immigrants, but they were just as eager to get to know the country which had become their home.

The result was that the 1930's saw several studies of the American character which took their starting point from conceptual keynotes such as frustration, anxiety, and insecurity. Commentators either traced manifestations of these tendencies in American life or concerned themselves with attempts to determine the sources from which these traits had sprung, or both. Most of the refugee psychiatrists insisted that they were not specifically concerned with the United States but with Western society in general. In practice, however, they drew virtually all their illustrative material from American life. They stated or implied strongly that the trends they described were more intense in the United States than anywhere else, and they gave the impression that they believed that the United States was the most hospitable home for most of the pathological tendencies they were worried about.

For example, it was a commonplace of psychiatry that culture itself produced certain frustrations, that the process of socialization inevitably warped and distorted the individual to a certain extent, and that civilized life was, almost by definition, a life in which certain basic desires of the human animal were constantly frustrated.[7] In these new studies, however, American life seemed to be especially frustrating and seemed to impose greater pressures on the individual than any other culture imposed. This endemic frustration was manifested in several ways, perhaps most sensationally in a tendency toward aggressive behavior. According to a well-developed and extremely popular socio-psychological theory, frustration and aggression were often related as cause and effect; aggressive behavior was the means by which the frustrated individual relieved his accumulated tensions. If the frustrations were severe, the resulting aggression could be sharp,

[7] That civilization and the socialization process were productive of frustration was, of course, one of the key points in Freud's whole system. Perhaps its clearest expression was in *Civilization and Its Discontents* (London, 1922). For a purely American treatment of the same theme see Lawrence K. Frank, "Cultural Coercion and Individual Distortion," *Psychiatry* 2 (1939), 11–27, reprinted in *Society as the Patient: Essays on Culture and Personality* (New Brunswick, N. J., 1948), pp. 166–192.

almost explosive in character. The fact that Americans seemed to be addicted to actual violence in their political life and to vicarious violence in their entertainment and to exhibit a generalized rebelliousness and resistance to authority was interpreted as the natural consequence of their suffering from chronic frustration. The most frightening aspect of this disposition to violence was a persistent condition of political instability so serious as to endanger the political structure of the nation.[8] This was, after all, the era of Huey Long, Father Coughlin, and the Black Legion.[9]

Anxiety and insecurity were other dominant traits that the refugee psychiatrists noted in the American character. Karen Horney summed up the general position when she said, "Our culture generates a great deal of anxiety in the individuals living in it."[10] In a frantic search for a way to relieve this anxiety, Americans engaged in fierce economic and social competition; success established the individual's place in the world, provided him with an identity, and reassured him that he was a worthwhile human being and a valuable member of his community. But this means of resolving the problem was not satisfactory, for the emphasis on competition meant that those who did not succeed became even more insecure. Even those who were successful continued their frantic striving, driven by the fear that what they had might be snatched away from them. In the long run, therefore, the competitive nature of American life did not resolve anxiety but intensified it. It led ultimately to a desperate conformity, to an attempt, in the words of Erich Fromm, to escape from freedom, to an attempt to escape feelings of isolation

[8] John W. Dollard et al., *Frustration and Aggression* (New York, 1939), and Harold D. Lasswell, *World Politics and Personal Insecurity* (New York, 1935), pp. 223–225. It is significant that although Dollard was a sociologist and Lasswell a political scientist, both had made it a point to submit themselves to analysis. They were in the vanguard of the movement to apply psychiatric concepts to the study of society. See John W. Dollard, *Caste and Class in a Southern Town* (New Haven, 1937), and Harold D. Lasswell, *Psychopathology and Politics* (New York, 1930).

[9] Morris Janowitz, "Black Legions on the March," in *America in Crisis: Fourteen Crucial Episodes in American History*, ed. Daniel Aaron (New York, 1952), pp. 305–325.

[10] *The Neurotic Personality of Our Time* (New York, 1937), p. 59.

and ineffectuality by behaving exactly like everyone else, and to a willingness, even an eagerness, to submit to a powerful leader.

We can see in all of this not only the fact that the American character was being dissected with conceptual tools borrowed from psychiatry, but also that the personal experiences of the interpreters had a significant effect on their interpretations. They were intensely afraid of fascism. They had seen its triumph in Germany and Italy, had experienced its effects at first hand, and had been forced to flee from it. They wanted to prevent it from coming to the Western democracies. They saw themselves, at least half consciously, as the bearers of a message of warning to the rest of the world. They did not employ psychoanalytic concepts in the study of society simply because they were psychiatrists. The society and culture of Nazi Germany seemed to demand analysis in these terms. If ever there was a society which could be said to be "sick" in more than a metaphorical sense, that society was Nazi Germany. If ever there was a political system which seemed to be the institutionalized expression of psychological abnormalities, that system was the Third Reich. German fascism was not only a political system but also a case study in abnormal psychology on the social, rather than the individual, level.

The result of this combination of influences was a series of studies of the American character which seemed to be based on the proposition that America was threatened by fascism and that the threat was internally caused and immediately present. Implicit in them was a constant comparison between the United States and Nazi Germany. The refugee intellectuals would certainly not have denied that America was a far better place to live than Germany; after all, they had spent much money and expended much effort to move to America. Yet their treatments did not stress the superiority of America over Germany or the differences between the two regimes, but rather the points of similarity between them. Because they feared fascism they looked for it. Because they looked for it they tended to see it everywhere. They seemed deliberately to seek out and to emphasize those traits in the American character whose existence would provide support for their contention that the United States was in danger of succumbing to fascist totalitarianism.

III

They found the source of this dangerous tendency in the American character in certain features of the economic system. Erich Fromm expressed the general view most clearly. He maintained that the breakdown of the feudal order had made man independent, but it had also isolated him from his fellows and given him feelings of powerlessness and anxiety. In throwing off the old external restraints on his freedom, man had merely substituted a new set of internal restraints. He had freedom of religion but was unable to believe anything that could not be proved "scientifically." He had freedom of speech but nothing original to say. He was independent of external authorities but terrified of public opinion and the thought of being "different." He felt this way because the economic system under which he lived had turned him into an interchangeable cog in a vast, mechanistic society. The consequence was that he felt lost, insignificant, and powerless.[11] His chief weapon in his unremitting struggle against insecurity and the feeling of ineffectuality was competitive success, measured by the accumulation of property. But the drive for success landed him in the midst of a vicious psychological circle, for success required competition, competition engendered feelings of hostility, and hostility produced fear, fear of others and especially fear of failure. This fear in turn bred a desperate conformity and also made it impossible for the individual to relax; competition itself became a psychological necessity in a competitive society.[12] Nor was this all. The drive for success exacted another psychological toll in that it required a kind of thinking and behavior that were flatly contradictory to the ideals of brotherly love and humility. Further, though individual freedom was highly valued in the abstract, in practical affairs the individual had to conform to achieve the success required of him by the society and by his own psychological needs.[13]

In short, American society was beset by disjunctions which led to psychological disturbances in the American people. Law-

---

[11] *Escape from Freedom* (New York, 1941), pp. 104–105, 241–255.

[12] This trend of thought was most clearly expressed by Lawrence K. Frank in his essay "The Cost of Competition," *Plan Age*, 6 (1940), 314–324, reprinted in *Society as the Patient*, pp. 21–36.

[13] Horney, *Neurotic Personality*, pp. 288–289.

rence Frank expressed the underlying thoughts of the entire school when he maintained that there was a serious breakdown in American culture, manifested in the lack of a unified body of ideas and beliefs relevant to the current scene. Individual deviance and disturbance arose "from the frantic efforts of individuals, lacking any sure direction and sanctions or guiding conception of life, to find some way of protecting themselves or of merely existing on any terms they can manage in a society being remade by scientific research and technology."[14] In other words, the society was changing so fast that it was outrunning the ability of individuals to find appropriate psychological adjustments to new ways of thinking and acting. The problem was cultural lag, differential rates of social change in different parts of the social body, particularly between the economic organization on the one hand and the general value system on the other.

Franz Alexander elaborated the theme in some detail. His treatment of the American character was essentially a restatement of the Frontier Thesis in the language of psychiatry and applied to a society in which the formative influence of the frontier existed only as a painful anachronism. The persistence of the frontier ideal "explained the most common conflict of American neurotics, the thwarted ambition of people trained to admire individual achievements, as their ancestors had done in the days of the Open Frontier, yet situated in a standardized industrial civilization which imposed uneventful routine and offered no real security in return." The primary conflict in the American character and the source of those painful dislocations and disharmonies in American life which produced mental disease was that "the individualistic ideological tradition of the expanding Frontier period conflicts with the changed economic structure of an industrial society which is in the process of consolidation."[15] These conflicts produced in the American personality a deepseated conflict between ambition and dependence, between the driving desire to make a success in the competitive world and the desire to stop and rest, between the desire to assert one's superiority and the desire to escape the fears and insecurities

[14] *Society as the Patient*, p. 5.
[15] *Our Age of Unreason: A Study of the Irrational Forces in Social Life* (Philadelphia, 1942), pp. 10, 293.

produced by the competitive race by retreating into childish dependence. Alexander summed up his findings this way:

> The answer is to be found in the culturally determined internal inconsistency of our social standards; the traditional one-sided worship of individual success in a complex interdependent society and the exaggerated emphasis on independence in terms of great insecurity. . . . The prestige attached to independent achievement on the one hand and the longing for security, love, and belonging to somebody or some group on the other are the two poles between which patients are torn in a futile struggle. . . . The analyst sees his patients . . . engaged in a Marathon race, their eager faces distorted by strain, their eyes focused not upon their goal, but upon each other with a mixture of hate, envy, and admiration.[16]

This concern with the economic roots of psychological maladjustment in the American character was closely connected with the experience of the Depression. The vehemence with which the success ethic was criticized had an obvious relationship to the fact that the current economic crisis made its evil effects especially apparent, since those who believed in it were especially likely to be seriously frustrated in their attempts to achieve the goals it set. But these commentators were disturbed not by a temporary derangement in the economic system but by its permanent and enduring features. If it was an economy in crisis, it was, in their view, a continuing crisis, one which existed not only in times of depression but also in times of prosperity when the economy was functioning normally. Indeed, one might almost conclude that Marx was as important an influence here as Freud, that the psychological contradictions emphasized in these treatments of the American character were simply special cases or particular manifestations of the economic contradictions in capitalism postulated by Marx. The effect of the Depression, which made Marxism seem more relevant to the American experience than it had seemed in the past, combined with the presence on the American intellectual scene of a large number of

[16] *Ibid.*, pp. 308–310.

European scholars to whom Marxism was probably more familiar and more congenial than it had been to thinkers on this side of the Atlantic, produced a climate of opinion in which one can detect substantial Marxist influences.

The extent of the Marxist influence, however, should not be exaggerated. In many ways the psychiatric interpretations of the American character were simply reworkings of themes which had already been well developed. Croly had pointed out contradictions between American ideals and American realities; striving for success had been widely condemned in the 1920's and earlier, though usually under the more general label of "materialism." The charges that were leveled by the psychiatrist-critics of American civilization in the 1930's were fundamentally no different from those of the artist-critics of the 1920's, except that they were directed toward psychological rather than artistic problems and were stated in psychiatric rather than aesthetic terms. The general basis was the same: Americans were so devoted to the pursuit of material gain that their characters had become seriously warped and one-sided. Needing a prop in an insecure world, they had developed a materialist obsession which had prevented them from being sufficiently flexible in their responses to the world. In both the 1920's and the 1930's, conformity and business civilization, materialism and insecurity, were thought to go hand in hand and to be the bases of the American character. It was not necessary to be a Marxist or to have lived through a depression in order to criticize the United States in this fashion. In the 1920's Babbitt had been isolated and described; in the 1930's he was psychoanalyzed.

IV

The culture and personality approach did not lead to any radically new conclusions about the American character, but it was a new approach, a new method of attack on an old problem. Because it was new and untried, it suffered from certain theoretical shortcomings.

Most treatments of the American character in this period attempted to understand America by discovering what was wrong with it. American distinctiveness was defined, for all practical purposes, in terms of the distinctive patterns of mental disease and disturbances that existed in the United States. The neurotic characteristics of American civilization were usually equated with the distinctively American characteristics of individual American neurotics. The operating assumption was that society was the patient and that neurotic personalities existed because of the neurotic characteristics of the society. Karen Horney summed up the prevailing view: "Hence in speaking of a neurotic personality of our time, I not only mean that there are neurotic persons having essential peculiarities in common, but also that these basic similarities are essentially produced by the difficulties existing in our time and culture."[17]

As a result, most of the studies of the American character made from the psychiatric point of view suffered from a conflict between the conceptual apparatus and the material to which that apparatus was applied. To assert, as most psychiatrists did, at least by implication, that society was the patient was to assert that their analyses were social, not individual; the national character, in other words, was the character of the nation, not of the typical individual. But the terms in which the discussion was conducted were the terms of psychiatry; the tendencies these students of American society discussed were tendencies toward mental disease manifested by individuals. To discuss a whole society in terms originally conceived to describe or explain mental disturbances in specific individuals was to stretch the original meanings of these terms almost beyond recognition. An individual may be neurotic, but to speak of an entire society as neurotic is to use the term in a purely metaphorical sense. Those who attempted to deal with the American character by applying psychiatric concepts to its study never resolved this conflict in their own minds; they could never quite decide whether they were speaking of American society as a whole or of the individuals within it.

If pressed for an explanation of what they were doing, they would probably have said that they were generalizing on the basis of their experiences with individual patients. But there is a real question whether this was their actual procedure. Even if it was, there remains the question of whether it is justifiable to generalize for an entire society on the basis of experiences with

[17] *Neurotic Personality*, p. 34.

its maladjusted members. Though it is comparatively easy to find social strains which produce neuroses in individuals, this does not prove that society is sick. Many people do not succumb to the psychological pressures of their society. People react differently to psychological strains; experiences which produce mental disease in one individual may have little or no effect on another. It is methodologically questionable in the extreme to infer national character solely from the individual characteristics of disturbed inhabitants of the nation.

The fact that these commentators on the American character were psychiatrists is partly responsible for their pessimism. By the very nature of their work, psychiatrists are brought most closely into contact with maladjusted personalities. They see the whole society, as it were, through the eyes of the psychologically unfit. They do not see the normal individual operating in a specific cultural context, but the maladjusted individual operating in a context which imposes strains on him that he cannot cope with.

To be sure, this is not a complete explanation of the profound pessimism of most of the writers in the culture and personality school. For one thing, not all of them were psychiatrists—Lasswell and Dollard, for instance, were not—and those outside the profession would not have had the continued exposure to maladjusted individuals that was presumably responsible for giving rise to the pessimism. Conversely, not all psychiatrists were unhappy with the American character. James S. Plant felt that a new kind of cultural pattern was evolving in the United States, an "individual-centered culture," which was replacing the older profit-centered culture in which the individual's importance was defined by what he contributed to the economic order. As far as Plant was concerned, the change was all for the better.[18]

What, then, explains why most of the interpretations made from the point of view of clinical psychiatry were so unfavorable? The answer lies in the fact that many of these commentators were refugees. Their extreme sensitivity to any evidence of fascism has already been discussed. It also must be remembered that they arrived in this country at a time when the nation was not at all prepared to receive callers—in the middle of a severe

[18] *Personality and the Cultural Pattern* (New York, 1937).

economic depression. With no first-hand knowledge of the "normal" state of American social and economic life to correct the impression left by the obviously deranged conditions that confronted them, they were not likely to be inspired with much confidence in the viability of the American way of life. Also, they were somewhat self-conscious. They were newcomers, true, but they were not the same sort of people who had come to the United States by the millions in the days of unrestricted immigration. They were not laborers or peasants, but sophisticated intellectuals, and they did not have the same kind of naive enthusiasm for their new home that their predecessors had had. Though they were grateful for having been given refuge, they were not going to allow their gratitude to obscure the clarity of vision with which they evaluated their adopted country. This very determination distorted their view. To look at a situation with "clear eyes" usually means to look at it with critical eyes, and the eyes of these refugees had already been jaundiced by their experiences in Europe. Finally, because they were relatively unfamiliar with the American scene, they were dependent upon previous analyses for an introduction to the subject and for basic categories of thought on it. They were at the mercy of the established myths concerning America and the American character. Since they were not Americans, one would not have expected to find them enmeshed in the agrarian myth, but in fact they were as firmly committed to Turnerian and Jeffersonian modes of thought as any native intellectual was. With this background, they tended to view America as the scene of a conflict between an orderly, harmonious, agrarian past and a disorderly, chaotic, industrial present. Their thinking ran down the old agrarian channel. They simply restated the Turnerian and Jeffersonian conclusions in psychiatric language.

7

THE AMERICAN
CHARACTER IN THE 1940's

AT WAR AND AT PEACE

I

The years during and after World War II saw a great upsurge of interest in the problem of national character. The national-character study was regarded by many as a practical instrument which could help in the winning of the war. It was thought to be an important and necessary part of America's "public relations" program in the war, an aid in the effort to understand American culture and customs in relation to those of America's allies so that there could be easy communication between them. It was also felt that a similar knowledge of America's enemies could be an important weapon against them. Margaret Mead said:

> In the United States, the study of national character as the application of anthropological and psychological methods to contemporary modern societies developed during World War II. It was the wartime situation—in which the United States was faced with the problem of waging a total war, including psychological warfare, against little-known and inaccessible enemies—which stimulated this special scientific development. . . .[1]

[1] "The Study of National Character," in *The Policy Sciences: Recent Developments in Scope and Method*, eds. Daniel Lerner and Harold D. Lasswell (Stanford, 1951), p. 70. See also Gregory Bateson, "Morale and National Character," in *Civilian Morale*, ed. Goodwin Watson (New York, 1942), pp. 71–91, and Otto Klineberg, "A Science of National Character," *Journal of Social Psychology*, 19 (1944), 147–162.

It would not be correct to interpret this as meaning that the war saw the *first* application of anthropological methods to contemporary societies—that, after all, had occurred at least as early as the 1930's—but it is unquestionably true that the pressures of war did stimulate interest in the problem of national character.

Not only were Americans driven to attempt to understand their enemies and allies, but it also seemed increasingly important to understand themselves. Since they were engaged in a bitter struggle with alien ideologies, they were naturally stimulated to pay some conscious attention to their own. As a consequence, studies from this period show a clear tendency to consider the American character in terms of values and underlying philosophical orientations. This approach had already been established, but the pressures of the ideological conflict probably speeded up the transition to a mode of attack on the problem of national character which defined the American by his outlook and assumed that the most important things that could be said of him would be contained in a description of his values—that the American *was* what he believed. After the war, interest in the problem continued, the wartime experience having established to the satisfaction of many that the investigation of the national character was a legitimate and fruitful mode of social analysis.

II

Much of the work of the group of social scientists who asserted that the study of national character could be an immensely practical tool in the war effort was purely theoretical. There were and are excellent precedents for adopting this line, for many social scientists take seemingly endless delight in elaborating possible new approaches to certain problems, recording the results of their intellectual labors for posterity in papers with titles such as "Fields of Research in . . ." or "Unanswered Questions in the Area of . . ." At least one member of this group, however, not only proffered advice but also followed it. In her book *And Keep Your Powder Dry*, Margaret Mead made a conscious attempt to evaluate America's human resources in the war effort, to arrive at an understanding of the strengths and weaknesses of the American character, in the hope that such an understanding would be useful as a guide to action in winning the war and in rebuilding the world after the war was over.

Her effort was not wholly successful, as she herself would undoubtedly have admitted. It was not the same kind of concentrated ethnographic study of alien cultures that she and other cultural anthropologists had engaged in, but rather a sparse and highly impressionistic account of a few major characteristics of the American value system and American culture: the emphasis on mobility and success, the overwhelming importance of conforming to the approved moral system, and the confusion and contradictions in the American code of prescriptions for coping with and justifying aggression and violence. Her scope was limited, and her findings were not scientifically verified. Perhaps they were not even scientifically verifiable. She recognized this, but offered her findings anyway, believing that since some kind of action had to be taken, it would be far better to have this action based on information and knowledge that were admittedly incomplete than on no information and knowledge at all.[2]

Mead did not try to make her work useful by turning it into a propaganda effort. Under the circumstances, one might reasonably have expected to find in her book a glorification of the American tradition, an extolling of American culture, a loving catalogue of the virtues of American civilization with comparisons to the vices of the cultures of America's enemies—in short, an apotheosis of chauvinism. Such expectations were to be disappointed. Mead's stated purpose was to evaluate both American strengths and American weaknesses. In practice, she devoted much more attention to American weaknesses. To be sure, she also offered some suggestions for remedial action, but for the most part they were vague and unspecific. Perhaps this was all she could have— or even should have—done. Specific suggestions should be based on thorough, detailed investigation, which she in effect admitted she had not been able to carry out. What does emerge from her discussion are the standard themes of the culture and personality studies of the American character: the psychologically destructive effects of the competitiveness of American society and the

[2] *And Keep Your Powder Dry: An Anthropologist Looks at America* (New York, 1942), pp. 13–14.

bitter frustration inevitable in a society that defined moral worth in terms of material success but at the same time offered few roads to such success for the majority of the people.

Unlike Margaret Mead, the economic historian John U. Nef did not make any explicit attempt to relate his interpretation to current world conditions, but nevertheless it bears the marks of contemporary struggles far more clearly than Mead's did. He, too, was disturbed by the American penchant for measuring all values by an economic yardstick, because he felt that this pervasive materialism threatened the older cultural, intellectual, and spiritual values of Western civilization. This must have seemed especially dangerous to him at a time when those values were under direct attack. Also dangerous, said Nef, was the complacent assumption that virtue was rewarded with material success; it was in effect a surrender to those forces in the world which were not at all concerned with virtue. To go on playing the game on the basis of such an assumption and according to the traditional rules would thus lead to the destruction of Western civilization and of what was best in man.[3]

Most wartime studies of the American character, however, were, as might be expected, substantially more optimistic than Mead's or Nef's. While Nef had seen trends in the United States that threatened the historic ideals of Western civilization, the Beards saw forces that would ultimately preserve that civilization from the threats which confronted it. Indeed, in their view the United States was almost synonymous with the idea of civilization itself: "We have reached the conviction that no idea, such as democracy, or the American way of life, expresses the American spirit so coherently, comprehensively, and systematically as does the idea of civilization." The Beards' definition of the idea of civilization was vague, but it bore a close resemblance to the idea of progress, the idea that man could and would improve his world and in the end "make the good, the true, and the beautiful prevail more widely, advancing civilization, amid divagations, defeats, and storms, toward its distant, ever-enlarging vision."[4] Since it was the American who was to do all this, the Beards' argument here is essentially a restatement of the old American idea of mission, the idea that America is the special

[3] *The United States and Civilization* (Chicago, 1942).
[4] Charles A. Beard and Mary R. Beard, *American Spirit*, pp. v, 672–674.

bearer of a message of salvation to the rest of the world, and that the American character was defined primarily by this missionary heritage. The relevance of this idea in the wartime situation is obvious.

There is good reason to believe that the war was the main factor in bringing about a change of mind, or heart, on the part of James Truslow Adams. In the 1920's his criticisms of American society, culture, and character were profound; in the 1940's he found much to praise, making the same conversion from prosecutor to defense attorney that Harold Stearns had made in the 1930's. Adams still found evidence of the traits that he had attacked in the 1920's: the materialism, the standardization, the conformity, the provinciality. But in his analysis in the 1940's these undesirable traits were played down and far more attention was given to the American's good qualities. Instead of dwelling on the conformist tendencies in American life, Adams emphasized the American's humor, hospitality, and friendliness; instead of criticizing America for its lack of devotion to the arts, Adams commented on the size of its museums; instead of condemning the American for his exclusive preoccupation with money-making, Adams extolled his generosity, his optimism, his versatility, his easygoing confidence in his own abilities; and instead of emphasizing the deadening effects of shortsighted practicality, Adams found that the American, "with all his Yankee 'notions,' his pioneer spirit, his mass production, and the rest . . . has ever been essentially the *dreamer*."[5]

This type of thinking was not confined to the period of the war itself, however. It persisted after the conflict had come to an end, at least in the work of Ralph Barton Perry. The direction that his interpretation of the American character was to take was clearly indicated by his wartime discussion of the American tradition, *Puritanism and Democracy*. He treated Puritanism and democracy as separate influences, but there are many indications that he believed them to work together and to be reflections of each other.[6] In Perry's hands, Puritanism was transformed from the anti-democratic force it had been in the 1920's to one of the principal sources of democratic ideas and feelings. The

[5] *The American: The Making of a New Man* (New York, 1943), pp. 384–385.
[6] (New York, 1944).

hints contained in this early work were made explicit after the war, in his book *Characteristically American*. Here Perry treated Puritanism as the doctrine from which Americans had derived their belief that man was a responsible and autonomous being, their belief in the power of the human will, and, in combination with Enlightenment thought, their belief in the theory of natural rights and the fundamental doctrines of American democracy. These ideas had been reinforced by the frontier experience, which had added to the American tradition a spirit that Perry called "collective individualism"—it was individualism, but it was modified and regulated; it was collective, but it did not result in any abject following of the crowd.[7] Perry went even further. As the self-appointed successor of William James, he maintained that the most nearly perfect expression of the American mind was pragmatism, which had left its mark on American life in many ways: in the American reverence for natural science, in the practical and experimental attitude with which Americans approached political and economic problems, in the general belief that the world was man's and that his environment existed to be manipulated by him and turned to his own purposes, and in the tendency of Americans toward moderation and the avoidance of fanaticism.[8]

An interesting feature of these favorable treatments of the American character is that the authors shared a tendency to view it as being composed of complementary opposites. Lee Coleman has made the point that writers on the American character tend to see it in terms of polar opposites: while one might see the American as a materialist, another would see him as an idealist.[9] This is perfectly correct, but Coleman has neglected to make room for the many other writers who would have described the American as a materialistic idealist. Perry combined two poles in his term "collective individualism," and in their description of the idea of civilization the Beards put individual liberty and the "social principle" side by side. Adams stressed those traits in the American character that enabled the American to work with his fellows at the same time that he was insisting that the American was not a conformist. A similar pairing in

[7] (New York, 1949), pp. 37–42.
[8] *Ibid.*, pp. 50–64.
[9] "What Is American?: A Study of Alleged American Traits," *Social Forces*, 19 (1941), 492–499.

the works of these authors is seen in their attention to what might be called "practical idealism." The Beards contended that creative intelligence could be applied to the practical realization of ideal objectives. Adams called the American a "dreamer," but a dreamer who had created and built a mass-production technology. Perry pointed out that the pragmatic spirit in America, with its moderation and avoidance of fanaticism, had given the world a vivid example of high ideals in action.

It is probable that these thinkers found justification for their views in the contemporary situation. The political experience of the New Deal and the necessities of the war, which had led people to accept, even demand, an increase of governmental power to defend the national interest, must have seemed to them a striking confirmation of their belief that individualism could be modified in a way that would promote not only the good of society as a whole but also the freedom of the individual. And the fact that in the New Deal and in the war Americans had devoted themselves to the task of finding practical defenses for their most deeply cherished ideals must have seemed to them a perfect illustration of practical idealism.

This tendency to think of the American character in terms of complementary opposites resulted in an exalted conception of it, for according to this formula the American could not be accused of being one-sided in his development; his virtues could not become defects by being exaggerated out of proportion. Idealism was something to be admired, but it was desirable to have it tempered by practicality. Individualism was a quality worthy of praise, but men had to live in society and get along with others. If the American was neither wholly materialistic nor wholly idealistic, neither a rampant individualist nor an abject conformist, he displayed a balanced collection of traits that was to be vastly preferred to a more one-sided development. People who adopted such a view of the American character were able to have their cake and eat it, too; the American character interpreted in such a fashion was immune to criticism from all directions.

III

After the war pessimism reappeared in interpretations of the American character. Since it was no longer necessary to view the

American character in a favorable light for the sake of the war effort, there was a return to the critical spirit which had prevailed widely before the war. F. S. C. Northrop criticized America's adherence to the rampant laissez-faire individualism of John Locke in terms that were reminiscent of the criticisms of America's "business civilization" current during the 1920's. Charles Morris feared that the overemphasis and overvaluation of those personality traits directed toward domination and mastery threatened the continued existence of America's open society. Clyde Kluckhohn catalogued the debilitating psychological effects of life in an excessively fluid, excessively mobile society.[10]

Gardner Murphy's treatment gave vivid expression to the underlying assumption upon which these writers had based their interpretations. Murphy maintained that the American character had been formed on the frontier and that it bore the imprint of the frontier experience. But when the frontier disappeared, "almost at one stroke there ceased to be a basis for the indefinite continuance of the personality type which had become dominant during nearly three centuries of American history." Thus, because of significant social changes in American life, a rift had developed between the traditional values of American culture and the situation in which those values were presumably embodied; people continued to adhere to traditional beliefs even though they no longer fit the present situation and the expectations they engendered were almost certain to be frustrated.[11]

The theme was often repeated. Northrop's objection to Locke's philosophy was not that it was inherently invalid, but rather that it was simply not suited to contemporary conditions of life in the United States. He felt that the unease and confusion of the American people were the predictable fate of a people who had become attached to a set of theoretical philosophical propositions that had been adequate in the seventeenth century but were totally inadequate in the twentieth. Morris

[10] F. S. C. Northrop, *The Meeting of East and West: An Inquiry Concerning World Understanding* (New York, 1946), pp. 66–164, and *The Taming of the Nations: A Study of the Cultural Bases of Foreign Policy* (New York, 1952), pp. 318–323; Charles Morris, *The Open Self* (New York, 1948), pp. 160–174; Clyde Kluckhohn, *Mirror for Man: A Survey of Human Behavior and Social Attitudes* (New York, 1949), pp. 178–195.

[11] *Personality: A Biosocial Approach to Origins and Structure* (New York, 1947), pp. 829–839.

maintained that the high value Americans placed on the dominant, masterful personality was rational and socially valuable in an underdeveloped area like the American frontier. But in a developed society, with no more "open spaces" in either the geographic or the economic sense, in a country in which the primary problem was not to build an economic machine but to exploit in a rational fashion a machine which had already been built, in such a situation the aggressive personality was an anachronism, and a dangerous anachronism at that. Kluckhohn questioned the suitability of frontier values to modern industrial society. He felt that American society suffered from what amounted to a mass neurosis, largely because the actual economic organization of society rendered success impossible for all but a few, while the cultural ideals preached the efficacy of hard work, education, and aggressiveness in overcoming all obstacles.

A comparison of the relatively optimistic works on the American character with those that were relatively pessimistic reveals that the differences between them were largely differences of emphasis and attitude rather than differences in the perception of fact. There was fundamental agreement on the basic traits of the American character and on the important formative influences: Puritanism, the frontier, and immigration. The main difference between them was usually seen in the way in which the interpretation was put forward. After noting the things that were wrong with the American character—materialism and conformity were the most frequent charges—the optimist went on to explain these deficiencies away or to turn them into positive advantages by including them as one half of a complementary pair of apparently contradictory traits. The pessimists, if they found anything at all to admire about America—and most of them did—noted these admirable qualities first, and then went on to catalogue all the limitations on American perfection that they could think of. What was thought to be right with the American character and what was thought to be wrong with it were frequently, even usually, identical. Often the difference between the optimist and the pessimist was, at least on the surface, only a difference in the order in which he presented the facts.

The question then becomes one of determining the reasons for the difference in presentation, and it appears that it was dictated most significantly by the fact that the optimists and the pessimists reacted in fundamentally different ways to industrialism. Practically all commentators on the American character would have agreed that the transition from an agricultural to an industrial economy had changed America profoundly. For the pessimists this change had been disastrous. Even those to whom the agrarian way of life and the Jeffersonian tradition were not sacred in themselves regarded their passing with discomfort, for they felt that American values were by and large the values of an agrarian society and did not work well in an urban and industrial setting.

Henry Bamford Parkes articulated a widely held view in an analysis of American history in which the main feature was the conflict between agrarianism and industrialism. He asserted that American institutions and the American character had been molded by an abundance of land and resources working within an agrarian economy, creating an American who was free, independent, optimistic, self-confident, and individualistic. These characteristics had made it possible for the American people to build an industrial society, but they also made it almost impossible for Americans to live in that society once it had been built. There developed a monumental divergence in American life between the ideals of America's agrarian past and the realities of its industrial present. The American people, in short, had gotten themselves into a psychological trap. The conditions of their life in the developmental phase of the nation's history had created a character structure and a set of values that emphasized domination, power, and mastery, and this emphasis was completely inappropriate in the modern setting.[12]

It is somewhat paradoxical that Parkes made so much of the fact of cultural lag and the persistence beyond the bounds of common sense of the agrarian tradition, for he seemed just as reluctant as anyone to give up the tradition. In itself, the cultural-lag hypothesis does not enjoin adherence to any particular ideal of society, but in fact it concealed an implicit faith. Parkes did not insist that America was an agrarian society, but it is quite clear that he wished it were. He assumed, tacitly at least, that industrialism was incompatible with economic democracy and

[12] *The American Experience: An Interpretation of the History and Civilization of the American People* (New York, 1947).

opportunity for all. He invariably painted agrarian society in pleasant terms, industrial society in unpleasant terms. It would seem, therefore, that if he were to propose a program to correct the radical disharmony between American traditions and American social realities he would have insisted upon adhering to the tradition and trying to restructure social institutions so that they would conform to the pre-existing ideal.

Parkes's attitudes were characteristic of many of those who were unhappy with the results of their investigations of the American character. Generally speaking, they were unhappy largely because they saw the United States as an industrial nation, and they distrusted industrialism. Mead was somewhat unusual among this group in that she felt that the American character had begun to change under the impact of necessity—most of the other pessimists felt that the primary difficulty was that it had *not* changed—but she did agree with the rest in her dislike of industrialism. She saw an American character that was changing, but she did not like the changes she saw. The success ethic, unattractive though it was, still had certain admirable qualities in Mead's view, especially its emphasis on personal responsibility and on intelligent experimentation as a means of solving problems. The type of character that Mead saw replacing the older success-dominated American, a type distinguished by fear of responsibility and by a defensive cynicism, was, for all its greater compatibility with social realities, not a type which she admired. Morris felt that the problem of cultural lag was to be solved by developing social institutions that would preserve the Jeffersonian ideal, by restructuring society instead of the ideal itself. Murphy welcomed the persistence of the frontier character in modern society despite the fact that he had defined it as anachronistic. This inconsistency reveals the powerful emotional hold of the agrarian ideal, a hold so strong that even those writers who noted the divergence between ideal and reality insisted on adhering to the ideal and on changing the social system to conform to the pre-existing and pre-established ideal.

IV

There were writers who did not fit into this pattern. F. S. C. Northrop, for instance, perceived a tension between America's philosophical traditions and its social realities; however, he did not want to improve the situation by changing society, but rather by changing basic philosophical preconceptions. Much of the emphasis on the restructuring of American institutions was probably a product of the New Deal experience. The New Deal technique of saving capitalism by modifying some of its cruder manifestations was analogous to the desire of the agrarian-minded interpreters of the American character to preserve the fundamentally agrarian ideals of the United States by changing the situation in which those ideals had to function. This was not true of Northrop. He was not a social scientist or a political analyst, but a philosopher. He focused on ideas, emphasized their intrinsic importance, and assumed that they could be changed rationally. Charles Morris, of course, was also a philosopher, but he came from the pragmatic tradition. As a pragmatist he tended to see ideas as social products while Northrop was more inclined to view them as independent variables.

Northrop was not directly concerned with the conflict, postulated by the writers who upheld the agrarian ideal, between an admirable agrarian past and a disjointed industrial present. Other writers made a more direct attack on the agrarian position.

Erik H. Erikson, though unhappy about many aspects of American life and character, was willing to concede the possibility that the people of the United States could make a creative adjustment to the pressures of industrialism. Much of his treatment, to be sure, was devoted to an analysis of the twin derangements of the American character which he called "Momism" and "bossism." The former denoted the tendency to be dominated by maternal authority in family situations; the latter, the tendency to surrender to external authority in economic and political affairs. Momism was the result of the autocracy of nature in a new continent, a product of the frontier experience and the Puritan heritage. Bossism was the product and the basis of the autocracy of the machine, industrial and political. To the extent that the American was dominated by bossism, he was a slave of the machine and machine processes. Yet it is significant that Erikson did *not* feel that industrialism had been responsible for the psychological enslavement of the American in the first instance. Momism, after all, was a product of Puritanism and the frontier. Erikson also felt that while the American showed a tendency to let himself be overwhelmed by the machine, he also demonstrated an uncanny affinity for industrial processes. In the end, therefore, Erikson seemed to accept the machine. Though he noted that submission to it could be dangerous, he implied that the American might be skillful enough to make the machine submit to him, thus freeing himself from the twin dependencies of Momism and bossism by providing himself with an outlet for, and thus a stimulant to, his individual initiative. In effect, the instrument of his enslavement might prove to be the tool with which he achieved his freedom.[13]

Others were more forthright in their acceptance of industrialism as a new, and better, way of life for the United States. Even during the war Arthur M. Schlesinger had noted: "This long apprenticeship to the soil made an indelible impress on the developing American character, with results which the modern age of the city has not wholly effaced." He felt that this agrarian character was in the process of being modified, and modified for the better, by the growth of the city and urban institutions. Urbanism tempered the original agrarian character of the United States, smoothing off some of the rough edges, correcting some of its excesses. For instance, it substantially modified the unbridled individualism which had been characteristic of rural America and created the necessity and the opportunity out of which grew the social attitudes of the New Deal. There is little doubt that Schlesinger regarded this as a thoroughly desirable modification.[14]

Clyde Kluckhohn maintained that there was little reason to be disheartened by the passing of the frontier. Noting that perhaps the most significant trait of the frontier character was flexibility, he argued that the persistence of the frontier character had made the transition from agrarianism to industrialism smooth and efficient. Americans had become so accustomed to change that the switch from agriculture to industry had not produced a great psychological wrench. The difficulties that existed in American life were simply a result of the fact that American industrialism had begun to develop too fast and too far. Even the adaptable

---

[13] *Childhood and Society* (New York, 1950), pp. 247–282, 355.
[14] "What Then Is the American, This New Man?," *American Historical Review*, 48 (1943), 225–244, reprinted in *Paths to the Present* (New York, 1949), pp. 1–22.

American character could not assimilate all the changes it had produced in American society. Implicit in his treatment was the assumption that the American people could learn to live with industrialism. He saw the United States desperately trying to achieve a new cultural equilibrium; it had not yet come about, but there was nothing in Kluckhohn's treatment to indicate that he believed it was unattainable. Indeed, in a later essay, he seemed to be saying that this equilibrium was being achieved. He found that there had been shifts in values as Americans had adjusted to the necessities of life in a highly developed industrial society. He welcomed these changes, not only because they brought the American value system into closer harmony with American society, but also because they were intrinsically desirable. He seemed to be saying that industrialism had neither destroyed the American character nor degraded it, but had in fact improved it.[15]

The new orientation could also be seen in Ernest W. Burgess' remarks on changing family patterns in the United States. He believed that the American family was changing from a predominantly rural to a predominantly urban type, and he liked the change. Family patterns were becoming increasingly democratic; a new ideal of companionship was replacing the older paternalistic pattern. Burgess felt that these changes were both cause and effect of increasingly democratic tendencies in American society as a whole.[16] It is clear that Burgess would not have accepted the Jeffersonian view that industrialism and democracy were incompatible. Indeed, his argument, pushed to its logical conclusion, was that industrialism was injecting a new vitality into the democratic tendencies in American life.

John A. Kouwenhoven made the clearest statement of the proposition that industrialism was one of the primary sources of

[15] "Have There Been Discernible Shifts in American Values During the Past Generation?," in *The American Style: Essays in Value and Performance*, ed. Elting E. Morison (New York, 1958), pp. 145–217.

[16] "The Family in a Changing Society," *American Journal of Sociology*, 54 (1948), 118–125. It is instructive to contrast Burgess' views with those presented by Arnold W. Green in his essay "Why Americans Feel Insecure," in *The Scene Before You: A New Approach to American Culture*, ed. Chandler Brossard (New York, 1955), pp. 161–179. Green, too, felt that family patterns were changing from a rural to an urban type, but Green deplored the change, feeling that it had produced uncertainty, insecurity, dissatisfaction, and frustration.

American democracy. He based his treatment on the belief that industrialism was as important a part of the American heritage as agrarianism. Indeed, America was distinctive, according to him, because it represented more clearly than any other nation a highly developed industrial society. It was distinguished from other nations because it was the only major one to have developed as a political and cultural unit at the same time that industrial technology was developing. America and the Industrial Revolution had been born at the same time. One feels that Kouwenhoven regarded America as virtually synonymous with industrialism. It is certain that he felt that industrialism and democracy were the two great forces which had shaped America and that the alliance between them was not merely fortuitous, but necessary. Democracy had given the American industrial system its special characteristics, and American industrialism had laid the economic basis for the health and fruition of democratic social and political institutions.[17]

Thus, while many of the agrarian commentators on the American character had worked from the assumption that there was a necessary contradiction between democracy and industrialism, there were those who found nothing at all incompatible between them, who argued that industrialism was the source and strength of American democracy, not its antithesis. The Jeffersonian tradition persisted, but it was coming under increasing attack.

[17] *Made in America: The Arts in Modern Civilization* (New York, 1948).

8

THE AMERICAN CHARACTER AND THE COLD WAR

THE ERA OF SELF-CONSCIOUSNESS

I

In a discussion of American culture in the 1950's, Richard Hofstadter remarked that for the first time a sense of tragedy was developing in the United States. He felt that this new perception of tragedy had been precipitated by the Korean War,

> because we had fully engaged in a world conflict and committed millions of men and then discovered that we were still confronted with the same unsolved problem. For the first time, and in an extremely dramatic way, the American feeling that problems are something you always solve— rather than that there are problems you may just have to live with—was irrefutably controverted in the Korean experience.[1]

William A. Williams noted that there had been a general loss of self-confidence in American foreign policy, that by 1957 Americans had come to reject their previous conviction that they could lead the world more or less as they wished.[2] He dated this change in attitude somewhat later than Hofstadter did, possibly because he was speaking of active political figures rather than intellectuals, and politicians tend to cling to old assumptions and attitudes longer than intellectuals. In any case there was a growing suspicion, largely a product of the Cold War, that the

[1] See Hofstadter's remarks in *American Style*, ed. Morison, p. 309.
[2] "American Century: 1941–1957," *Nation*, 185 (1957), 297–301.

people of the United States were not as completely the masters of the world as they had liked to believe. This suspicion produced a questioning, evaluating attitude and an almost painful self-consciousness in studies of the American character.

It was revealed in two general ways. First, American intellectuals began to evaluate the American character, American beliefs, and American values from the point of view of their usefulness, their applicability, and their relevance to the problems America faced in the world. Their studies of the American character centered on the problem of trying to determine just what it was in the American character that made America's relations with the rest of the world so confused and American foreign policy so inept. Second, there was an attempt on the part of many intellectuals to discover, define, or invent an American ideology, a statement of American beliefs which would be competitive with communist dogma, which would provide, for our enemies, our allies, the uncommitted, and ourselves, a set of working principles, a definition of fundamental beliefs. Americans who had previously been inarticulate about the American creed suddenly found it necessary to become articulate, to try to define for themselves just what it was that made America distinctive and presumably superior.

II

The attempt to define a working ideology for the United States was an attempt to solve some of the problems raised by the Cold War, but first the problems had to be stated. In the post-war decade there were many who argued that the main problem was that Americans were simply not prepared, intellectually or emotionally, to play the role required of them by modern world conditions. It was not only that they lacked the necessary intellectual and emotional equipment. That would have been bad enough, but, worse, Americans were encumbered with values, assumptions, and responses that were truly detrimental to the performance of their role. It was not that they did not know their lines, but rather that they knew the lines for the wrong play. Once again the central theme was cultural lag: the American character was thought to be incapable of coping effectively with its surroundings because it reflected conditions of life and thought that were simply not applicable to the existing situation.

If the cultural-lag hypothesis was a relatively old idea, it was now being applied to a new problem in the post-war years, the problem of foreign affairs. It had usually been applied to the conflict between an agrarian character and an industrial society. Now, with the increasing concern over America's world position occasioned by the Cold War, the conflict was transformed into one between an isolationist and arrogantly self-confident character and a world situation in which arrogance was out of place, isolation was impossible, and there was considerable reason to doubt the justification for any degree of self-confidence.

Gabriel Almond's analysis provides a convenient point of departure for a consideration of this trend in studies of the American character. He said nothing new about the American character in itself. His description was, as he admitted, abstracted from the writings of previous commentators. But in applying those descriptive findings to the problem of America's conduct of its foreign affairs, he stated many of the themes that were to be developed by others. He maintained that because Americans were concerned with their own material affairs, their approach to public problems tended to be perfunctory and based upon momentary moods rather than reasoned attitudes and opinions. He argued that the Americans' emphasis on practicality and common sense and their rejection of intellectualism led them to oversimplify the problems they faced. And when their policies proved unsuccessful—as they were all too likely to do, given the deficiencies in their approach—they tended to react with impatience, irritability, and a pessimism out of all proportion to the magnitude of the setback they had suffered. So sure were they of success that any failure, no matter how trivial, was a disaster to them. Such failures also made Americans deeply suspicious of the motives of other peoples; the American was not blessed with a high tolerance for difference in the first place, and failure made him even more intolerant. Uncertain of his place in society, he tended to exhibit wide changes in his self-evaluations from superiority to inferiority. Judging others by his own standards and values, he assumed an attitude of cultural arrogance that was often merely protective coloration designed to mask unconscious feelings of inferiority.[3]

[3] *The American People and Foreign Policy* (New York, 1950), pp. 29-65.

Almond's ideas were widely echoed. Americans were accused of approaching practical problems without mature reflection or of formulating theories that were irrelevant and inapplicable in practice. Their unwarranted self-confidence inhibited their search for meaningful solutions to the problems they faced. They were the prisoners of their own inflexibility. In short, Americans were too firmly committed to their own way of thinking and acting, too certain of the absolute righteousness of their cause, too convinced of their own impeccable morality, too self-centered, too provincial, and too confident of their own ability to know and to do the right thing. Earlier commentators had usually pointed with pride to the American traits of self-confidence and optimism. Now, however, students of the American character were placing these traits on the debit side of the ledger. The Americans' past optimism had been rooted in a firm sense of their own superiority. They believed that they had succeeded because they were right and that those who had failed were wrong. This attitude not only made it impossible for them to understand and deal sympathetically with underdeveloped nations striving for improvement; it also created all sorts of traumas when they found that they had been less than completely successful in their dealings with the rest of the world.

The idea that Americans suffered from an erroneous overconfidence in their own abilities had already been vigorously propounded by Reinhold Niebuhr. The attention that Niebuhr began to receive in this post-war period is perhaps the most impressive indication of the increasingly troubled state of mind of many American intellectuals. As early as 1932 he had argued that the traditional American attitude that human intelligence was equal to every task was not only wrong but also dangerous.[4] He never changed this basic tenet of his thought; the inability of the human being to deal with human problems solely with human intelligence remained the heart of his work, both theological and sociological. He was not in any sense the founder of a "school"; he represented no one but himself. After the war, the times caught up with him; attitudes that he had been expounding for twenty years took on a relevance they had not had before,

[4] *Moral Man and Immoral Society: A Study in Ethics and Politics* (New York, 1932).

and his basic point, that there were certain problems which might simply prove to be insoluble, suddenly struck a responsive chord in many other American minds.

Niebuhr maintained that Americans were not able to face up to their world responsibilities in a constructive way because they assumed that man in general and the American in particular could control the course of history and that virtue and prosperity were necessarily interrelated. These beliefs had grown out of the historical experience of America:

> Faith in the forward march of history had not been limited to the New World, but here a threefold convergence has caused it to flourish. The frontier provided freedom; great untouched natural resources provided near-perfect raw material for the emerging technology; and the idealism of a society that had recently broken with tyranny provided the needed psychological dynamic. Having as a people experienced a situation in which for a number of generations time visibly brought improvement, we came to assume that the connection was intrinsic.[5]

This historical experience had been so pleasant and Americans had had things so easy that they were unprepared to cope with a world where things were not pleasant and the responsibilities of leadership were not at all easy. Nevertheless, they clung to their assumptions that progress was inevitable and that man could control the course of history, despite the increasingly obvious absurdity of both propositions. They remained so convinced of their own wisdom and virtue that they found it impossible to understand why people did not like them, and their policy was crippled by this lack of understanding:

> The fact that the European nations, more accustomed to the tragic vicissitudes of history, still have a measure of misgiving about our leadership in the world community is due to their fear that our "technocratic" tendency to equate the mastery of nature with the mastery of history would tempt

[5] "From Progress to Perplexity," in *The Search for America*, eds. Huston Smith, Richard T. Heffron, and Eleanor Wieman Smith (Englewood Cliffs, N. J., 1959), p. 135.

us to lose patience with the tortuous course of history. We might be driven to hysteria by its inevitable frustrations. We may be tempted to bring the whole of modern history to a tragic conclusion by one final and mighty effort to overcome its frustrations.[6]

Obviously sharing the fears he attributed to European nations, Niebuhr was openly apprehensive that the Americans' low threshold of tolerance for frustration might lead to a nuclear disaster. He felt profoundly that Americans would have to learn to accept frustration and to do away with their old optimistic preconceptions if they were not to plunge the world into an atomic holocaust.[7]

The philosopher Abraham Kaplan elaborated on other themes. He was particularly concerned with the dangers inherent in American self-righteousness and with the discrepancy between American values and the situation in which those values were supposed to provide guides to action. American moral principles, Kaplan said, were so highly generalized and abstract that they had no relation to the practical requirements of everyday life. There was thus an inevitable conflict between ends and means. In addition, Americans assumed that moral principles had an a priori existence; as a consequence, they tended to be moral absolutists, to believe that values were unconditional, that morality was a matter of black or white, and that their particular values were beyond question. Americans were also guilty of moralization, the ritualistic use of verbal formulas in a semi-magical way to ensure the morality of a particular action. Their habit of defining morality solely in terms of verbal protestation instead of examining it rationally made moral standards trivial. Propriety became righteousness, and conformity was the order of the day.

[6] Niebuhr, *The Irony of American History* (New York, 1952), pp. 145-146.

[7] Niebuhr's contention that traditional American optimism was not only outmoded but even positively dangerous was echoed by Robert L. Heilbroner in *The Future as History: The Historic Currents of Our Time and the Direction in Which They Are Taking America* (New York, 1959), especially pp. 16-18, 49-54, 55-58, 175-181. On p. 178 he says: "Optimism as a philosophy of historic expectations can no longer be considered a national virtue. It has become a dangerous national delusion."

Kaplan felt that these traits of the American mind poisoned the relations of the United States with the rest of the world. Since Americans believed that the welfare of others consisted in their being as much like Americans as possible, they felt bewildered and threatened by the existence of moral systems different from their own. Unable to appreciate the moral positions of their opponents and their allies, they were accordingly rendered incapable of dealing effectively with them.[8]

David Potter also examined the American propensity for a merely verbal morality, arguing that it was a manifestation of a desire to avoid moral responsibility:

By invoking a morality of principle rather than a morality of responsibility, we have, in effect, abdicated our duty to decide questions on their merits and with reference to their consequences. When we say that we will do what is right and leave the event in the hand of God, we are really contriving to make the deity responsible for the way our decisions turn out and are indulging ourselves in the pretense that we are not answerable for the results of our acts. We invoke what purports to be an automatic process—the application of fixed moral law—to avoid the obligations of power and the responsibility for consequences.[9]

W. W. Rostow argued that an inconsistency between theory and practice was the basis of what he called "the American style." It was the style of the operator, the active man, the doer. The most brilliant American performances in all fields tended to be *ad hoc* responses to crisis situations rather than carefully organized assaults on well-defined problems. But this rampant empiricism was accompanied by a devotion to extremely vague high-order generalizations, at least on the verbal level. What

[8] "American Ethics and Public Policy," in *American Style*, ed. Morison, pp. 3–110. See also Joseph S. Roucek, "The Geopolitics of the United States," *American Journal of Economics and Sociology*, 14 (1955), 185–192 and 287–303, in which the author argues that Americans had difficulties in world affairs because of an inexperience caused by their isolationist past and because of their tendency to view world conflicts in moralistic terms.

[9] "Commentary: Theory Versus Practice in American Values and Performance," in *American Style*, ed. Morison, p. 327.

Rostow seemed to be saying—it is somewhat difficult at times to determine his precise meaning—is that this tension between vagueness in theory and hard-headed empiricism in practice resulted in an inability to apply theoretical principles to practical problems. Like many of his contemporaries, Rostow felt that this constituted a serious defect in the American character, for he thought it questionable that the American style, successful only in dealing with relatively familiar problems in situations in which there was time for the experimental testing of proposed solutions, could handle the new and unfamiliar problems that the world situation presented. Consequently, he believed that there was a real danger that Americans' lack of a general theory and their militant empiricism would lead ultimately to destruction.[10]

All these arguments are strongly reminiscent of the critical treatments of the American character that were prevalent during the 1920's. The same dissociation of theory and practice noted by Kaplan, Rostow, and others had been the basis of Brooks's formulation of the high-brow–low-brow dichotomy. And the many writers who were troubled by America's adherence to an abstract and verbal moral system might easily be taken as modern supporters of the attack on Puritanism that had been launched in the 1920's.

The atmosphere of the two periods, however, was different. Richard Hofstadter had said that a sense of tragedy was developing in the United States. Now, the basis of the critical treatments we have just considered was that the American did not have a sense of tragedy, that he was entirely too sure of himself. Nevertheless, Hofstadter was correct in a certain sense, for the existence of these critical works indicates that at least certain American intellectuals were becoming aware of the increasing moral complexity and ambiguity of the modern world. And most of these intellectuals seemed to feel that the American people, too, were beginning to question their own easy complacency. Behind the detailed exposition of America's deficiencies there lay a sense of purpose and a hope for better things to come. The pessimism of the Cold War was far more positive in its tone

[10] "The National Style," in *ibid.*, pp. 246–313. See also J. Robert Oppenheimer, "Theory Versus Practice in American Values and Performance," in *ibid.*, pp. 111–123.

and far more responsible than the pessimism of the 1920's. One gets the impression that the "young intellectuals" of the 1920's would have been bitterly disappointed if they had not been able to find something to complain about. The critics of the Cold War period, on the other hand, gave the impression that something could be done to improve the situation. In other words, their criticism was not destructive; they detailed the defects in the American character so that they could be corrected, and they seemed to feel that they could be, or even were being, corrected. Even Niebuhr, despite his conscious pessimism, seemed to feel that things were looking up, that Americans were finally beginning to accept their responsibilities. These critics, then, felt that Americans were confused and bewildered and unprepared for the crisis that faced them, but also that they were beginning to show some limited signs of coping with their confusion, of ending their bewilderment, and of preparing themselves to face the crisis.

III

The negative approach, concentrating on America's inadequacies, was balanced by a more positive kind of thinking, devoted to the task of discovering a distinctive American tradition, an ideology which would make "Americanism" explicit so that it could be used consciously and effectively in competition with foreign systems of thought and belief. Many commentators felt that the keynote of this ideology was liberalism. The emphasis on liberalism as *the* distinctive American creed became the basis for several interpretations of American history and politics.

Louis Hartz's treatment of the American political tradition provided the most explicit formulation of the proposition that America was distinctive because of its liberalism. Taking as his motto a quote from De Tocqueville to the effect that Americans were born free in the sense that they did not have to fight a revolution in order to attain democratic political institutions, Hartz maintained that all American political ideas which had actually been put into effect were simply variations on the single theme of Lockean liberalism. This American tradition arose purely and simply out of the early settlers' devotion to liberalism and their freedom from feudal institutions. American democracy was not the product of the frontier, for frontiers existed in other nations. Nor was it the product of industrialism and the rise of an urban proletariat, for these developments were not distinctively and uniquely American either. And Puritanism had had a home in Britain before it was transmitted to the United States, so the source of the American tradition was not Puritanism. What was left after all this was a devotion to Locke fostered and intensified by its existence in the midst of a politically and intellectually empty continent. This was the real source of the American tradition.[11]

Hartz asserted that the validity of his thesis could not be destroyed by comparative analysis, and in this he was correct. Not only can it not be destroyed by comparative analysis, it cannot be destroyed by any kind of analysis at all, since it merely restates in another form the very fact that it is trying to explain. To say, as Hartz did, that democracy was "inherent" in the American situation is to explain nothing at all. It may be correct, but by itself it is insufficient, for it begs an obvious question: Why was democracy inherent in the American situation? Hartz did not answer this question beyond stating that democracy grew up in the power vacuum created by the lack of feudal institutions in America. Again, this is insufficient. Why did *democracy* of all possible forms of government grow up in the United States? Granting the absence of feudal institutions, why was it not possible for them to grow as democracy did? It is not sufficient to assert that democracy grew because it was the only available alternative. It is necessary to determine *why* it was the only available alternative, and in order to do so it still seems necessary to resort to the Frontier Thesis or some other comparable historical generalization that will withstand the comparative test, for although it is possible to accept the justice of Hartz's criticisms, the alternative he offered is no more satisfying than the explanations he rejected.

Daniel Boorstin also attempted to find a distinctive American tradition. He was concerned with the "genius" of American politics, and he found it to consist in the common acceptance

[11] *The Liberal Tradition in America: An Interpretation of American Political Thought Since the Revolution* (New York, 1955), pp. 95–96.

of the general axiom that "institutions are not and should not be the grand creations of men toward large ends and unspoken values; rather they are organisms which grow out of the soil in which they are rooted and out of the tradition from which they have sprung."[12] Because they accepted this assumption, said Boorstin, the American people were remarkably inarticulate in politics. They did not theorize, because they believed that they already had a theory, a theory which grew naturally and inevitably out of their immediate situation. Boorstin called this the sense of "givenness," the sense that values and institutions were automatically defined by and implicit in the environment. This sense of givenness was the basis of American political thought or, rather, since Americans avoided explicit theorizing, of American political attitudes.

At the same time, Boorstin detected signs that the sense of givenness, created in the American past and persisting through it, was beginning to decline in the present. Americans were beginning to wonder if it might not become necessary for them to think about their political values and institutions: "More than ever we feel that we are cast in a great role, but for the first time, we begin to wonder if we ourselves may not have some responsibility for composing the plot." Boorstin placed the beginning of the decline in the sense of givenness at the end of the nineteenth century, specifically with the Frontier Thesis, "more an autopsy than an anatomy of our institutions." The effect of the disappearance of the frontier, one of the primary sources of the American sense of givenness, was reinforced by American involvement in world politics on a large scale, and "with each national crisis of the twentieth century the demand for explicitness has recurred."

Boorstin tried to cope with the decline in the sense of givenness by pointing out the ideas that were latent and implicit in it. First, there was no ideology. The American experience had led to the destruction of romantic illusions about the possibilities of man's remaking himself by remaking his institutions, for in America for the first time in human history it became *possible* for man to remake his institutions as he wished, and he quickly realized that the expected utopian consequences did not ensue.

[12] *The Genius of American Politics* (Chicago, 1953), p. 6.

What the sense of givenness did include was in the first place a tendency to see things as wholes, both in space and in time. Society was assumed to be an organic growth, and social and political institutions were believed to grow naturally out of their environment and to be intimately related to it. It also included the perception of continuity through time, the perception of the roots that the present had in the past.[13] It would seem, therefore, although Boorstin never said so in so many words, that the American character was basically conservative, founded as it was upon a belief that institutions were organic and that institutions and practices were continued from the past.

Whereas Hartz emphasized the dominance of the liberal tradition in America and Boorstin pointed out the conservative components of the American tradition, Clinton Rossiter in effect combined the two approaches. Americans, he argued, agreed on the fundamentals of their political beliefs, and those fundamentals were, because of the Americans' historical experience, basically liberal:

> Thoughts of liberty—bold, optimistic, adventurous thoughts—came naturally to men who lived in the American environment. . . . America was a land in which men could literally behold opportunity. There were forests uncut, soil unplowed, rivers untravelled, resources untapped. The frontier beckoned and, beckoning, touched both those who answered and those who did not. The results are chronicled in words like "enterprise," "energy," "achievement," "individualism," "progress," and "mobility," the only words that can describe the astounding pilgrimage of a new race of men more concerned with getting ahead than with holding their own. The American political mind has been a liberal mind, for change and progress have been the American way of life.[14]

Liberalism was not, however, the only important force that Rossiter saw in American political life. He pointed out that America was a happy and prosperous nation; Americans liked

[13] *Ibid.*, pp. 161–189.

[14] *Conservatism in America, the Thankless Persuasion* (2nd ed.; New York, 1962), p. 69.

their country and were well contented with the way things were done. This feeling of contentment had given rise to a strong conservative impulse, but conservative with a difference: Americans were conserving a liberal tradition; they were devoted to the past, but a past characterized by freedom and liberty and not by remnants of feudalism. The American tradition emphasized optimism and progress, but Americans also admired the traditionally conservative values of unity and loyalty. The American emphasis on constitutionalism and the belief that politics should be guided by religious principles—the "higher law"—were other examples that Rossiter gave of the conservative orientation of the American people. "While our tradition remains Liberal, we are ever more insistent that it is just that: a tradition."[15]

Just as American liberalism had a strong conservative component, so American conservatism had strong overtones of the dominant liberal philosophy. American conservatism differed from that of other countries in that it was more optimistic, more materialistic, and more individualistic. In these respects, it was simply an *American* conservatism, partaking of the national characteristics. It was distinctively American because it had accepted, as other conservatisms had not, the triumph of democracy and industrialism. Rossiter pointed out that the triumph of industrialism in the United States—"nowhere in the world did it achieve so sweeping a victory over other ways of life and thought"— had in fact destroyed conservatism in the sense in which the word was usually used in the context of European politics. The American capitalist, who was the primary beneficiary of the system under which he lived and would thus be expected by all normal rules to be the natural bastion of American conservatism, could not really be a conservative because he was the most powerful agent of change the world had ever known. American conservatism, in fact, had become unflinchingly liberal in its economic philosophy, both in inducing widespread and radical changes and in accepting laissez-faire individualism. It had also succumbed to the American tendency to value action over thought and practice over theory, and because it had become so thoroughly enmeshed in the distinctive political atmosphere of the United States, it had failed as a philosophy; it did not offer a

[15] *Ibid.*, pp. 67–78.

real alternative to the dominant liberal spirit of American society.[16]

A comparison of these three commentators on the American political tradition reveals that the apparent differences between them are minimal, are differences in labeling which do not denote real differences in content. Boorstin's "conservatism" was not a political belief but a temperamental disposition; he was not describing American political doctrine but rather the reaction patterns that translated doctrine into a working political system. Hartz, on the other hand, was speaking of explicit political doctrine when he discussed American liberalism. It is true that Boorstin described the conservative tendencies of the American character in terms of warm approval while Hartz was profoundly disturbed by what he called "liberal absolutism," the tendency for American political beliefs to become rigid, hidebound, and, in effect, conservative.[17] Thus, Boorstin tended to value the conservative characteristics of the American political mind while Hartz deplored them. But they were agreed on what the American character *was*. Despite differences in terminology and attitude, they were in fundamental agreement with Rossiter; they, too, believed that while the American may have been a conservative in certain respects, he was bent on conserving a tradition that was profoundly liberal. They agreed further that there had been in the past and was still in the present a substantial consensus on political questions and that most Americans were agreed in their basic political views.

It was this emphasis on consensus which has caused some observers to regard the current of thought represented by Hartz, Boorstin, and Rossiter, among others, with suspicion. Arthur Schlesinger, Jr., for instance, asserted that these historians tended to overemphasize the extent of political agreement which existed and exists in America: "For, however much Americans may have united on fundamentals, there still remain sharp and significant differences."[18] Many commentators have, in fact, come to regard works in this vein as a part of the conservative revival itself. Rossiter took note of this tendency to equate discussion with advocacy and insisted that he was not to be taken as a con-

[16] *Ibid.*, pp. 200–217.
[17] Hartz, *Liberal Tradition*, pp. 228–283.
[18] *The Politics of Hope* (Boston, 1962), p. 65.

servative simply because he was concerned with the political theory of conservatism.[19] Thus, it would seem that William Newman's criticisms of the "neo-conservatives" were based upon a misapprehension. He criticized writers like Hartz and Boorstin because he believed they were trying to avoid conflict by simply arguing it out of existence. He felt that their emphasis on the American past, their search for a distinctive American tradition, constituted a conservative reinterpretation of American history.[20] Unfortunately, Newman tended to view any questioning of the "liberal" assumptions of the New Deal period as evidence of rank conservatism. It is true that the "neo-conservative" writers considered here did run somewhat desperately after evidence of political unity, in the hope that clinging to such symbols would somehow provide Americans with intellectual ammunition in their struggle with communism, but the fact that they might have been guilty of overstating their case should not be allowed to obscure the fact that they did have a case. The existence of conflict in the American past does not destroy the importance of the neo-conservative contention that America was distinctive because there had been *less* conflict here than in other nations. The implied—and sometimes explicit—comparison is of fundamental importance, and critics of the neo-conservatives frequently did not take it into account.

Hartz, Boorstin, and Rossiter were united in another significant respect. In their search for a distinctive American tradition, they all turned instinctively toward politics, assuming that the American identity could be most easily discovered in an analysis of political life and theory. This illustrates a continuing tendency in analyses of the American character in the twentieth century, a tendency to regard American politics not necessarily as the most distinctive thing about America but as the most distinctive *favorable* thing. When commentators praised the American character, their work was usually heavily weighted on the side of politics. This was certainly true of the neo-conservatives. Starting as they did with the purpose of discovering a distinctive American tradition, they searched, perhaps unconsciously, for something they could praise. Because of the fierce competition of the Cold War, they *wanted* to think well of their country, and

[19] *Conservatism in America*, pp. ix–x.
[20] *The Futilitarian Society* (New York, 1961).

they turned to politics in the hope of finding in American political life something they could be proud of, indicating their unconscious assumption that if there was an American tradition to be proud of, it was a political tradition.

Despite this attempt to discover grounds for pride in America, this "positive" approach to the American character had much in common with the critical, negative approach discussed earlier. The two approaches were not contradictory, but complementary. Both arose in response to the perception of a particular problem, America's difficulties in the Cold War, and both were attempts to find a solution to the problem. One group of thinkers tried to do it by analyzing American weaknesses so that they could be corrected; the other group tried to do it by discovering American strengths so that they could be exploited. Though they started from different positions, they tended to arrive at roughly the same destination.

The basis of the critical approach to the American character was the assumption that Americans were incapacitated by their own moral inflexibility. The same idea can also be found in the more favorable treatments of the American character. Hartz, for instance, maintained that America was possessed by a liberal absolutism that inhibited creative theoretical thinking in politics and made it impossible for Americans to appreciate the standards and norms of other people. He went so far as to say that America suffered from the lack of an effective socialist tradition which could provide a much needed counterweight to the dominant liberal philosophy.[21] Rossiter criticized American conservatism for precisely the same reason: it had been so profoundly influenced by the liberal ideology of America that it did not constitute an effective alternative. His call for a refurbished, responsible American conservatism was not a rejection of liberalism but an expression of his belief that conservatism was necessary to keep American liberalism alive and vital by providing the competition that would prevent it from degenerating into a set of unquestioned attitudes devoid of intellectual incisiveness and emotional force.[22] Boorstin thought that the decline of the sense of givenness in America was a tragedy. He wrote his book not

[21] *Liberal Tradition*, pp. 228–283.
[22] *Conservatism in America*, pp. 234–270.

to define an American ideology but to convince Americans that their ideology needed no definition, indeed, that to try to define it explicitly was a grave mistake. In putting forward this argument, Boorstin was stating a point of view that might seem to be antithetical to the pleas sounded by many of his contemporaries for a reconciliation between theory and practice, but it must be remembered that Boorstin had insisted that to define an American ideology in words was a mistake because Americans had already defined it in practice.

There was another important point of contact between Boorstin and the critics of the American's performance in foreign affairs. He insisted that Americans could not export their political theory or their political institutions, nor should they try to. The attempt would violate the most important principle of American political belief: that institutions and theories grow out of a particular environment and cannot be created by the arbitrary act of man. His analysis can be interpreted as an attack on the idea of mission, which had played an important role in American thought. To Boorstin and other analysts of the American character in the Cold War, this idea was dangerous. It represented a thoroughly illiberal kind of moral absolutism. Boorstin accurately summed up the basic attitude of the other students of the American character in the Cold War when he said: "We must refuse to become crusaders for liberalism, in order to remain liberals."[23] The fanaticism and moral inflexibility of the crusader were precisely the traits which were thought to be most unfortunate in the American character as Americans attempted to deal with the dangers that confronted them.

IV

The same distrust of fanaticism can be seen in another series of works on the American character, those concerned with the growth of a radical right in America. This concern was an obvious consequence of McCarthyism and the threats it posed to domestic political health. But it was by no means completely unrelated to the problems of the Cold War. For one thing, McCarthyism was thought to be damaging to the American

[23] *Genius of American Politics*, p. 189.

image abroad in the same way that the existence of racial discrimination was. It was argued that this blatant manifestation of political hysteria could not help undermining America's public relations efforts overseas. Second, it was widely believed that one of the important sources of McCarthyism was the frustration engendered by the apparent failures of American foreign policy to produce a definitive "victory" over communism. Cries of "treason" and "subversion" arose from those who believed that America should be victorious and who reacted to its defeats by insisting that they had to be the result of skulduggery. The existence of such feelings provided vivid proof that not all Americans had developed a sense of tragedy, that there were still many who believed that the United States could find immediate solutions to all the problems it faced in the world.

Those who tried to determine the sources of these attitudes usually laid considerable stress on the importance of frustration and anxiety. Richard Hofstadter, for instance, pointed to the characteristic social and economic mobility of the United States as significant factors, maintaining that living under such conditions made people uncertain of their identity. Yet the value system to which they gave allegiance imposed upon them the necessity of making a success. The conflict between personal insecurity and the drive toward material success produced a scramble for status and bitter frustration. The drift toward the radical right, with its overstated emphasis on loyalty and conformity, was the response of those who hoped by their insistence on those values to establish their own loyalty and conformity—and hence their own identity and place in the social system—beyond any shadow of a doubt.[24]

Seymour Lipset's account of the emergence of the radical right was slightly different. He placed far more emphasis on the importance of certain well-established and long-standing features of American political thought and behavior. As he saw it, the radical right in contemporary America was simply another in a long line of manifestations of political intolerance, the spiritual suc-

[24] "The Pseudo-Conservative Revolt," in *The New American Right*, ed. Daniel Bell (New York, 1955), pp. 33–55. David Riesman and Nathan Glazer also felt that the radical right had its origins in the status deprivations of the American middle class. See "The Intellectuals and the Discontented Classes," in *ibid.*, pp. 56–90.

cessor of the Ku Klux Klan, the Know-Nothing crusade, and other mass movements of intolerance. The American as a political animal showed strong tendencies toward intolerance in periods of relative prosperity, and the emergence of the radical right was only the current expression of a constant and continuing American trait. Lipset thought that this intolerance was the product of several factors: the persistence of a Puritan morality that induced a black-or-white view of the world, the lack of an aristocratic tradition that could serve to mitigate the harshness of American political rhetoric, a history of mass immigration that both threatened the stability of society and forced those already in the United States to impose intolerant assimilative requirements on the newcomers, the insistence of those newcomers themselves upon conformity as they strove desperately to prove their own Americanism, and the recurrent necessity, imposed upon Americans by historical conditions, of taking the law into their own hands, thus destroying civic discipline and giving rise to the vigilante spirit of mob action. Intolerance was rife also because "Americanism" was an ideology and a political creed, not a simple fact of residence or birth, and ideological conformity became one of the primary conditions of good citizenship. Lipset also noted that the openness of American society made it relatively easy for extremist groups to gain footholds in American society and thus to provide institutional outlets for such feelings of intolerance as existed in the community.

Lipset agreed that insecurity about status was an important contributory factor in the growth of the radical right. The movement drew support from old families afraid of declining prestige, from new Americans attempting to achieve status by adopting ultra-conservative attitudes in order to prove their Americanism, from *nouveaux riches* insecure in the possession of their wealth, from small businessmen who felt squeezed by modern economic conditions and government regulations, from the uneducated lower classes who tended to be intolerant anyway and who felt insecure because they had not succeeded while others around them had, from old-line isolationists who attempted to justify their past positions by attacking New Deal domestic and foreign policy and whatever resembled it in later days, and from those extremist right-wing organizations which had always existed in the United States and which, by providing scapegoats, represented outlets for various personality repressions and frustrations. The radical right, in other words, was not a special development but an almost normal—if one may use the word in a slightly special sense—outgrowth of American social, political, and cultural characteristics.[25]

These two essays on the "new American right" illustrate an important trend in studies of the American national character in the 1950's. In one, a historian used psychological and sociological concepts and vocabulary to analyze a contemporary political phenomenon. In the other, a sociologist undertook an extensive historical analysis in order to demonstrate the genesis and continuity with the past of the same political phenomenon. Better illustrations of interdisciplinary cooperation could hardly be found. Interdisciplinary analysis was not confined to this particular subject. In fact, it became something of a fad in the 1950's. It was not new, but its possibilities were explored far more widely than they had been before. As interest in interdisciplinary study grew, so did interest in the study of national character, for the simple reason that national character was the type of subject that was perfectly suited to the interdisciplinary approach. The national-character study involves generalization on a very broad scale and in areas of investigation that are not directly related to any single academic discipline. One of the reasons for the relative dearth of national-character studies by academicians in the years before the end of the war was probably their inability to decide just whose business such studies should be. And one reason for the upsurge of such studies in the 1950's was the eagerness to experiment with the interdisciplinary approach and to find topics suitable to it.

This, of course, was only part of the reason for the growth of interest in national character. More important, probably, was that America's position in the world seemed to demand an analysis of the nation, its people, and its culture, in the hope of coming to terms with the crisis that confronted the nation. America's isolation had ended. Americans were much more aware of Europe than they had been previously. Though they had always been concerned with Europeans' opinions, especially of the

[25] "The Sources of the 'Radical Right,'" in *ibid.*, pp. 166–233.

United States, now they had some knowledge to go with their concern. They had, in short, a basis on which to make comparisons with their own institutions. The necessities of the age combined with the opportunities thus provided permitted Americans to evaluate themselves more carefully and more rationally than they had been able to do before. This evaluation was expressive of a rather painful self-consciousness, a self-consciousness growing out of a sense of tragedy, as Americans attempted to come to terms for the first time with a world in which they *knew*—rather than only suspected—that they could no longer have their own way.

9

THE AMERICAN
CHARACTER IN THE 1950's

OLD PROBLEMS AND NEW HOPES

I

In the 1950's much of the discussion of the American character
came to revolve around the concepts elaborated in a single book:
The Lonely Crowd by David Riesman, Nathan Glazer, and
Reuel Denney.[1] It was one of those rare books which, though
intended primarily for a scholarly audience, enjoyed an enormous popular success.[2] It was probably even more popular and
influential outside the academic community than within it. For
non-academic intellectuals it became the basic document of social
analysis in the 1950's, and discussions of contemporary society
and culture frequently, if not usually, took place within the
frame of reference established by *The Lonely Crowd* and used
the vocabulary coined by the authors.

With hindsight, it is not difficult to explain the book's rather
surprising popularity. It is obvious that it struck a responsive

[1] *The Lonely Crowd: A Study of the Changing American Character*
(2nd ed.; Garden City, N. Y., 1954). I have used the abridged paper-
back edition of the book for this study since it is more accessible to
most readers than the original edition and because, at least for present
purposes, it is virtually identical with the original edition. I have also
taken the liberty of using the name "Riesman" as a convenient shorthand expression denoting not only Riesman himself, but also his co-
workers, Glazer and Denney, whenever they collaborated with him.

[2] See Eric Larrabee, "David Riesman and His Readers," in *Culture
and Social Character: The Work of David Riesman Reviewed*, eds.
Seymour Martin Lipset and Leo Lowenthal (Glencoe, Ill., 1961), pp.
404–416.

chord. Why? The easy answer would be that it verbalized the more or less inarticulate feelings of large numbers of people, that it systematized ideas that were in the air, that it said things that people were already thinking. Many analysts of the culture of the United States were not at all convinced that the American scene was as prosperous and cheerful as it appeared to be. Beneath the glittering surface they detected evidences of profound insecurity and uncertainty, due partly to the frustrations of the Korean War and also to the necessity of living in a world all too familiar with the destructive potentialities of modern weapons. Prosperity itself was sometimes regarded with suspicion, since it was based to a considerable extent on defense spending and was thus dependent on the continued existence of a substantial threat to the nation's very existence. Many commentators believed that Americans had paid dearly for their affluence; their society was in a considerable mess. Materialism, Coca-colonization, and the heinous crimes perpetrated by the mass media in the guise of entertainment all found a prominent place in their works. Paul and Percival Goodman summed up the general feeling:

> The critics have shown with pretty plain evidence that we spend our money for follies, that our leisure does not revive us, that our conditions of work are unmanly and our beautiful American classlessness is degenerating into a static bureaucracy; our mass arts are beneath contempt; our prosperity breeds insecurity; our system of distribution has become huckstering and our system of production discourages enterprise and sabotages invention.[3]

To use Henry Miller's telling phrase, America was usually pictured as an "air-conditioned nightmare."

Perhaps the most unpalatable feature of this depressing spectacle was conformity. In their frantic, even hysterical, search for security in a threatening and insecure world, Americans seemed to have made a massive retreat into conformity. American intellectuals launched what amounted to a concerted attack upon the problem. It was not, of course, a new problem—it

[3] *Communitas: Means of Livelihood and Ways of Life* (2nd ed.; New York, 1960), p. 5.

had been one of the keynotes of analyses of the American character at least since De Tocqueville—but in the 1950's it was discussed with an intensity and on a scale rarely if ever approached before except possibly during the 1920's, the heyday of the critics of Babbittry. And it was discussed not only by disaffected litterateurs but also by social scientists. It came to be regarded as *the* American characteristic, the besetting American sin; commentators on the nation's life found in all areas of that life new evidences of the mindless conformist tendencies of the American people. Mark Twain's remark about the weather could very justly have been applied to conformity.

That there were several parallels between the social criticism of the post-war period and that of the 1920's is undeniable, but there was also one important difference: in the 1950's the villains were not so easy to identify. In the 1920's the targets had been satisfyingly concrete. All those who were unhappy with American civilization had been able to join in the game of Puritan-baiting or pioneer-baiting. In the 1950's, however, the culprit seemed to be the diffuse entity called "mass society" or "mass culture." Assaults on the public taste were legion, but they were launched by institutions whose impersonality gave their critics some difficult moments. "We are only giving the public what it wants" turned out, dishearteningly, to be true enough to rob the critics' barbs of much of their sting. Their efforts were frustrated and frustrating. The situation seemed to call for the wholesale reform of the "public" mind, a task which would have been virtually impossible to accomplish even if someone had succeeded in determining precisely who, or what, the public was.

The Lonely Crowd found a ready response because it appeared to offer a tidy solution to this dilemma. It would be easy at this point to become involved in a discussion of one of the possible variations of the debate over the Great Man theory of history —did the book define the thinking of the time, or was it a product of the *Zeitgeist?*—but for the present let it merely be noted that it filled an important niche in the current intellectual framework. It seemed to offer a reasonably precise conceptual scheme for the analysis of contemporary American society with historical and sociological evidence to support it.

Riesman's main point was that a fundamental change was taking place in American life, a characterological shift from what he called "inner-direction" to what he called "other-direction." These terms were used to denote the different ways in which the mechanisms of social authority were brought to bear upon the individual to secure from him the conformity necessary to maintain social order and stability. In the case of inner-direction, these mechanisms were implanted in the individual early in his life by his parents or other elders, so that throughout the rest of his life he was directed by internalized rules of conduct that appeared to come from "inside" him. In the case of other-direction, the necessary social authority over the individual was exercised by his peer group, and the individual was thus directed by forces which were exerted by "others."[4]

Riesman maintained that the United States was distinctive among the nations of the world because the other-directed character type was more prevalent and more highly developed in the United States than in any other nation. But he did not feel that it was the only character type which existed in the United States. In fact, he insisted that inner-direction was still the dominant component in the characterological composition of the nation.[5] The transition from inner-direction to other-direction was still in process; it had not been completed.

II

As stimulating and provocative as Riesman's analysis of the American character was, perhaps even more interesting was the response it evoked. His book was almost universally misinterpreted. Indeed, it had the impact it did precisely *because* it was misinterpreted, and the way in which it was misinterpreted reveals much about studies, past and present, of the American character.

Most of Riesman's readers, already concerned with conformity, saw in his analysis a sociological confirmation of their beliefs. In fact, "other-direction" fulfilled the same function for critics of American society in the 1950's that "Puritanism" had fulfilled in the 1920's. It was both the name and the cause of everything they found distasteful. But they suffered from two

---

[4] *Lonely Crowd*, pp. 29–32, 34–40.
[5] Riesman and Glazer, *Faces in the Crowd: Individual Studies in Character and Politics* (New Haven, 1952), p. 5.

misapprehensions. First, they tended to assume that other-direction was the dominant mode of social conformity in the United States, while Riesman had said quite pointedly that it was not. They also tended to feel that other-direction was an exclusively American phenomenon. Riesman had implied very strongly that while there were more other-directed people in America than in any other nation, other-direction existed everywhere and would spread as socio-economic conditions in the rest of the world came to resemble those in the United States.

Second, and more interesting, is the fact that Riesman's readers tended to assume that inner-direction and other-direction were synonyms for individualism and conformity respectively. They were not. Both inner-direction and other-direction were modes of conformity, and the sole difference between them was in what the individual was conforming to. The inner-directed person *seemed* more individualistic than the other-directed person, but only because the pressures to which he conformed were less obvious. He had no more rational freedom of choice than the other-directed person. He himself was likely to be deluded into thinking that he was following his own self-determined course, but Riesman insisted that this *was* a delusion.[6]

It is therefore incorrect to assume that Riesman put a higher value on inner-direction than on other-direction. In many specific instances, in fact, he appeared to value it far less. What he did value was a state of mind and being that he called "autonomy," a state in which the individual transcended both inner-direction and other-direction and achieved a position in which he was able to make free choices about what he would conform to and, indeed, whether he would conform at all. He was not inevitably a rebel; he could choose to conform, to submit to social pressures, but if he did, it was because he had made a free, rational decision. His acceptance of authority, if he chose to accept it, was only provisional and did not indicate that he had abandoned the right or the ability to reject authority in other circumstances.[7] If any of Riesman's character types deserve

[6] Riesman, *Individualism Reconsidered and Other Essays* (Glencoe, Ill., 1954), pp. 101–102.

[7] *Lonely Crowd*, pp. 282–286. See also Riesman's essay "The Saving Remnant," in *Individualism Reconsidered*, pp. 99–120, where he makes he same point at greater length and in a slightly different terminology.

the name "individualist," therefore, it is the autonomous individual and not either the inner-directed or the other-directed one.

Despite Riesman's discussion of autonomy, most of his critics and commentators have persisted in assuming an exact correspondence between inner-direction and individualism on the one hand and between other-direction and conformity on the other. To be sure, the concept of autonomy is somewhat vague; there is no precise way to determine in any individual case whether a person's submission to external pressures is the result of rationality or rationalization. Still, the ambiguity is not so great as to cause the concept to be ignored completely. Inner-direction and other-direction are also rather vague, after all, and they were certainly not ignored. The mystery is deepened when it is pointed out that if Riesman was in fact talking about individualism as opposed to conformity, he went to excessive lengths in attempting to define inner-direction and other-direction. The fact that he was at some pains to devise a new vocabulary should have indicated that he did not intend to talk about individualism and conformity but about something quite different. However, it is possible that people had become so hardened to the unnecessary proliferation of jargon in the social sciences that it did not seem strange that a social scientist would coin new words when there were perfectly suitable old ones; after all, it had happened fairly frequently in the past. And because Riesman's labels were so popular, because they were seized upon so eagerly and talked about so widely, many people probably felt entitled to use them without ever having read *The Lonely Crowd*.

Many who read the book with some care, however, were still led astray. Seymour Lipset, in most ways a remarkably astute analyst of the American scene, criticized Riesman's contention that there had been a change in the American character, pointing out that many nineteenth-century commentators had stressed conformity as a distinctive American trait.[8] In other words, he also assumed that Riesman's other-direction was identical to the simple conformity stressed in so many previous treatments of the American character, and this was not the case. Conformity implies the maintenance of certain standards of external behavior,

---

[8] "A Changing American Character?," in *Culture and Social Character*, eds. Lipset and Lowenthal, pp. 141–156.

whereas other-direction describes a psychological condition and a value system. It is not mere behavioral conformity, for the autonomous individual may also conform in that sense.

Lipset's analysis raises another point. The concept of national character is by its very nature comparative. To establish his basic assumption that the nation he is dealing with is distinctive in certain respects, the analyst of national character must compare it to other nations, at least by implication. Now, much of the evidence upon which Lipset based his contention that other-direction was a distinguishing American trait in the nineteenth century was drawn from the observations of foreign travelers, and the traits they regarded as distinctively American were those which stood out as the result of comparisons, stated or implied, between the United States and Europe. Thus, they were saying in effect that nineteenth-century America was more other-directed than nineteenth-century Europe. Even granting that what they noted in the nineteenth century *was* other-direction and not simple conformity, this does not contradict Riesman's contention that the American character was more other-directed in the twentieth century than it had been in the nineteenth.

Riesman himself must bear part of the blame for this inability of his critics to deal with his work. For one thing, his choice of labels for his character types was unfortunate and probably led to considerable misunderstanding. "Inner-direction" and "other-direction" do not have the exotic flavor of many of the more unusual terms employed by social scientists. They sound fairly familiar and seem to be the kind of words one might use with reasonable comfort in ordinary speech. Perhaps Riesman chose them for this very reason, hoping to avoid the appearance of unnecessary jargonizing. But the apparent familiarity of these terms was an unintended trap for his readers, for it seemed to make it unnecessary to determine their precise meanings. Many people were probably misled into thinking that terms which sounded so familiar meant exactly what they appeared to mean. Unfortunately they appeared to mean something far different from what Riesman had intended them to mean. To people brought up to value individualism, at least on the level of verbal affirmation, inner-direction must have seemed much more palatable than other-direction and to have an aura of moral superiority about it. One can easily see an individual who is unaware of the precise meanings of the terms gladly admitting that he is inner-directed or indignantly denying that he is other-directed. Inner-direction just sounds better.

Nor is this all. Riesman admits that he consciously modifies his ideas to suit the specific context in which he happens to be presenting them, that he consciously adopts different positions before different audiences. He is also prone to cast arguments in the form, "While it is true that . . . , nevertheless. . . ." And he may reverse the order of the clauses from one work to the next. Consequently, it is often quite difficult to discover precisely what he thinks on any given question. It might almost be said that he forestalls all criticism by taking the critic's position himself before anyone else has a chance to. His changeableness might almost be taken for a mild form of intellectual dishonesty were it not for four facts: one, he usually adopts a position likely to win him more critics than disciples; two, playing the role of devil's advocate is a very good way of getting people to think; three, the practice of adapting one's remarks to suit one's audience is nearly universal, and Riesman differs only in that he does it consciously and admits it openly; four, he does not use his own modifications of his remarks as a protective hedge, but stands behind what he has written, at the same time showing a greater readiness than most to admit that he has been wrong and has changed his mind. The fact remains, however, that this flexibility, admirable though it may be in many respects, does make it difficult to deal with his work as a whole and to comprehend it as a finished product.[9]

Lipset may thus have been led astray by Riesman himself, for Riesman did talk at times as if he felt that other-direction and conformity were synonymous. While there may be some justification for identifying other-direction with conformity, there is none at all for identifying inner-direction with individualism or for assuming that Riesman valued inner-direction more than other-direction. Yet Carl Degler did just that in his commentary on *The Lonely Crowd.* "Translated into more familiar words," he said, "the inner-directed personality is individualistic and self-reliant." Criticizing Riesman for what seemed to him to be

[9] See Riesman's essays "Values in Context" and "Individualism Reconsidered," in *Individualism Reconsidered*, pp. 17–25, 26–38.

an inaccurately laudatory treatment of the nineteenth century, Degler commented, "Undoubtedly to anyone with a spark of inner-direction in his personality the nineteenth century as depicted in *The Lonely Crowd* is almost too good to be true."[10] But the quotations which Degler cited to prove that Riesman preferred the nineteenth century to the twentieth really do nothing of the kind. If, as Degler said, "In *The Lonely Crowd* the decisive, ruthless, brusque, self-confident robber baron is taken as typical of the nineteenth century,"[11] it is difficult to see how it is possible to argue that Riesman believed nineteenth-century society to be admirable. Degler also quoted Riesman's use of words like "gloomy," "grim," and "stern" in reference to the people and culture of the past. Of course, Degler is quite correct in saying that Riesman found much to approve of in the nineteenth century, and it is obvious that he found much to disapprove of in the twentieth. However, the other-directed character, for all its deficiencies, did have certain redeeming features in Riesman's view: tolerance, sympathy, and insistence on fair play. Thus, it is possible to find in Riesman evidence that he liked certain features of the inner-directed style of the nineteenth century but disliked others, and that he disliked certain features of the other-directed style of the twentieth century but liked others. On the whole, therefore, it does not seem that Degler's argument has enough force to contradict Riesman's explicit declarations that he did not value the inner-directed past any more than he valued the other-directed present.

How can we explain this misreading of Riesman's work, a misreading more glaringly revealed in various "popular" treatments than in the work of academicians like Lipset and Degler? David Potter has pointed out—and the evidence of this study also reveals—that interpretations of the American character tend to fall into one or the other of two broad groups: they portray the American either as a materialistic conformist or as an idealistic individualist.[12] When Riesman announced the distinction between inner-direction and other-direction, therefore, Americans

[10] "The Sociologist as Historian: Riesman's *The Lonely Crowd*," *American Quarterly*, 15 (1963), 483–497. The quotations are on pp. 485 and 487 respectively.

[11] *Ibid.*, p. 485.

[12] "Quest for the National Character," in *Reconstruction of American History*, ed. Higham, pp. 197–220.

brought up on the conflict between conformity and individualism, and accustomed to thinking in these terms, were deluded by the apparent similarity of Riesman's concepts to the older ideas and simply assumed that they *were* the older ideas slightly refurbished.

An analysis of the types of society with which Riesman linked each of his character types provides another perspective on the problem. The inner-directed personality was created in and suited to a society characterized by a state of "transitional population growth," while the other-directed personality was the product of a society in a state of "incipient population decline." This use of demographic labels should not be taken too seriously, for Riesman admitted that he used them only as a brief way of denoting a number of specific institutional characteristics.[13] Thus an inner-directed society was characterized above all by expansiveness in population, production, and space. Other-directed societies were characterized by capitalism, industrialism, urbanism, and material abundance.[14] The state of "incipient population decline" seems identical, for all practical purposes, to the state of society usually referred to by the phrase "mature industrial society." It is here that the difficulty lies.

When Riesman spoke of the inner-directed personality of the nineteenth century, his readers, regardless of Riesman's actual description, insisted on seeing Turner's individualistic frontiersman and contrasting him with the conformist security-seeker of the twentieth century. In other words, they saw in Riesman not what he actually said but what they wanted and expected him to say. They assumed that he condemned other-direction and praised inner-direction because, with their allegiance to Jeffersonian and Turnerian models of thought, *they would have done so themselves.*[15] But in fact Riesman showed a small but unmistakable preference for the industrial society of the present, feeling that such a society provided the greatest opportunities

[13] *Lonely Crowd*, pp. 23–24.
[14] *Ibid.*, pp. 28–40.
[15] This was not true of Lipset and Degler. They went astray not because they were trapped by the agrarian myth but because they assumed that Riesman was. It was an understandable mistake. Most native commentators on the American character were trapped.

for the development of autonomous personalities, the type he really valued.[16]

III

Riesman's attitudes concerning the American character were echoed by David Potter. Potter made material abundance the main explanatory principle in his study, and, like Riesman, he was not at all dismayed by his recognition of the importance of industrialism in the formation of the American character. Indeed, this attitude was the most distinctive thing about Potter's work. The emphasis on abundance was not new in itself, as Potter pointed out. He reinterpreted the work of Horney, Riesman, and Mead, arguing that their formulations were not inconsistent with the idea that material abundance had been of great importance in shaping the American character. Turner, too, had noted the fact of abundance, and Turner's followers had emphasized the molding effects of the rich American continent, the plentiful resources, and the resulting high standard of living. Potter's theory of abundance was in a sense a variation on Turner's thesis, but he went one step further than Turner, and it was a significant step. He maintained that Turner had defined abundance too narrowly, limiting its incidence to the geographical, and thus agrarian, frontier. He had not, said Potter, paid sufficient attention to the existence of "frontiers" in science, industry, and technology. In effect, Potter criticized Turner for mistaking the part for the whole, for being so tied up in his agrarian preconceptions that he could not see that the importance of agrarian abundance was not that it was agrarian but that it was abundance. Free land was important only because it was the most immediately available of America's vast store of natural resources, resources which were less important in themselves than the desire and the ability to exploit them effectively. Thus when the frontier disappeared, indeed even before it had disappeared, that desire and that ability had been transferred to industrial pursuits without affecting the fundamental determinants of the American character in the slightest.[17]

The work of Potter and Riesman broke new ground in studies

[16] *Lonely Crowd*, pp. 285–286.
[17] *People of Plenty*, especially pp. 142–165 on the Frontier Thesis.

of the American character. Both maintained, in essence, that whatever had been true in the past, America was distinctive in the present because it was the most highly developed industrial nation in the world. This was not new in itself. American industrialization had been noted and commented upon by many previous students of the subject. What was different about Riesman and Potter was that they were not at all unhappy about American industrialism. It had usually been described in words of contempt, fear, and foreboding; Jeffersonian and Turnerian preconceptions were so firmly ingrained in the American mind that most students of the American character simply could not consider industrialism dispassionately. They assumed that the United States was an agrarian nation and that to destroy its agrarian character was in effect to destroy the nation itself, or at least the institutions which had made it distinctive and great. Now both Riesman and Potter recognized, accepted, and even welcomed industrialism, thus providing if not a new analysis at least a fundamentally new attitude toward the old facts.

It is interesting to note that the most bitter attacks on American civilization and culture were made by non-academic intellectuals. Academicians, on the whole, tended to be considerably happier and more hopeful. Riesman was misinterpreted mostly, and most egregiously, in mass-circulation magazines. The contrast is revealed not only by the work of Riesman and Potter but more clearly by the fact that even such an intransigent viewer-with-alarm as Peter Viereck saw *some* room for hope.[18]

There is one book that does not properly fit this generalization. William H. Whyte, Jr., was an assistant editor of *Fortune* when he undertook the research that resulted in *The Organization Man*. The character of the organization man was not the national character; Whyte did not feel that he was typical of the whole population, but he did feel that the organization man was becoming more prevalent and more dominant in society. What is most relevant for present purposes, however, is Whyte's contention that there had been a substantial shift in American values from the Protestant Ethic of thrift, hard work, and self-denial to what he called the social ethic:

[18] *The Unadjusted Man, a New Hero for Americans: Reflections on the Distinction Between Conforming and Conserving* (Boston, 1956), pp. 329–332.

By social ethic I mean that contemporary body of thought which makes legitimate the pressures of society against the individual. Its major propositions are three: a belief in the group as the source of creativity; a belief in "belongingness" as the ultimate need of the individual; a belief in the application of science to achieve the belongingness. . . . Man exists as a unit of society. Of himself, he is isolated, meaningless; only as he collaborates with others does he become worth while, for by sublimating himself in the group, he helps produce a whole that is greater than the sum of its parts. There should be then, no conflict between man and society. What we think are conflicts are misunderstandings, breakdowns in communication. By applying the methods of science to human relations we can eliminate these obstacles to consensus and create an equilibrium in which society's needs and the needs of the individual are one and the same.[19]

Whyte felt that the increasing acceptance of this social ethic was symptomatic of a general and dangerous loss of individualism in America.

It is also important to appreciate the things that Whyte did *not* say about the organization. Much as he worried about it, he did not advocate its abolition. He maintained that the central problem was to ensure the continued existence of individualism within the organization or its preservation in a world dominated by the organization. His attitude is revealed by comparing it with the attitude of the Goodmans. Feeling that the American standard of living was absurd and that a modest reduction would do no real harm, they advocated a program which would mean, in essence, the abolition of many of the institutional mechanisms of modern society—a highly decentralized productive system, involving even a return to domestic industry, so that it would be possible to regain the sense of accomplishment in work which had been lost with the advent of the machine.[20]

Whyte advocated no such utopian solution. To him, the really disturbing element in the present situation was not the organization itself, but the social ethic which had grown up with it. He was not condemning a social system, but a value system. He did not want to retreat from industrialism, but to reorganize men's

19 (Garden City, N. Y., 1957), pp. 7–8.
20 *Communitas*, pp. 153–186.

thinking so that they could find individual freedom within an industrial system. Whyte was disturbed because he felt that the social ethic was too faithful a reflection of current social realities. His argument was almost a perfect reversal of the cultural-lag hypothesis. The social ethic embodied a system of thought and belief which involved a surrender to the pressures of the organization instead of providing the individual with the necessary intellectual and emotional defenses to protect his individuality. Whyte wanted a value system that would teach people to fight the organization, not give in to it. The social ethic asserted the compatibility of man and society; Whyte called for a recognition of their fundamental incompatibility. The implication was that once this had been accomplished—and he seemed to feel that it was possible, even by such apparently trivial acts as "cheating" on personality tests—the organization could be made to serve man, and that life with all the powers of the organization turned to man's service instead of his domination might be wonderful indeed. Life in Park Forest, after all, had some very pleasant features.

Thus, along with the highly critical attitude adopted by many commentators on the American character, it was also possible to detect a persistent strain of optimism, a belief that the present situation, difficult as it was, still contained potentialities for the greatest advance in the development of the human individual that the world had ever seen. For all the critical emphasis on conformity, for all the condemnations of mass culture and its effects, the intellectual atmosphere of the 1950's was, therefore, different in one respect from that of the 1920's. The 1950's were marked by an attitude which did not exist in the 1920's: a steady and considerable undercurrent of hope, called forth not by the belief that present circumstances would be completely changed, but that they would be modified. For the first time, some commentators on the national character seemed disposed to come to terms with America's industrial heritage on a wide scale, to recognize its importance, and to welcome rather than condemn its effects. The attitude was still ambivalent; there was still concern about the undesirable effects of the organization, but for the first time the vast potentialities of industrialism for human as opposed to material development were widely recognized.

AFTERWORD

Perhaps the most striking fact that emerges from a study of American conceptions of the American character during the twentieth century is the remarkable similarity among them. Though there have been certain changes over the course of several decades, those studies that are roughly contemporaneous with one another exhibit surprising degrees of congruence. Given the wide variety of backgrounds, opinions, and predilections of those who have written on the subject, and given its enormous complexity, one would expect to find substantial differences between one author and the next. On the whole, this is not the case. Studies of the American character have consisted for the most part of variations on a strictly limited number of themes. The variations that do exist are variations of attitude, emphasis, and focus, revealing much about the personal idiosyncrasies of the authors, but adding little that is new about the subject itself. (A qualification must be entered here. Recent attempts by social scientists to describe the American character are different from the older treatments, which, in general, suffered from a lack of sociological awareness.) The usual style of the commentator on the American character is to make a simple declarative statement, then to say "but" and go on at far greater length. The final features of the picture thus presented, especially the favorable or unfavorable impression that the picture is intended to leave, are often dependent only on the order in which the data are presented; the data themselves are almost always the same.

It would be possible to argue, of course, that this remarkable consensus is dictated by the facts of the subject—that is, that the American character is in fact precisely what these commentators have said it was and that they have agreed simply because they have all perceived the truth. This explanation is unsatisfying. The United States is a large, heterogeneous nation. Variations among social classes, geographical sections, and racial, ethnic, and religious groups are so wide that the concept of a *national* character which presumably includes all or most of them is questionable. It certainly could not have any predictive value whatever: a knowledge of the American character would not allow an outsider to predict how any individual American might react in any given situation. This does not necessarily rob the concept of all validity, but it must be obvious that whatever validity it has, when applied to a nation as heterogeneous as the United States, is only the validity of a vague, extremely high-order generalization to which there are many individual exceptions and qualifications. Such generalizations cannot be called true or false with any certainty, any more than a poetic metaphor can be called true or false. They may be insightful, stimulating, provocative, but they are not scientific laws and cannot be evaluated according to the canons of the scientific method. The construction of any outline of the American character cannot be made simply through the proper alignment of relevant statistics, but only through the creative structuring and interpretation of such facts as the analyst has available. The national character, therefore, is largely a product of the perceiving mind. If propositions concerning national character were like simple arithmetical statements of addition and subtraction, one would not be surprised to find substantial agreement. But the national character is neither an eternal truth nor a mathematical law, and the agreement that has existed among American commentators on the American character, especially in view of the diversity of their backgrounds and interests, cannot be explained in such a fashion.

Rather, it is a product of their willingness, at least up to the recent past, to avoid the knotty problems involved in making a precise, systematic determination of the fundamental traits of the American character. Indeed, they have usually not even attempted to define with any rigor what they mean by "American character" in the first place. They have taken the concept as given and have largely agreed with each other that certain traits are, and have been for some time, the distinguishing features of the American character, differing only on the question of which traits deserve emphasis and which can be dismissed as unimportant. Except for these differences of emphasis and attitude, they have been quite content, for the most part, to accept the traditional, prevailing, comfortable view of what traits make a person "American."

One might almost say that they have been forced to accept the traditional view. Most students of the American character have been very poorly equipped for the task of systematic social analysis and description on a wide scale. Before the last twenty years, most of them were not social scientists but novelists, poets, literary critics, literary historians, travelers, and, generally, just interested citizens who wanted to understand their nation and express their opinions of it. Lacking the necessary qualifications to make original investigations of American traits, they were driven, almost inevitably, to accept the views of others.

Another important factor here is that most of those who have written on the American character have not been interested in it in itself, but in other things. They have been interested in attacking immigration, in defending the immigrant, in criticizing the "official" custodians of the nation's culture, in asserting the necessity of making substantial social changes to cure significant social ills, or in accomplishing any one of several other aims. The national-character study was simply a vehicle for the delivery of opinions on the contemporary scene, and the national character itself was relatively unimportant. Consequently, the picture of the American character presented by tradition was quite good enough. Writers were willing to accept traditional conclusions as long as they could use them as the basis for their own generalizations. They were content to repeat what others had said and to interpret it to suit themselves.

Perhaps under the circumstances it would be more accurate in certain respects to substitute for the term "national character" the term "national caricature." The caricaturist selects and emphasizes—or exaggerates—certain elements in the physiognomy of his subject. The student of national character, especially in a nation like the United States, must do the same thing. He is confronted with a reality that includes tens of millions of individuals, from different social classes, following different occupations, professing varying values and beliefs and adhering to them with varying degrees of consistency, and from this hodge-podge he must construct a coherent picture of the national character. To perform his task at all, he must select and emphasize those elements which seem to him to be most important and most revealing.

Of course, there is an apparent difference of purpose between the caricaturist and the student of national character. A caricature is a conscious, purposeful distortion; its function is not simply descriptive, it is also editorial; the artist is not only depicting his subject, he is also commenting upon it. He is, in effect, using his portrayal of a particular subject as a platform from which to deliver opinions on the subject and possibly on a variety of related themes as well, for the caricature can have a symbolic value that portraits of specific individuals do not often possess. The national-character study differs in that editorializing is not, or should not be, its primary purpose. The student of national character is presumably trying to arrive at a reasonably close approximation to objective truth. The realization that the full attainment of this goal is impossible does not relieve him of the obligation of striving to get as close to it as he can. In fact, however, the editorializing function has been dominant in most treatments of the American character. This is not unjustifiable in itself; "editorial" comment is not out of place even in the most scholarly works, and the scholar should not be denied the privilege of making value judgments if he feels inclined to do so. He will in any case, and it is better that he and his readers are fully aware of what he is doing. The caricaturist, however, *knows* that he is distorting reality when he does it; he does it consciously and for a purpose. But most students of the national character do not seem to have been aware of their editorializing; they have distorted their subject while offering their conclusions as if they were unquestioned truths determined with the strictest scientific exactitude, without giving explicit recognition to their motives for undertaking a study of the American character in the first place.

The most profound of these motives, in the majority of cases, was to give expression to a chronic distrust of industrialism. For the most part, commentators on the American character have refused to come to terms with modern industrial realities. For roughly the first half of the twentieth century, they were trying to assess a phenomenon that they disliked and that they were not equipped to interpret. So firmly committed to agrarianism were they that they were rendered incapable of seeing exactly what industrialism was and what it had done and was doing to the United States.

The impact of commentaries by foreign travelers—De Tocqueville, Bryce, Dickens, Arnold, Mrs. Trollope, and their many colleagues—reinforced the anti-industrial bias of native efforts to interpret the American character. To many of these Europeans, the American and his industrial civilization appeared crass, crude, and vulgar. Many Americans have taken such criticism to heart, apparently on the totally unwarranted assumption that those who advanced it, being outsiders, were disinterested and objective. Even if they were not deluded in this way, they might well have been trying to compensate for their own cultural inferiority complex by demonstrating that they, too, saw the horrors of American civilization and were themselves capable of the refined sensibilities of the European critics—even if the majority of their countrymen were not. Those who did not accept the strictures of the Europeans—and there have been many who have begun their treatments of the American character with fervent statements to the effect that most foreign analysts have been wrong—nevertheless tended to share the underlying assumption of most European works, in that they maintained or implied that industrialism was an undesirable form of social and economic organization. Though they did not share the Europeans' low opinion of the United States, they did accept the major premise of the European attack: that industrialism produced a disreputable, vulgar, coarse, and unenlightened civilization. Their defense of their native land, therefore, had to attempt to prove that the United States was not an industrial nation; they were forced to argue from a premise that was patently false, at least during the twentieth century. The tension can be seen in most treatments of the American character as "enforced optimism," a favorable view that seems, on the basis of the writer's own evidence, to have little or no justification.

This is especially true of American liberals who were trying to defend the United States as the home of democracy and liberalism against attacks from foreigners who, for the most part, were neither democrats nor liberals. Distrust of industrialism would seem to be a conservative political attitude, and in European politics it has been. In the United States, however, it is the liberals who have launched the strongest attacks on it; American liberalism has been a predominantly agrarian philosophy, while American conservatism, gaining its natural allies among the relatively wealthy, has found its political home largely on the side of the industrial system which has produced wealth. The classical European pattern has been reversed in the United States; American liberals have been raised on Jeffersonian doctrine, and American liberalism has been equated with Jeffersonianism.

Recently, however, there are signs that this situation is changing. Native writers on the American character are beginning to accept industrialism much more warmly than they did before. Willing to accept the verdict that America has come to symbolize industrialism, they now find in this grounds for hope, not despair. They have awakened to the potentialities of industrialism. They have begun to question the assumption that the acceptance of industrialism leads to the abandonment of democracy. Events of the past two decades have probably contributed strongly to the change of opinion. During World War II, the industrial might of the United States, the arsenal of democracy, had much to do with the preservation of freedom in the world. Later experience with the Marshall Plan and other aid programs and with various agencies of the United Nations seemed to indicate that political democracy was difficult to establish and preserve unless certain minimum standards of affluence could be maintained for a significant proportion of the population. Consequently, industrialism, since it was the most efficient producer of wealth in the modern world, was no longer regarded as the enemy of democracy, but as its strongest bastion.

This kind of revisionism in historical attitudes is inevitable. What is interesting about studies of the American character is not that traditional views have been revised, but rather that the views of one man have persisted for so long. American analysts of the national character have been extremely reluctant to give up the categories of thought that found their definitive expression in the Frontier Thesis. The agrarian biases of Turner's work have also continued in most subsequent treatments of the American character. The consistent fear of industrialism which has marked these treatments up to the recent past is clear evidence of the persistence of the attitudes from which the Frontier Thesis originally grew. Even when commentators question its agrarian biases, even when they appear willing to accept industrialism, they do so largely because they seem to feel that industrialism constitutes a new frontier. The "frontier" as an operative concept is so deeply ingrained in American thinking that it is almost impossible for American intellectuals to think about their country as a whole without it. If they realize that it no longer makes sense—if it ever did—to talk about an agrarian frontier as the essential element in the creation of the American character, they talk instead about an industrial or a scientific frontier. Their frontier is not Turner's, but they owe a considerable intellectual debt to Turner. In bringing the frontier to the consciousness of American intellectuals, he did more than give voice to the agrarian presuppositions of the American tradition. In his conception of America as a nation characterized uniquely by creative responses to specific challenges, he invented a compelling symbol of expansion, challenge, and change. The original Frontier Thesis stressed the challenge of an empty continent. Though that challenge no longer exists, Americans still like to think of their nation as a frontier nation, as a nation successfully responding to whatever challenges might exist in the world.

ANNOTATED BIBLIOGRAPHY
OF CITED WORKS

PRIMARY SOURCES

Abbott, Lyman. *America in the Making.* New Haven, 1911.
  A series of lectures on the responsibilities of citizenship in the course of which Abbott finds the mainsprings of the American character to lie in the principle of free choice.
Abbott, Wilbur C. *The New Barbarians.* Boston, 1925.
  A discussion of various subversive tendencies in the radical ideas imported into the United States by immigrants. The first chapter contains an extended discussion of the American character.
Adamic, Louis. *From Many Lands.* New York, 1940.
  An exalted treatment of the part played by immigrants in the building of the United States and a plea for cultural pluralism as the proper concept around which to organize American culture and American life in general.
Adams, Charles Francis, Jr. *Imperialism and the Tracks of Our Forefathers.* N.p., n.d.
  The text of an address delivered before the Lexington, Massachusetts, Historical Society on December 20, 1898. Adams argues that imperialism is contrary to American traditions and threatens their existence.
Adams, George Burton. "A Century of Anglo-Saxon Expansion," *Atlantic Monthly,* 79 (1897), 528–538.
  A plea for the Anglo-Saxon race to reunite, to undo the damage done by the American Revolution, and to begin the task of establishing a world empire built upon the superior political sagacity and ambition of the Anglo-Saxon peoples.
Adams, James Truslow. *The American: The Making of a New Man.* New York, 1943.
  An historical survey of the American character and how it got to be the way it is. It is considerably more optimistic in tone than the book Adams did on the same subject in the 1920's.
———. *Our Business Civilization: Some Aspects of American Culture.* New York, 1929.

A statement of the proposition that American culture is dominated by the standards and values of business, which is to say that it is acquisitive, materialistic, anti-intellectual, and thoroughly undesirable. The book expresses the feelings of alienation experienced by many American intellectuals in the 1920's.

Addams, Jane. *Twenty Years at Hull House.* New York, 1910.

Jane Addams' autobiography, interesting in the present context for its analysis of the relationship between immigration and political corruption and for her unconscious but very real sense of discomfort in an urban atmosphere.

Agee, James. *A Death in the Family.* New York, 1957.

Agee's highly evocative prose poem "Knoxville: Summer 1915" is printed as a prologue to this novel. It is a very moving picture of small-town life in the United States.

Alexander, Franz. *Our Age of Unreason: A Study of the Irrational Forces in Social Life.* Philadelphia, 1942.

Alexander was one of the many psychiatrists who fled Nazi persecution in the 1930's. Once in the United States, he began to analyze the American character by applying psychiatric concepts to the frontier experience.

Almond, Gabriel A. *The American People and Foreign Policy.* New York, 1950.

An analysis of the American character in terms of its assets and liabilities in the task of conducting a rational and effective foreign policy in the post-war world. Almond feels that the liabilities outweigh the assets.

Anderson, Sherwood. *Puzzled America.* New York, 1935.

A series of brief, impressionistic sketches of Anderson's travels around the country, mostly devoted to portraying the feelings of bewildered anger among the "ordinary" people of America.

Antin, Mary. *They Who Knock at Our Gates: A Complete Gospel of Immigration.* Boston, 1914.

A defense of immigrants and an attack on those who would restrict immigration, based on the proposition that immigrants have not harmed America and the American character but have improved both.

Asch, Nathan. *The Road: In Search of America.* New York, 1937.

An account of the author's trip through the country and a vivid example of the "documentary" style of social criticism prevalent in the 1930's.

Babbitt, Irving. *Democracy and Leadership.* Boston, 1924.

An attack on the American character for its lack of firm moral and cultural standards.

Barzun, Jacques. *God's Country and Mine: A Declaration of Love Spiced with a Few Harsh Words.* Boston, 1954.

An analysis of the contemporary scene in the United States in which the concept of national character does find a place despite Barzun's previous attacks on it as invalid and dangerous.

————. *Race: A Study in Modern Superstition.* New York, 1937.

A study of race-thinking, its assumptions and characteristics, reflecting the distrust of Nazism which led to a fear of broad generalizations concerning large groups of people.

Bates, Ernest Sutherland. *American Faith: Its Religious, Political, and Economic Foundations.* New York, 1940.

A description of the "American creed" and the relations between the religious, political, and economic aspects of that creed, in which the author gives first place and primary significance to the religious factor, deriving other features of American thought from it.

Beard, Charles A., and Beard, Mary R. *The American Spirit: A Study of the Idea of Civilization in the United States.* New York, 1942.

A statement of the Beards' belief that America is unique because it is uniquely devoted to the idea of civilization, an idea they never define with any precision, but which seems to be directed at bottom toward creating a full and satisfying life, materially and spiritually, for all people.

Bell, Daniel (ed.). *The New American Right.* New York, 1955.

A series of essays by various authors on the sources and manifestations of right-wing extremism. Many of the authors regard this type of political thinking as an extreme, but consistent, manifestation of certain traits in the American character.

Beveridge, Albert J. *Americans of To-Day and To-Morrow.* Philadelphia, 1908.

An analysis of the American character in terms of its suitability to realize a glorious imperial destiny.

Bierstadt, Edward Hale. *Aspects of Americanization.* Cincinnati, 1922.

A collection of essays on various aspects of Americanization based on the premise that most methods of Americanization are worse than useless and that the immigrants are far closer to the original spirit of America than native Americans.

Boas, Franz. *The Mind of Primitive Man.* New York, 1921.

In many ways, the summary of Boas' whole system of thought. The main point of the book is that such differences in behavior and mental organization as may exist between groups of men are due to differences in social organization and experience and are not the product of innate, hereditary mental characteristics.

Boorstin, Daniel J. *The Genius of American Politics*. Chicago, 1953.

A history and analysis of American political thought in which the author argues that its fundamental distinguishing characteristic is a profound belief in "givenness," the idea that political institutions are the inevitable product of geographical and historical conditions, not of conscious thinking.

Bourne, Randolph. "The Heart of the People," *New Republic*, July 3, 1915, p. 233.

A brief essay, in the guise of a movie review, on the dangers of a standardized culture.

Boutwell, George S. *Problems Raised by the War*. Washington, D. C., 1898.

A vigorous attack on imperialism based upon the belief that the Philippines are incapable of self-government and that they cannot be effectively governed by the United States.

Bowers, David F. (ed.). *Foreign Influences in American Life*. Princeton, 1944.

A collection of essays by various authors on the contributions made by immigrants.

Brooks, Van Wyck. *The Ordeal of Mark Twain*. New York, 1920.

An analysis of Mark Twain's work in terms of the conflict Brooks perceived between his artistic instincts and his surrender to the materialistic, moralistic values of the Gilded Age.

———. *Three Essays on America*. New York, 1934.

A one-volume edition of "America's Coming of Age," "Letters and Leadership," and "The Literary Life in America." The theme of all three essays is the same: the undesirable state of American literature resulting from Americans' exclusive preoccupation with the materialistic tasks involved in conquering and exploiting the American continent.

Brossard, Chandler (ed.). *The Scene Before You: A New Approach to American Culture*. New York, 1955.

A collection of essays by various authors on various aspects of life in modern America. The essay by Arnold W. Green on patterns of American family life is especially noteworthy.

Brown, Francis J., and Roucek, Joseph Slabey (eds.). *One America: The History, Contributions, and Present Problems of Our Racial and National Minorities*. New York, 1937.

A collection of essays by various authors on various aspects of the problems created by the presence in America of several imperfectly assimilated ethnic and racial minorities. Generally speaking, the authors in the book favor cultural pluralism rather than the melting-pot theory of assimilation.

Brown, Rollo Walter. *I Travel by Train*. New York, 1939.
An account of the author's trip through the United States. A good example of the "documentary" approach to social analysis and of the frequent connection between this documentary approach and political radicalism.

Bunker, John. "Nationality and the Case of American Literature," *Sewanee Review*, 27 (1919), 82–91.
Bunker comes to the conclusion that American literature is not better than it is largely because the American character is more oriented toward practicality than artistry; he is not particularly disturbed by the fact.

Burgess, Ernest W. "The Family in a Changing Society," *American Journal of Sociology*, 54 (1948), 118–125.
Burgess argues that much of what appears to be dislocation and disorganization in American family life is the result of a transition from an older, more authoritarian family to a newer, more democratic type of family life. He is not as disturbed, therefore, as most commentators on the American family have been, by these changes in American family life and structure.

Burgess, John W. *The Foundations of Political Science*. New York, 1933.
This is a republication of those parts of Burgess' great work *Political Science and Comparative Constitutional Law* that relate to the nation and the state and elaborate one of Burgess' favorite themes: the peculiar political genius and consequent responsibilities of the "Teutonic" peoples.

———. "Germany, Great Britain, and the United States," *Political Science Quarterly*, 19 (1904), 1–19.
An article devoted to the proposition that the three great Teutonic powers of the world should devote themselves to the cause of creating friendly relations among themselves to make effective leadership in the world possible.

———. "The Ideal of the American Commonwealth," *Political Science Quarterly*, 10 (1895), 404–425.
A discussion of American political beliefs and behavior and the direction that the American people should try to make them take in the future. In the course of the discussion, Burgess expresses his fervent belief in the distinctive political genius of the American people.

———. *Recent Changes in American Constitutional Theory*. New York, 1923.
A survey of American constitutional history from 1898. The

major emphasis is the steady increase in the power of the government as opposed to that of the individual, a development about which Burgess is not at all happy.

———. *The Reconciliation of Government with Liberty*. New York, 1915.

The title of the book reveals Burgess' chief concern and main point: that government and liberty are inherently incompatible and that recent increases in governmental power in the United States are threats to liberty.

Butler, Nicholas Murray. *The American as He Is*. New York, 1908.

In these lectures Butler was attempting to explain the American character to a foreign audience. Not surprisingly, the picture he paints is quite rosy.

Canby, Henry Seidel. *Everyday Americans*. New York, 1920.

Canby's book bears the imprint of the uncertainty of the 1920's, in that he is concerned about the apparent aimlessness of American life, but he comes to the conclusion that the nation is in fairly good shape and that things are improving.

Commander, Lydia Kingsmill. *The American Idea: Does the National Tendency Toward a Small Family Point to Race Suicide or Race Development?* New York, 1907.

One of the many expressions of dismay about the possibility of "race suicide" in the early twentieth century, and a plea for the restriction of immigration so that the American type would not be bred out of existence by the less worthy racial strains among the immigrants.

Commons, John R. *Races and Immigrants in America*. 2nd ed. New York, 1920.

Considerably more judicious in tone than many of the other arguments for the restriction of immigration, but interesting in that it shows that even those who were politically liberal were not immune from nativist intolerance.

Conant, Charles A. "The Economic Basis of 'Imperialism,'" *North American Review*, 167 (1898), 326–340.

A brief statement of the theory that developed capitalist nations resort to imperialistic expansion in order to find new places to invest surplus capital. Conant also feels, however, that the United States is impelled toward imperialism by its racial destiny.

Croly, Herbert. *The Promise of American Life*. New York, 1909.

Croly's insistence that the promise of American life would not be fulfilled unless the American people rid themselves of their outworn social and political ideas represents one of the few instances in which an American intellectual argued consciously and coherently for an industrial instead of an agrarian way of life in the United States.

Dollard, John W. *Caste and Class in a Southern Town*. New Haven, 1937.

A study of racial relations in a southern community. One of the classic, pioneering attempts to apply psychiatric concepts to the study of society.

——, *et al. Frustration and Aggression*. New York, 1939.

A clear statement of the now commonplace psychological theory that frustration tends to lead to aggressive behavior.

Dos Passos, John R. *The Anglo-Saxon Century and the Unification of the English-Speaking People*. New York, 1903.

An argument for the unification of the United States and Great Britain so that these nations, with their birthright of superior political wisdom, can more effectively lead the rest of the world to political stability and lasting peace.

Drachsler, Julius. *Democracy and Assimilation: The Blending of Immigrant Heritages in America*. New York, 1920.

An argument for cultural pluralism as the proper road to the solution of the problems raised by immigration instead of the attempts made by most adherents of the Americanization movement to reduce the immigrants to absolute identity with the American population and each other.

Eggleston, Edward. *The Transit of Civilization from England to America in the Seventeenth Century*. New York, 1900.

In this historical analysis of the first century of American life, Eggleston insisted that the similarities between America and Britain were cultural and not, as most of his contemporaries would have had it, racial.

Eliot, Charles W. *American Contributions to Civilization and Other Essays and Addresses*. New York, 1907.

In his address "Five American Contributions to Civilization," Eliot expatiates on the traditional themes of American opportunity, individualism, love of liberty, etc., which constituted the standard picture of the American character around the turn of the century.

Erikson, Erik H. *Childhood and Society*. New York, 1950.

A study by a psychiatrist, who specializes in work with children, of the way in which social pressures act upon the infant to produce certain types of personality configuration. Much of his illustrative material is drawn from contemporary American life and constitutes, in effect, a commentary on the American character, whose chief distinguishing traits he finds to be domination by mothers and bosses.

Erskine, John. *Democracy and Ideals: A Definition.* New York, 1920.
A collection of essays on various subjects. Two are devoted
to attempts to define the ideals of democracy and the American character.

———. *Prohibition and Christianity and Other Paradoxes of the
American Spirit.* Indianapolis, 1927.
A collection of essays on various subjects, one of which,
"American Aristocracy," takes America to task for its compla-
cent assumption of moral superiority.

Foerster, Norman (ed.). *The Reinterpretation of American Literature: Some Contributions Toward the Understanding of Its
Historical Development.* New York, 1928.
A series of essays on American literature and its historical
backgrounds from the "new humanist" point of view, with
primary emphasis upon the frontier and Puritan influences.

Frank, Lawrence K. *Society as the Patient: Essays on Culture and
Personality.* New Brunswick, N. J., 1948.
A series of previously published essays on various aspects of
the relationship between culture and personality, most of
which are extremely critical of the cultural patterns of American civilization and the personality types to which they give
rise.

Frank, Waldo. *Our America.* New York, 1919.
The "our" of the title refers to American intellectuals and
artists, who the author feels are being dominated by a
culturally, intellectually, and spiritually sterile America born
of the frontier and Puritanism and maintained by the machine.

———. *The Re-Discovery of America: An Introduction to a Philosophy of American Life.* New York, 1929.
A repetition, in slightly more mystical language, of most
of the fundamental ideas of *Our America.*

Freud, Sigmund. *Civilization and Its Discontents.* London, 1922.
Freud's classic statement of the proposition that civilized
life by its very nature prevents or restricts the expression
of certain natural drives and thus leads to frustration and
possibly to mental disease.

Fromm, Erich. *Escape from Freedom.* New York, 1941.
A study of the conflicts and insecurities besetting the individual who lives in a modern industrial society.

Giddings, Franklin H. "The American People," *International
Quarterly,* 7 (1903), 281–299.
Giddings was one of those who felt that the American character was likely to be improved by the racial intermixture resulting from immigration.

————. "What Shall We Be: Comments on the Foregoing," *Century Magazine*, 65 (1903), 690–692.

A commentary on an article by another sociologist, in which Giddings again expressed his opinion that the United States had nothing to fear and much to gain from the introduction of new racial strains into the American population through immigration.

Gilman, Charlotte Perkins. "Is America Too Hospitable," *Forum*, 70 (1923), 1983–1989.

The author answers the question in the title with a resounding "yes," arguing that the United States must restrict immigration to preserve its distinctive national character.

Goodman, Paul, and Goodman, Percival. *Communitas: Means of Livelihood and Ways of Life*. 2nd ed. New York, 1960.

Some "utopian" speculations on the future of American cities, city plans, and culture. The authors are thoroughly dismayed by the present state of all three.

Gould, Charles W. *America, a Family Matter*. New York, 1922.

A long historical account of racial rise and fall designed to prove that "pure" races have made all the significant contributions to the advancement of civilization, that racial intermixture is therefore bad in itself, and that the United States must restrict immigration or the American character will degenerate.

Grant, Madison. *The Conquest of a Continent, or the Expansion of Races in America*. New York, 1933.

America was established by Nordics, its culture and institutions are distinctively Nordic, and this culture and these institutions are threatened by the introduction of non-Nordic elements into American society. It is every bit as ridiculous as Grant's other works.

————. *The Passing of the Great Race, or the Racial Basis of European History*. 4th ed. New York, 1921.

Grant's major work, in which he attempts to show that the "Nordic" race is generally superior in all fields to all other races.

Hall, Prescott F. *Immigration and Its Effects upon the United States*. New York, 1906.

One of the earliest large-scale attacks on the "new" immigration of the 1890's and its deleterious effects upon American ideals, institutions, and character.

Hankins, Frank H. *The Racial Basis of Civilization: A Critique of the Nordic Doctrine*. New York, 1926.

The effectiveness of Hankins' attack on European and

American racists is somewhat compromised by his own adherence to some of the questionable doctrines of the eugenists.

Hansen, Marcus Lee. *The Immigrant in American History*. Cambridge, 1940.

A collection of essays on the effects of immigration upon American history. Fundamentally, Hansen sees immigration as a force which extended, intensified, and modified the frontier experience.

Hartz, Louis. *The Liberal Tradition in America: An Interpretation of American Political Thought Since the Revolution*. New York, 1955.

Hartz maintains that American political thought, at least when it has been translated into effective political action, has been nothing more than a set of variations on the single theme of Lockean liberalism and that American political thought is distinctive because of this extraordinary liberal consensus.

Heilbroner, Robert L. *The Future as History: The Historic Currents of Our Time and the Direction in Which They Are Taking America*. New York, 1959.

A consideration of the problems currently facing America and the difficulties that are likely to occur in attempts to solve these problems because of the conflict between American optimism and a situation in which optimism is no longer rationally tenable as a philosophy of life and a guide to policy.

Horney, Karen. *The Neurotic Personality of Our Time*. New York, 1937.

A study of the characteristic mental diseases produced in modern society because of its distinctive social and cultural patterns.

Ireland, Alleyne. *Democracy and the Human Equation*. New York, 1921.

An analysis of the current ills of American government, for which the author blames the distinctive social and cultural patterns of modern society.

Jordan, David Starr. *Imperial Democracy*. New York, 1899.

A collection of essays devoted to the theme of anti-imperialism in which the author argues that imperialism is contrary to American traditions and dangerous to the American character.

Josephson, Matthew. *Portrait of the Artist as American*. New York, 1930.

A literary history of the United States oriented around the theme of the mechanization of American life and the way in which this development has made it impossible for artists to live here. Accordingly, they have fled to other countries, to hermit-like existences here, or to imaginative worlds of their own creation.

Kallen, Horace M. *Culture and Democracy in the United States: Studies in the Group Psychology of the American Peoples.* New York, 1924.

The classic argument for cultural pluralism, in the course of which Kallen analyzes the American culture and character and its deficiencies, deficiencies which are presumably to be compensated for by the qualities of immigrant cultures.

Kardiner, Abram. *The Individual and His Society: The Psychodynamics of Primitive Social Organization.* New York, 1939.

One of the pioneering studies of the relation between culture and personality, important chiefly for the enunciation and application of the concept of basic personality structure.

Kellor, Frances. *Immigration and the Future.* New York, 1920.

A discussion of the problems of immigration and assimilation. Kellor is somewhat doubtful about the methods of the more extreme Americanizers, but she is also insistent that assimilation is the only possible solution to the immigration problem.

————. *Straight America: A Call to National Service.* New York, 1916.

Americanization here becomes an important part of the preparedness movement. She blames the native American rather than the immigrant for the dangerous lack of unity in national life, but her proposed remedy is an Americanization campaign which will ride roughshod over immigrants' cultures.

Kluckhohn, Clyde. *Mirror for Man: A Survey of Human Behavior and Social Attitudes.* New York, 1949.

A general introduction to the assumptions, concepts, and methods of cultural anthropology including, more or less by way of illustration, an analysis of the American value system and the American character.

Kouwenhoven, John A. *Made in America: The Arts in Modern Civilization.* New York, 1948.

A discussion of the distinctive American tradition in art, in terms of its adherence to the "vernacular"—the characteristics and qualities of common objects of everyday use, designed and created for their efficiency, their cheapness, and their ease of manufacture. He argues that by thus adhering to the vernacular, American culture has borne the stamp of industrialism to a far greater extent that any other culture in the world.

Lasswell, Harold D. *Psychopathology and Politics.* New York, 1930.
The classic and justly famous attempt to apply psychiatric concepts to the analysis of political behavior.
———. *World Politics and Personal Insecurity.* New York, 1935.
A discussion of the American political scene in psychiatric terms.

Linton, Ralph (ed.). *The Science of Man in the World Crisis.* New York, 1945.
A collection of articles on various aspects of anthropology, including several that relate to culture and personality theory.

Lipset, Seymour Martin, and Lowenthal, Leo (eds.). *Culture and Social Character: The Work of David Riesman Reviewed.* Glencoe, Ill., 1961.
A collection of essays on Riesman's work, most of them quite stimulating, but also reflecting the ways in which Riesman's work has been misinterpreted by most of his critics.

Lowell, A. Lawrence. "The Colonial Expansion of the United States," *Atlantic Monthly*, 83 (1899), 145–154.
A discussion of America's problems as a colonial power, and an enunciation of the theme that American imperialism developed from the necessity of finding an outlet for expansionist urges after the closing of the frontier.

Lynd, Robert S. *Knowledge for What?: The Place of Social Science in American Culture.* Princeton, 1939.
A consideration of the possibilities of using the social sciences in a rational attempt to create the good life in America. The discussion is prefaced by an extended consideration of the American value system and its inherent contradictions.

———, and Lynd, Helen Merrell. *Middletown: A Study in American Culture.* New York, 1929.
The classic community study.
———, and ———. *Middletown in Transition.* New York, 1937.
A sequel to *Middletown*, designed to see how this "typical" American community had been changed by the Depression.

Mandlebaum, David G. (ed.). *Selected Writings of Edward Sapir in Language, Culture, and Personality.* Berkeley, 1949.
A collection of essays on various topics by the man who did more than any other single individual to define the culture and personality approach to the study of man.

Mathews, Shailer. *The Validity of American Ideals.* New York, 1922.
A definition of major American ideals and values and a diatribe against various kinds of "radicalism" which threaten to undermine them.

Mead, Margaret. *And Keep Your Powder Dry: An Anthropologist Looks at America.* New York, 1942.

An analysis of American culture and the American character using the approaches and concepts of the culture and personality school.

Mencken, H. L. *A Book of Prefaces.* 2nd ed. New York, 1918.

A collection of literary essays, one of which, "Puritanism as a Literary Force," is one of the classic expressions of the anti-Puritan crusade mounted by American artists and intellectuals in the 1920's.

———. *Prejudices, Second Series.* New York, 1920.

A collection of brief essays in which Mencken delivers himself of various scathing opinions on the state of American culture, politics, and intelligence.

———. *Prejudices, Fourth Series.* New York, 1924.

Another collection of incidental essays.

Michaud, Gustave. "What Shall We Be: The Coming Race in America," *Century Magazine*, 65 (1903), 683–690.

An analysis of the effects of immigration and racial intermixture on the American character. He feels that some of the results will be beneficial, others will not.

Morison, Elting E. (ed.). *The American Style: Essays in Value and Performance.* New York, 1958.

A collection of essays by various authors on American culture and the American value system, most of them devoted to the problem of the discrepancy between theory and practice, values and realities, in American life.

Morris, Charles. *The Open Self.* New York, 1948.

A discussion of the problems faced by contemporary man, especially the problem of maintaining America's open society under modern conditions which have made the frontiersman, who created and maintained that society, an anachronism.

Mumford, Lewis. *The Golden Day: A Study in American Experience and Culture.* New York, 1926.

Another attack on American culture, its Puritanism and materialism, in the guise of a history of American literature and philosophy.

Murphy, Gardner. *Personality: A Biosocial Approach to Origins and Structure.* New York, 1947.

An extended definition and discussion of the concept of personality, part of which is devoted to a discussion of American culture and personality, or national character.

Nathan, George Jean, and Mencken, H. L. *The American Credo: A*

Contribution Toward the Interpretation of the National Mind. New York, 1920.

A caustic analysis of the American character, the chief traits of which would seem to be conformity, timidity, and an abject fear of public opinion.

Nef, John U. *The United States and Civilization.* Chicago, 1942.

Nef argues that modern Western man, with the American in the van, has sold his cultural and spiritual birthright for a mess of materialistic pottage.

Niebuhr, Reinhold. *The Irony of American History.* New York, 1952.

A study of American history based on the assumption that the American people have been spoiled by their historic experiences into thinking that they are able to control the course of history. This delusion has made Americans unable to deal effectively with the problems they face in the modern world.

————. *Moral Man and Immoral Society: A Study in Ethics and Politics.* New York, 1932.

One of the earliest expressions of the basic premise underlying all Niebuhr's work: that the unaided human intelligence is not equal to the task of building a rational social order.

Northrop, F. S. C. *The Meeting of East and West: An Inquiry Concerning World Understanding.* New York, 1946.

A consideration of the primary philosophical orientations of several contemporary civilizations, including that of the United States. He concludes that America's outlook has been defined by John Locke, but that America's exclusive dependence on Locke's philosophy serves it ill in the contemporary world.

————. *The Taming of the Nations: A Study of the Cultural Bases of Foreign Policy.* New York, 1952.

The conclusions of *The Meeting of East and West* are here applied to a consideration of the problems of foreign policy.

Panunzio, Constantine. *Immigration Crossroads.* New York, 1927.

A study of immigration and the movement to restrict it devoted to proving that the assumptions which underlie the restriction movement are invalid.

Park, Robert E., and Miller, Herbert A. *Old World Traits Transplanted.* New York, 1921.

A study of the psychological problems faced by immigrants in their attempt to move from one cultural system to another. It contains a repudiation of the concept of "immigrant gifts," based upon the authors' contention that the concept assumed that cultural functions were determined by heredity, an assumption they would not grant.

Parkes, Henry Bamford. *The American Experience: An Interpretation of the History and Civilization of the American People.* New York, 1947.

A general history of the United States couched in terms of the conflict betwen agrarianism and industrialism. The author's sympathies incline unmistakably toward the former.

Parsons, Talcott. *The Social System.* Glencoe, Ill., 1951.

Parsons here discusses, among other things, the way in which the concept of the basic personality structure may be used in the analysis of social systems.

———. *The Structure of Social Action.* New York, 1937.

In this work, Parsons outlines a general theoretical scheme of social analysis based upon the consideration of values as the feature of primary significance in any social system.

Perry, Bliss. *The American Mind.* Boston, 1912.

A study of American literature organized around the theme of the accuracy with which it expresses the American mind. It is, in essence, the Frontier Thesis applied to a study of American literature.

Perry, Ralph Barton. *Characteristically American.* New York, 1949.

As the title implies, a study of the distinctive elements of American civilization and culture. Perry devotes most of his attention to an examination of the American system of values, which he seems to regard as synonymous with the American character.

———. *Puritanism and Democracy.* New York, 1944.

A description and analysis of the two primary forces in the formation of the American character.

Plant, James S. *Personality and the Cultural Pattern.* New York, 1937.

One of the many psychiatrically oriented studies of the American character which appeared in the 1930's. Unlike most of his contemporaries, Plant seems to be quite pleased with the American character.

Potter, David M. *People of Plenty: Economic Abundance and the American Character.* Chicago, 1954.

A theoretical consideration of the problem of national character, and an analysis of the American character based on the premise that the primary force in determining it was economic abundance. It is also a repudiation of the agrarian preconceptions of Turner's work.

Proctor, John P. "Isolation or Imperialism," *Forum*, 26 (1898), 14–26.

An argument for imperialistic expansion by the United States in cooperation with Britain, based on the assumption that the Anglo-Saxon peoples are uniquely endowed with political capacity and therefore have a right and duty to bring civilization and political stability to less fortunate peoples.

Riesman, David. *Individualism Reconsidered and Other Essays.* Glencoe, Ill., 1954.

A collection of previously published essays, many of which discuss in detail and in relation to specific and fairly limited areas of American life concepts treated in broader outline in *The Lonely Crowd.*

————, and Glazer, Nathan. *Faces in the Crowd: Individual Studies in Character and Politics.* New Haven, 1952.

A series of individual interviews designed to test the conceptual framework established in *The Lonely Crowd.*

————; Glazer, Nathan; and Denney, Reuel. *The Lonely Crowd: A Study of the Changing American Character.* 2nd ed. Garden City, N. Y., 1954.

The famous study of the transition in the American character, just as important for the many comments it has provoked as for its intrinsic ideas.

Ringel, Fred J. (ed.). *America as Americans See It.* New York, 1932.

A series of very brief, and usually superficial, essays on various aspects of American life and civilization, comparable in general outline to Stearns's *Civilization in the United States,* but neither as unified nor as incisive.

Roberts, Peter. *The New Immigration: A Study of the Industrial and Social Life of Southeastern Europeans in America.* New York, 1912.

Roberts is sympathetic to the problems of the immigrants, and he is opposed to restriction, but he insists categorically that immigrants must make themselves conform to pre-established American values and ideals.

————. *The Problem of Americanization.* New York, 1920.

Ostensibly a handbook for workers in the field of Americanization. The point of view is fundamentally identical to his earlier opinion that immigrants should be poured into the American mold.

Rorty, James. *Where Life Is Better: An Unsentimental American Journey.* New York, 1936.

The travel diary of a self-confessed "radical" as he traveled through the United States reporting his experiences. A good example of the documentary style of social comment prevalent in the 1930's.

Ross, Edward A. "The Causes of Race Superiority," *Annals of the American Academy of Political and Social Science*, 18 (1901), 67–89.
A discussion of the various factors involved in racial superiority. Ross finds that the American rates high in all the areas he isolates, but he also points out the dangers of race suicide.

————. *The Old World in the New: The Significance of Past and Present Immigration to the American People*. New York, 1914.
A vigorous plea for restriction, asserting that if immigration is not stopped America will be radically changed for the worse.

————. *What Is America?* New York, 1919.
A general discussion of American society in relation to questions of social structure, including some brief remarks on national character.

Rossiter, Clinton. *Conservatism in America, the Thankless Persuasion*. 2nd ed. New York, 1962.
A study of conservatism and its place in the American tradition of political thought and action. Rossiter maintains that American conservatism is distinctively American—more willing to accept change, less devoted to tradition than European conservatism—but that it has to struggle against a political tradition that is unremittingly liberal.

Roucek, Joseph S. "The Geopolitics of the United States," *American Journal of Economics and Sociology*, 14 (1955), 185–192, 287–303.
An analysis of American foreign policy in terms of American history and the American national character.

Royce, Josiah. *Race Questions, Provincialism, and Other American Problems*. New York, 1908.
A series of essays on various subjects: the inadequacies of racist theories, the necessities of maintaining and developing local peculiarities of thought and behavior in the United States, the distinctive characteristics of American idealism.

Royce, Monroe. *The Passing of the American*. New York, 1911.
Royce, like many of his contemporaries, felt that immigration was a danger to American institutions and character, but he was unusual in that he felt that it was unfortunate not because of the characteristics of the immigrants, but because the presence of immigrants created in native Americans a disposition to laziness and sloppiness and an aversion to discipline.

Santayana, George. *Character and Opinion in the United States.* Garden City, N. Y., 1956.

A discussion of the primary characteristics of the American mind based partly upon analyses of the author's colleagues at Harvard, partly upon general reflections on the American scene. This book was first published in 1920.

Sapir, Edward. "Personality." In E. R. A. Seligman (ed.). *Encyclopedia of the Social Sciences.* 15 vols. New York, 1930–1934. Vol. 12, pp. 85–88.

A brief article on personality, mostly in its relations to the culture in which it exists and in which it was formed.

Schlesinger, Arthur M. "What Then Is the American, This New Man?," *American Historical Review,* 48 (1943), 225–244.

Schlesinger argues for a modified version of the Frontier Thesis in which the formative influences of the frontier are altered by urban influences.

Schultz, Alfred P. *Race or Mongrel.* Boston, 1908.

One of the more extreme racist works. Schultz argues that the product of a mixed racial background is always and inevitably inferior to the racially "pure" individual.

Seldes, Gilbert. *The Years of the Locust: (America, 1929–1932).* Boston, 1933.

A trenchant study of the worst years of the Depression, focusing on the sense of shock, bewilderment, and general paralysis of mind that afflicted the American people as a result of the crash of 1929.

Shaler, N. S. "European Peasants as Immigrants," *Atlantic Monthly,* 71 (1893); 646–655.

Argues that immigration should be restricted because the immigrants are mostly peasants and thus, because of the experience of centuries of oppression, not good material for democracy.

Sherman, Stuart P. *Americans.* New York, 1922.

A series of essays on leading American literary figures. It begins with a vigorous attack on Mencken.

———. *The Genius of America: Studies in Behalf of the Younger Generation.* New York, 1923.

This collection of essays reveals why Sherman became the symbol of the Old Guard for the rebel intellectuals of the 1920's. His pose of fervent moral exhortation is more than a little ridiculous.

———. *The Main Stream.* New York, 1927.

Chiefly important in the present context for Sherman's essay "Middle-Class Strategy," in which he presents a view of the American character that is squarely in the tradition of the optimistic view that prevailed at the turn of the century.

———. *Points of View*. New York, 1924.

When he talks about literature, Sherman manages to make sense. However, in his essay "Towards an American Type" he is again speaking directly to the younger generation, and whenever he does that he makes himself look silly.

Smith, Huston; Heffron, Richard T.; and Smith, Eleanor Wieman (eds.). *The Search for America*. Englewood Cliffs, N. J., 1959.

A collection of essays by various authors on the current American scene and American problems, including an especially stimulating essay by Reinhold Niebuhr on the idea of progress in America and its relation to America's role in the current world situation.

Speek, Peter. "The Meaning of Nationality and Americanization," *American Journal of Sociology*, 32 (1926), 237–249.

An attempt to define nationality and the forces which create it in relation to the Americanization problem. In discussing America, Speek in essence repeats the Frontier Thesis.

Speranza, Gino. *Race or Nation: A Conflict of Divided Loyalties*. Indianapolis, 1923.

A plea for restriction and rapid and thorough Americanization of immigrants already in the nation, because of the dangers of having large numbers of people with divided loyalties here.

Stearns, Harold E. *America: A Re-Appraisal*. New York, 1937.

This book reflects a fundamental re-evaluation of the strongly critical stance Stearns had adopted in the 1920's.

———. *America and the Young Intellectual*. New York, 1921.

A series of essays on various subjects, most of them having to do with the sad state of American civilization and culture, especially the stifling of American arts and ideas.

———. (ed.). *America Now: An Inquiry into Civilization in the United States*. New York, 1938.

A sequel to *Civilization in the United States*, differing from the earlier volume in that there is less unity in the points of view expressed by the various authors and, with some exceptions, less of a disposition to criticize American civilization with severity.

——— (ed.). *Civilization in the United States: An Inquiry by Thirty Americans*. New York 1922.

This collection of essays by various authors established most of the themes of the criticism of American life by

American intellectuals which were to become general in the 1920's.

Steiner, Edward A. *Introducing the American Spirit*. New York, 1915.

An attempt to defend America from the criticisms of a foreign traveler.

———. *The Making of a Great Race: Racial and Religious Cross-Currents in the United States*. New York, 1929.

A study of immigration and Americanization based on the proposition that immigration has been and will continue to be of enormous benefit to the United States.

Stoddard, Lothrop. *The Rising Tide of Color Against White World-Supremacy*. New York, 1920.

Stoddard predicted that the white races of the world would be overwhelmed in competition with the colored races unless preventive action were taken.

Straus, Oscar. *The American Spirit*. New York, 1913.

An ecstatic account of the basic outlines of American culture and institutions, interesting chiefly because of Straus's insistence that immigration has been one of the chief sources of America's strength.

Strunsky, Simeon. *The Living Tradition: Change and America*. New York, 1939.

An analysis of American civilization oriented around the idea that the real American tradition is change and that change is the most important constant in American life.

Thompson, Robert Ellis. *The Hand of God in American History: A Study of National Politics*. New York, 1902.

A sketch of the history of the United States designed to show that it has been influenced at decisive points by divine Providence. Thompson also argues that the United States has a God-given mission, not, surprisingly, imperialist expansion, but rather the enlargement of private privileges for the enjoyment of everyone.

Turner, Frederick Jackson. "The Problem of the West," *Atlantic Monthly*, 78 (1896), 289–297.

An elaboration of the character of the Western American, concentrating mainly on his expansiveness.

———. "The Significance of the Frontier in American History." In American Historical Association, *Annual Report* (Washington, D.C., 1894), pp. 199–227.

The classic elaboration of the Frontier Thesis.

Twain, Mark. *Innocents Abroad*. 2 vols. New York, 1869.

Twain's satirical account of a foreign trip in which he

manages to poke fun not only at Europe but also at America and Americans.

United States, *Congressional Record*, vol. 28, March 16, 1896.
   A speech to the Senate by Henry Cabot Lodge advocating a literacy test as the proper mode of restricting immigration, a policy he deemed necessary because of the threat immigration posed to the American character.

Viereck, Peter. *The Unadjusted Man, a New Hero for Americans: Reflections on the Distinction Between Conforming and Conserving*. Boston, 1956.
   An attack on conformity in which Viereck pleads for a reasoned adherence to traditional standards instead of slavish aping of current fads and fancies.

Walker, Francis A. *Discussions in Economics and Statistics*. 2 vols. New York, 1899.
   One of the opening guns in the battle for immigration restriction around the turn of the century and one of the first enunciations of the "race suicide" theory.

Whyte, William H., Jr. *The Organization Man*. Garden City, N. Y., 1957.
   The best-selling account of the way in which the pressures of the organization are destroying individualism in America.

Williams, William A. "American Century, 1941–1957," *Nation*, 185 (1957), 297–301.
   An analysis of the growing realization among the formulators and executors of American foreign policy that they could not expect to have things their own way in the Cold War era.

Williams, William Carlos. *In the American Grain*. New York, 1925.
   An imaginative reconstruction of certain events and persons in American history, the main theme of which is that the chief shaping force in the creation of America has been fear.

Woodruff, Charles Edward. *The Expansion of Races*. New York, 1909.
   One of the more extreme statements of the racist position.

SECONDARY WORKS

Aaron, Daniel (ed.). *American in Crisis: Fourteen Crucial Episodes in American History*. New York, 1952.
   Contains an essay by Morris Janowitz on the "Black Legions" of the 1930's, one of the most vivid expressions of the political extremism of the decade.

Bowers, Claude G. *Beveridge and the Progressive Era*. Boston, 1932.
   A biography of Beveridge, chiefly valuable in the present

context because it contains transcripts of some of Beveridge's more important speeches.

Burns, Edward McNall. *The American Idea of Mission: Concepts of National Purpose and Destiny.* New Brunswick, N. J., 1957.

A study of the various manifestations of the American feeling that their country is endowed with a special mission to the rest of the world.

Coleman, Lee. "What Is American?: A Study of Alleged American Traits," *Social Forces*, 19 (1941), 492–499.

A study of studies of the American character, but designed only to discover what traits have been assigned to it most frequently.

Cowley, Malcolm (ed.). *After the Genteel Tradition: American Writers Since 1910.* New York, 1937.

A series of essays by various authors on the major literary figures of the 1920's, important largely because it includes substantial excerpts from the writings of the men discussed.

Degler, Carl N. "The Sociologist as Historian: Riesman's *The Lonely Crowd*," *American Quarterly*, 15 (1963), 483–497.

A recent instance of the way in which Riesman's work has been misinterpreted by most of those who have discussed him.

Fairchild, Henry Pratt. *Race and Nationality as Factors in American Life.* New York, 1947.

A general discussion of the place that race and nationality have had in the development of American life, including a definition of "nationality" to fit the American context, a definition similar to what others have often called "national character."

Gottschalk, Louis (ed.). *Generalization in the Writing of History: A Report of the Committee on Historical Analysis of the Social Science Research Council.* Chicago, 1963.

Includes an essay by Walter P. Metzger concerning the practical and theoretical problems involved in the historian's use of the concept of national character.

Griswold, A. Whitney. *Farming and Democracy.* New York, 1948.

Questions the Jeffersonian assumption that democracy and industrialism are incompatible.

Haller, Mark. *Eugenics: Hereditarian Attitudes in American Thought.* New Brunswick, N. J., 1963.

A general history of the eugenics movement in the United States.

Higham, John (ed.). *The Reconstruction of American History.* New York, 1962.

A series of essays on present trends in historical interpretation and the ways in which present interpretations differ from those of the past. Includes an essay by David Potter on the general qualities of studies of the American character.

———. *Strangers in the Land: Patterns of American Nativism, 1860–1925.* New Brunswick, N. J., 1955.
By far the best secondary account of American nativism, its origins and effects.

Hofstadter, Richard. *Anti-Intellectualism in American Life.* New York, 1963.
A general history of the origins and development of anti-intellectual attitudes in America.

Hsu, Francis L. K. (ed.). *Aspects of Culture and Personality.* New York, 1954.
A series of essays on various problems in the culture and personality approach to the study of man.

Kazin, Alfred. *On Native Grounds: An Interpretation of Modern American Prose Literature.* Garden City, N. Y., 1956.
A stimulating treatment of American literature and an attempt to place this imaginative literature within the political, economic, and social context in which it was written.

Klineberg, Otto. "A Science of National Character," *Journal of Social Psychology,* 19 (1944), 147–162.
A discussion of the various objections to the national-character concept and of the ways in which those objections may be met so as to establish the study of national character on more rigidly scientific foundations.

———. *Tensions Affecting International Understanding: A Survey of Research.* Social Science Research Council Bulletin, no. 62. New York, 1950.
A survey of research on various problems relating to international understanding, one of which is the question of how the concept of national character may be used in specific studies to help contribute to international good will.

Kluckhohn, Clyde, and Murray, Henry A. (eds.). *Personality in Nature, Society, and Culture.* 2nd ed. New York, 1953.
Many of the articles in this excellent anthology are related to the problem of national character in one way or another.

Kohn, Hans. *The Idea of Nationalism: A Study in Its Origins and Background.* New York, 1944.
Important in the present context chiefly for its theoretical discussions of nationality and national character.

Kouwenhoven, John. *The Beer Can by the Highway: Essays on What's "American" About America.* Garden City, N. Y., 1961.
In this series of essays, Kouwenhoven makes a few brief

remarks concerning previous studies of the American character.

Lasch, Christopher. "The Anti-Imperialists, the Philippines, and the Inequality of Man," *Journal of Southern History*, 24 (1958), 319–331.

In this article, Lasch shows that there was a strong current of racist thought in the arguments of the anti-imperialists.

Lerner, Daniel, and Lasswell, Harold D. (eds.) *The Policy Sciences: Recent Developments in Scope and Method.* Stanford, 1951.

Contains an essay by Margaret Mead on the theoretical problems of the study of national character.

Lipset, Seymour Martin, and Bendix, Reinhard. *Social Mobility in Industrial Society.* Berkeley, 1959.

A comparative discussion of rates of social mobility in various industrial societies. The authors' findings call into question the traditional assumption that the United States has a distinctively high rate of social mobility.

May, Henry F. *The End of American Innocence: A Study of the First Years of Our Own Time, 1912–1917.* New York, 1959.

May argues that the immediate pre-war period saw the beginnings of a basic change in the orientation of most American intellectuals, a loss of optimism, a questioning attitude toward the idea of progress, and a repudiation of idealism. These changes reached their full development in the 1920's.

Mills, C. Wright. *The Sociological Imagination.* New York, 1959.

Important in the present context chiefly for its discussion of the overwhelming importance of the nation-state in any meaningful discussion of contemporary social structures.

Newman, William J. *The Futilitarian Society.* New York, 1961.

A decidedly unsympathetic treatment of contemporary American conservatism.

Paxson, Frederick L. "A Generation of the Frontier Hypothesis: 1893–1932," *Pacific Historical Review*, 2 (1933), 36–48.

A discussion of reactions to Turner's theory.

Polsby, Nelson W. "Power in Middletown: Fact and Value in Community Research," *Canadian Journal of Economics and Political Science*, 26 (1960), 592–603.

Criticizes the Lynds for allowing their Marxist orientation to lead them into ascribing more power and influence to the business class of Middletown than the actual facts they unearthed warranted.

Schlesinger, Arthur M., Jr. *The Politics of Hope.* Boston, 1962.

A collection of essays on various topics, including one on the place of conservatism in American political thought which is critical of recent attempts by American historians and political scientists to find a "consensus" in the American past.

Shafer, Boyd. "Men Are More Alike," *American Historical Review*, 57 (1952), 593–612.
Argues that historians' concentration on national history does a serious disservice to the ideal of history.

Smith, Henry Nash. *Virgin Land: The American West as Symbol and Myth*. New York, 1957.
A study of the continuing hold of the agrarian tradition upon the American mind and heart.

Wallace, Anthony F. C. *Culture and Personality*. New York, 1961.
An illuminating introductory discussion of the concepts and the literature of the culture and personality movement.

Warner, W. Lloyd, and Abegglen, James C. *Big Business Leaders in America*. New York, 1955.
A study of the social backgrounds of business leaders which concludes that there are more self-made men at present than there were in the past.

———. *Occupational Mobility in American Business and Industry*. Minneapolis, 1955.
Concludes that social mobility has increased significantly in recent years.

Watson, Goodwin (ed.). *Civilian Morale*. New York, 1942.
Includes an essay by Gregory Bateson on the problem of morale as it relates to the American character.

Weber, Max. *The Protestant Ethic and the Spirit of Capitalism*. Translated by Talcott Parsons. New York, 1958.
The classic statement of the theory that the development of capitalism owed much to the intellectual and emotional atmosphere created by the Protestant Reformation.

INDEX

Adamic, Louis, 112
Adams, Henry, 17, 33
Adams, James Truslow: views in 1920's, 101; views in 1940's, 139, 140, 141
Addams, Jane, 44, 67–68
Agee, James, 96n
Agrarian philosophy: persistence of, 9–10, 36–37, 95, 97–98, 133, 144–145, 184, 191–193; attacks on, 11, 33, 146–149
Alexander, Franz, 123, 128–129
Almond, Gabriel A., 153–154
Americanism: definitions of, in immigration controversy, 63–64; as ideology in Cold War, 159–167; as ideology in Lipset's view, 169
Anderson, Sherwood, 102
Anglo-Saxon school. See Germ theory
Anthropology: development of culture and personality theory in, 120–121; applied to study of national character, 135–136
Antin, Mary, 62
Asch, Nathan, 109

Babbitt: as typical American, 74, 109–110, 130, 175
Babbitt, Irving, 82
Barzun, Jacques, 104, 105
Basic personality structure: defined, 121; deficiencies of, 122; relation to national character, 122
Bates, Ernest Sutherland, 111n
Beard, Charles A.: Butler's reaction to, 27n; and idea of civilization, 106n; on American character,

138–139; compared with Ralph Perry and James Truslow Adams, 140–141
Beard, Mary R. See Beard, Charles
Bendix, Reinhard. See Lipset, Seymour Martin
Bettelheim, Bruno: mentioned, 123
Beveridge, Albert J.: on American character, 20–21; and racism, 25; and determinants of American character, 28; compared with Monroe Royce, 55
Bierstadt, Edward Hale, 63
Boas, Franz, 69n
Boorstin, Daniel: on American political tradition, 160–162; compared with Hartz and Rossiter, 164–165; emphasis on politics, 165–166; on foreign affairs, 167
Bourne, Randolph, 82n
Boutwell, George S., 46n
Brooks, Van Wyck: on American character, 85–89; attacks small town, 96; mentioned, 97, 112, 158
Burgess, Ernest W., 148
Burgess, John W.: on American character, 17–18; on arts, 22; on immigration, 38
Burlingame, Roger, 114
Butler, Nicholas Murray: and racism, 25; and economic interpretation, 27n; and determinants of American character, 28

Canby, Henry Seidel, 94
Climate: as determinant of national character, 2, 27–28, 46–47